MY STORY

D0755585

MY STORY
The Duchess of York
Her Father and Me

Lesley Player

with William Hall

Grafton
An Imprint of HarperCollins*Publishers*

*A special dedication to the most
precious person in my life, Antony.*

Grafton
An imprint of HarperCollins*Publishers*
77–85 Fulham Palace Road,
Hammersmith, London W6 8JB

A Grafton Original 1993
9 8 7 6 5 4 3 2 1

A catalogue record for this book
is available from the British Library

ISBN 0 00 255239 6

Set in 10/12 point Garamond

Printed in Great Britain by
HarperCollinsManufacturing Glasgow

Speak your truth quietly and clearly

Desiderata

This is to set the record straight

Lesley Player, 1993

To my best friends in my life whom I love.
And to God who loves me.
Who forgives and empowers me.
And never betrayed me.

For permission to reproduce photographs the publisher and author thank:

Rex Features; Associated Press; Galbraith; Solo Syndication; Press Association; Kaphart; Mike Roberts; Camden Graphics; Dafydd Jones; Chanrai.

CONTENTS

FOREWORD

Why am I writing this book?

Quite simply, to clear my name.

I am standing on the wooden patio of a small beach-house on the outskirts of Cape Town, staring out at the restless sea. This is close to the spot where two great oceans meet, and where you can actually see the murky waters of the South Atlantic to the west link up with the clear blue of the Indian Ocean to the east, the two kept apart by some magic dividing line.

My friend Diana, who kindly loaned me the use of her home when I fled from the turmoil of London, is away for a month, so I can collect my thoughts – and make my decision.

Only a few months ago the idea of writing a book that might cause hurt to other people would have been completely alien to me. But the revelation of my affair with Major Ronald Ferguson, and the accusations of my having defrauded a charity and posed at being a lady-in-waiting to the Duchess of York, have all but ruined me, losing me my home, my health, two businesses – and almost my sanity.

Branded a scarlet woman, I became a social outcast in the rarefied world of polo and the glamorous society figures who move within it.

The reality is, of course, that I had an affair with the Major. And, by denying it when so many within royal circles and elsewhere knew it to be true, I only made things worse.

The official itinerary for the royal tour of Palm Beach listed me as Sarah's lady-in-waiting. With one call – instead of an unwarranted denial – she could so easily have put matters right, as the Charity Commissioners did to exonerate me completely from any misconduct.

I thought I had found true friends in Sarah and her father after they had welcomed me so warmly on numerous occasions to Sunninghill Park House, the home of the Duke and Duchess of York. I was wrong. When I needed them, at the lowest time in my life, they turned their backs.

I was tried and sentenced by the Press, with no opportunity of defence – until now.

All I ever wanted on the day I met Major Ronald Ferguson was to organize a polo tournament, and to rebuild my life after separating from my husband. Instead, I found myself pursued obsessively by a man nearly twice my age, and caught up in the web of intrigue and deceit that surrounded the fall of the House of York.

In writing a book to describe what really happened, I can at least offer an explanation to those willing to give me a fair hearing. One thing it will not do is to put any further clouds on the horizons of the 'real' Royal Family, who do so much for this country.

But now, here is the truth behind the headlines.

My diaries show the date, the place and the time where it all began:

Friday 9 November 1990. The Royal County of Berkshire Polo Club, Ascot. Noon.

I had arrived promptly on time. Not a minute early, not a minute late. That way, they had told me at my business psychology courses, nobody can pre-judge you before you've even started a meeting.

Through the windows of the Secretary's office I could see the sleek outlines of my Silver Spur Rolls-Royce parked in the drive. The jet-black limousine had brought faces to the windows of the clubhouse as I drove up to the main entrance for the encounter that would change my life.

I was used to questioning looks. Just who was this petite young woman in the smart navy-blue Chanel suit walking briskly through the hallowed portals of one of the world's most exclusive Establishment male bastions?

A place where wealth, prestige and power preside. And where you are judged by your skill in the saddle as you wield a four-foot bamboo mallet in passionate pursuit of a hard white ball the size of a small cantaloupe melon.

Smooth green fields of conflict, six of them, guarded by lines of hefty oak trees, stretched away to the misty ramparts of Windsor Castle.

Beyond a handful of BMWs, Porsches and Range-Rovers parked near the goalposts, a Sikorsky helicopter squatted on its pad like a giant insect.

Inside this inner sanctum that has been described as 'England's ritziest polo club' I was nervous as a kitten, but refused to show it. I sat in a comfortable chair opposite the big desk and tried to radiate the confidence of someone about to make the Club an offer it couldn't possibly refuse.

At least the office was reassuringly untidy – the desk piled high with papers and programmes, ballpoint pens and paperclips, and filled with the sound of phones that never seemed to stop ringing. Assistants popped in and out, and the atmosphere was positively crackling with energy.

As a businesswoman who had been dealing with the very top strata of industrialists and banks, I knew what the sweet smell of success was all about – and this was a heady scent indeed.

The door opened again, and a very tall, strongly built man with rugged features and bushy eyebrows walked in. He marched up to me without a pause and stuck out his hand. His voice boomed out.

'Hello, you must be Miss Player. Let me introduce myself. I'm Major Ferguson. Just what can we do for you?'

CHAPTER ONE

Early Days

In the beginning, who could have known? Certainly not me. When I was a little girl growing up in a warm, happy household in the stockbroker belt near Maidenhead, I dreamed of handsome princes and ivory towers – but then, they were only dreams.

As a baby I had a mass of dark curls, wide brown eyes, and a smile that won me first prize at a local baby show when I was just twelve months old.

My father called me his 'little Princess', and absolutely doted on me. Even when I was naughty, I could do no wrong.

But life is full of surprises, and mine started early. The first unexpected thing that happened to me was actually on the day I was born. Not so much when – that *was* expected – but where. My mother, Irene Lamont-Black, the wife of a wealthy businessman, was desperate to have me at home.

But on a September day in 1958, her own mother died. The shock of it so distressed Mummy that two weeks later, on 14 September, the birth pangs started and she was rushed to the local Redhill hospital where I came into the world at 3.00 a.m. I was a month premature, and a forceps delivery – quite a small baby, weighing just 6 lbs, but healthy, bubbly and cheerful. I'm told that I gurgled a lot in my cot, but I hardly ever cried.

My parents were delighted to have a daughter. Daddy – who was chairman of a catering firm – already had a son by his first marriage. It had all been planned for weeks and weeks. The nursery was ready, with bright new wallpaper full of colourful flowers and animals. My mother was terribly excited because I was her very first baby.

Granny went into hospital in Crawley, Sussex, to have a routine operation on her gall bladder – but what no one realized was that she was allergic to general anaesthetic. It was so routine that no one even bothered to go in with her when she was admitted. She insisted: 'Don't bother. I'll be all right.' She was an indomitable old lady, and the last thing she wanted was a lot of fuss.

My mother was Daddy's second wife. He hails from Scotland – Alan Veitch Lamont-Black was proud to boast of his own clan, and of our own tartan in green, cream and brown, with the emblem of an open right hand in a wreath and the family motto, 'Neither spear nor dispose.'

In the end they got divorced – and Daddy went on to marry again. As I grew up I came to realize what a child he was at heart, like a little boy who constantly needed reassuring and mothering. He had had a bad first marriage, which ended in blazing rows and shouting-matches, and was very hurt from it. But while Mummy was strong-willed, she instinctively knew his weaknesses and was able to be the wife he wanted. He was very much in love with her.

As a result my own childhood was normal, loving and secure. I also saw for myself how a woman of strong character could attract a weak man, yet be happy enough to make a life together. It was something I would experience at first hand for myself years later.

My mother's maiden name was Hamecher, of German origin, and she was wealthy in her own right before they met. She owned her own restaurant and ran a dancing-school before joining my father's catering company based in Richmond, Surrey, which specialized in frozen foods. It had been founded by his father Alan, who had revolutionized the freezing process – making a fortune for the family.

Mummy swiftly made her own mark, rising through the departments to become regional manager. That was how she met the boss, fell in love with him, and married him.

I was the apple of my father's eye, a cherubic little thing who seemed to find the world a funny old place even from the start, because I was always chuckling away happily in my cot. Well, that's what they told me later. My mother also told me it was my smile that gained me first prize in the Hanworth baby show at the age of one.

Daddy had always wanted a daughter, and I was a real cutie! He adored me so much that he took me everywhere – to company parties, to sports meetings and cricket matches, showing me off to his friends and business colleagues as if I were the most precious thing in the world. And to him, I really think I was.

The marriage fell apart four years after I was born. My grandfather died in a sailing accident in a dreadful storm in a race off the coast of Cornwall. My grandmother was so upset, poor lady, that she passed away two months later. It was really so strange. Eight weeks previously she had been a fit, healthy woman – but after that terrible day she just didn't want to go on any more. They had been immensely close, and without him she just gave up living. It was so sad.

The doctor came round to our house and told us: 'I have to put down the cause of death on the certificate as a heart attack. But unofficially I think she died of a broken heart.'

We believed it. I think it happens all the time with people who have lived close to one another all their lives. When one goes the other just fades away.

But those twin deaths would break up our own family. Suddenly my father came into a huge amount of money from the estate – and he wasn't mature enough to handle it. He sold his firm to a big conglomerate and all at once he found himself with millions in the bank. I mean *millions* – and that was in the fifties.

He got himself a secretary named Ivy. He also got her pregnant, and Mummy didn't like that one little bit. She realized what was going on when she found a lipstick in my father's jacket pocket – he must have been very silly, or just plain careless!

She confronted him, and he admitted it. He told her: 'Yes, I've gone with other women.' She threw him out of the house! He promptly went off and married his secretary, and that started a whole financial hullabaloo which of course I was too young to understand.

I was told later that Daddy was moving his money around frantically from place to place to stop Mummy catching up with it, and there must have been some high old fun and games going on.

There was a court case; she won custody – and ended up with just £16 a week maintenance, even though he was a multi-millionaire. By that time I also had a younger brother, Neil, who was adopted when my mother thought she could never have any more children – and a sister, Nicola, who was born a year later, when Mummy found she was wrong!

Despite the fact that we had to watch the purse-strings, our early life was really happy, and we were a close-knit family. We moved from Maidenhead to West Green in Sussex, where I went first to West Green Junior School in Crawley, then to the Holy Trinity Church of England School.

In Maidenhead I had gone to an infant school, a private establishment for girls, with only twenty-five pupils. We all wore striped blazers, and flounced around in navy-blue skirts and straw boaters with pink ribbons like little moppets out of a Hollywood musical.

I have always said that I was a born leader. If anyone doubts it, look what happened when I was just three years old. One morning my mother got a frantic phone call from the headmistress to say that the whole school was missing! The distraught teacher was phoning round every parent to say: 'They've all gone! We don't know where they are. When we hear anything, we'll let you know.'

My mother later told me: 'Funny, I had a *feeling* about it.' And ten minutes later, what did she see? A file of tiny schoolgirls, marching two-by-two in through the front gate and up the drive – with me in the lead. I'd said to them: 'Line up! I'm taking you home for lunch!'

It was just awful, kidnapping an entire school. Well, unusual at least. But my mother was wonderful, and rallied round at once. She rang the headmistress and told her: 'My daughter's brought the whole school home. Don't worry. I've got them all here. I'm giving them beans on toast and sending them back ...'

I was a proper little madam, a real bossy-boots even at that tender age. We'd crossed a main road, walked for at least ten minutes in a neat crocodile with me keeping them in line like a sergeant-major. My mother didn't have the heart to tell me off, though the headmistress's attitude was slightly different. When we moved away I rather think my infants teacher was quite happy to see me go.

My first memory of life is one I wish I could blot out. I believe that very young children really do know what's going on with their parents, which is why you've got to be so careful how you behave in front of them. But the first thing I can ever remember is my mother and father having a fight. It happened in the hall at the foot of the staircase of our house in Maidenhead, and they were screaming and yelling at each other, with Daddy grabbing Mummy by her sleeves and pulling her violently around.

I was about four years old, and I remember getting between them, pushing myself between their legs with tears streaming down my face, pleading: 'Mummy! Daddy! Stop ...'

They ended up cuddling each other, and cuddling me too.

After that I seemed to become much more aware of what was going on around me. I felt my mother was being extra-protective, probably because of the tensions building up between them. But we kids were happy enough, though I was the naughty one and frequently got into trouble.

Our house was one of those large, attractive Tudor houses you find in stockbroker territory – I always seem to have lived in big houses, and never felt lost or afraid in them. This one had lots of rooms. It also had a big, open coal fire in the living-room. My mother warned me: 'Don't ever touch the poker or go near the fire, understand?'

I understood, but that didn't necessarily mean obey.

One day, when the room was empty, I picked up the cast-iron poker and began prodding the red-hot coals. Of course, the poker became hot too, and I dropped it on the carpet. In my panic I trod on it with my bare foot – and my screams filled the house. My parents ran from room to room trying to find me – and finally my father burst into the lounge, swept me up in his arms, and rushed me off to hospital. I had a huge bandage on my foot for days, but at least both my parents were too relieved to scold me.

At breakfast I would always pile sugar on my porridge, and sometimes I'd go too far. 'No more sugar,' my mother ordered – and I'd sneak another spoonful when I thought she wasn't looking. When I got caught, I'd have to stay indoors while Daddy took the other two to the sweet-shop down the road to buy them penny chocolate bars – and I'd be left with my nose pressed to the window forlornly watching them go hand in hand up the drive without me.

If we were basically a normal, happy group of children growing up together, I still sensed all was not quite right. Something seemed to be missing in the family, though I had no idea what it was.

In the end, after only five years, it was my father. One day he just went away and didn't come back.

Mummy called the three of us into the kitchen, sat us down, and told us gently: 'Daddy's had to go away for a while. I'm not sure when we'll see him again. But remember – he loves you, and always will.' In fact she had thrown him out, and I wouldn't see my father again until I was twelve years old.

Strangely enough, that day none of us cried when she broke the news.

Another memory still haunts me – but in my dreams. One bright summer's day the circus came to town, and there we were hand in hand with Daddy taking us across the village green for a surprise treat. In among the fairground barkers and noisy side-shows we skipped and ran – until we reached the Big Top. That's when I started screaming.

I was suddenly faced with the sight of a huge teddy bear standing at the entrance to the Big Top. It scared me stiff when a voice rumbled through: 'Hello, little girl!' I just threw a fit of hysterics, yelling my head off – which rather startled the clown inside. Daddy bundled me up in his arms, apologized profusely to the bear, and hurried me past into the arena.

From that day I started having nightmares – one in particular, which is still recurring. I'm lying on the bare floor of a loft, waking from a drowsy sleep, to find myself trapped in the dust and cobwebs – with dozens of teddy bears sitting around staring at me with their little beady hostile eyes.

I still have that dream today. It ends with me trying to run away – but it's one of those dreams where you can't run; you always stay in the same place however hard you try. And when I really wake up I often find the bed bouncing up and down on its springs because I've been struggling so hard to escape.

I know I'm running away from something – but what? I suspect it's my inner feelings, because I'm a very emotional person, and when I get involved with something – whether it is a person or a project – I give all of myself to it.

In West Green we lived in my granddad's house. My mother's father, John Hamecher, was a cantankerous old man who had lost a leg, and couldn't stand us boisterous kids running around. But the house was a rambling old cottage with a huge garden where we could play for hours and keep out of his way.

As I grew older I watched him become more and more frail and helpless. By the time I was ten I was being woken by my mother at three in the morning to help carry Granddad to his commode, as she wasn't strong enough to do it on her own. I'm sure he felt ashamed of his granddaughter seeing him in such a condition, but Mother refused to put him in a home, and somehow we looked after him until he died.

At school I was a loner. Not shy – just withdrawn, always in a world of my own, creating my own dreams and fantasies. I always felt remote from the other girls in my class – though academically I was judged to be 'extremely bright'.

Halfway through my first term at West Green junior school my form-mistress rang my mother and said: 'Look, Lesley has a problem making friends. I think she should go to a psychiatrist.'

We went along to a child-psychiatrist in Crawley, and a very kind man sat me down at a table and gave me lots of wooden squares and objects to work out and assemble. I kept thinking: 'What am I *doing* here? This is ridiculous!'

There were two other children in the same room, and when I got a chance I whispered to them: 'Why are you here?'

The first one said: 'I hate spiders.' The other girl replied: 'I hate snakes.'

They both asked me why I was there, and I could only answer: 'I don't know.' I quite like spiders, and I'm not afraid of snakes.

At the end of the day the psychiatrist invited us into

his consulting-room and said to my mother: 'This child has no problem. She's just getting over losing her father. That's all it is. She's growing up and realizing there's a gap in her life. While other girls are talking about their fathers, Lesley hasn't got one – and she's feeling it.'

A month later my father came back.

Although he had behaved badly to my mother, Daddy had also been terribly hurt at not being able to see his children and being kept apart from us for so many years. But finally my mother relented – maybe that session with the psychiatrist did the trick. And there on the doorway one autumn morning was my father.

I remember a tall figure standing in the mist-shrouded garden with the wet leaves all around his feet, and his arms stretched out to us as we hurled ourselves at him, all three of us, shouting: 'Daddy! Daddy!' Somehow there was no holding back, no shyness – just a great feeling of joy and somehow relief that he was still part of our young lives, even if he wasn't living under the same roof.

Whatever had gone on behind the scenes between them, Mummy had never said anything bad about him in our presence. He was still our Dad!

My life at school changed from that day. I made friends with other girls who are still my close chums even today. When I was moved to Holy Trinity Church of England School in nearby Gossops Green at the age of twelve, I had completely broken out of my trauma. I entered into everything I could – and became captain of the school hockey team, the netball team, head girl of the monitors, and deputy head girl of the whole house.

Holy Trinity was a mixed school, and I was a member of a gang – twenty-six of us. When we were around sixteen years old we would frequent a pub called The Lambs in the nearby village of Rusper. There was a phone box outside, and one day someone suggested we should all try to get into it. With a lot of huffing and puffing and squeezing we managed twelve – but after that it became a challenge. Every Friday evening for months we piled into that wretched box, but we never got more than twelve stuffed into it. I still see some of the gang, and we laugh over those mad evenings.

I used to get up to all sorts of pranks. Silly things – such as when I was a Brownie, and put drawing-pins on Brown Owl's chair just before she sat down. I got a severe ticking-off for that – she just knew it had to be Lesley.

They say schooldays are the happiest days of your life, and to some extent I'll go along with that. I was totally in tune with my school, and I made the most of every day. Two weeks before we were due to leave, with our A-levels behind us, I turned to my best friend, a girl called Zoe, and said: 'You know, we're really going to regret leaving this place.'

She said: 'Don't be so stupid. I can't wait to get away.'

'Think of it,' I said. 'We're protected, we have long holidays, we have fun. The real world is on another planet somewhere out there beyond the gates. And now we're going to have to join it.'

She scoffed at me. 'You say such crazy things!' But I knew I was right – and I was ahead of my time.

Academically I was no slouch either. Every year I won some award or other. Mathematics, Religious Education, Home Economics ... My school reports bordered on the ecstatic! Headmaster Mr David Eynon wrote: 'Lesley's creative writing indicates she has a pleasing sensitivity to her environment ... she is a very reliable, hard-working girl who always produces her best ...'

Even though we had been reunited, and I had become more adjusted, Daddy was hardly ever there. He would write to us, and phone occasionally. But his visits were few and far between. Mother felt she had done enough by allowing him occasional access, but it was never like the real relationships that my other friends enjoyed. As I grew older I noticed his absence more. They say fathers and daughters are very close, and mothers and sons – and that would have been true if only I'd had the chance to make it happen.

The worst part was the end of term. Other girls would be rushing around excitedly on the last day, squealing: 'My Dad's come to take me out to dinner.' Or: 'We're going off shopping to buy me a new dress.' I never had any of that.

I thought: 'Right, if I'm going to be left out like that, I'll show them!' I set out to be the best at everything, where no one could hurt me inside. I had A's on all my reports. I'd go around the house spouting Shakespeare. I astounded my mother with my brilliance!

The only other thing lacking was boyfriends ...

After I had taken my O-levels, I hung around the front door waiting for the postman to arrive the week the results were due out. I had taken eleven subjects. Finally he came trudging up the garden path – and I had the front door open and my hand outstretched before he got there.

My mother appeared, and I gave her the envelope. 'Go on,' I said. 'You tell me.'

She opened it, and her eyes widened. 'Eleven O-levels,' she said. 'Grade A in nearly every one! What can I say?'

'How about "Well done"!' I said cheekily, with what I can only describe as a smirk of satisfaction.

'I'm just so proud of you,' she said. 'We all are.'

For a fleeting moment I longed for Daddy to be part of that 'all' – and be there to tell me he was proud of his 'little Princess' too.

Two years later, I had gone on to pass three A-levels, in Home Economics, Biology and English Literature.

After that I started noticing boys.

CHAPTER TWO

High Jinks

I talked it over with my mother. For a start, I had no one else I could really discuss my life with, and she had always wanted the best for me. What should I do? Where could I go?

I was eighteen years old, there had been no young men in my life whatever – and now she could sense my restlessness. I had been a home bird for too long, and now it was time to flee the nest.

Mummy said: 'I think you should go away. The atmosphere here is too claustrophobic for you. What do you want to do – have you any idea?'

I already knew. 'Medicine,' I said firmly. 'Something in the medical field. Don't ask me why.' I was learning to trust my instincts. 'I just feel it's right for me. But first I'd like to improve my languages.'

The result was that I found myself on a plane to Zurich, with a study course in German ahead. At Gatwick Airport we were all in tears – my mother, brother and sister – clinging on to each other and to me by the departure gates and crying: 'We don't want you to go.' And I was crying right back at them. 'I don't want to go either – but it's too late now.' What a sight we must have been!

But it was too late. We had enough money to afford it. And off I went for a year, during which I had the time of my life! Not too much work, but a whirl of parties and socializing in the heady atmosphere of Switzerland. My new friends were the rich kids who ostensibly were there to study and in fact were there to have fun and spend their parents' money.

In the end I only stayed for nine months. But in that time I had acquired my first boyfriend. Kevan was a languages graduate from Cambridge who was 'between years', taking his second year off for practical experience abroad before going back to finish his course. I became part of that practical experience – and was lucky to find a warm, tender and sensual lover as my first real boyfriend.

We spent a lot of evenings in a pub called Oliver's in the old cobbled part of the town opposite the famous Chocolate House where the calorie count is measured in thousands. It was known as the 'English pub' because of all the British students who frequented it.

It was brilliant to meet Kevan. We got talking in the pub, and everything just happened from there. We found we had a lot in common, and always had so much to talk about. We just swung into an easy, uncomplicated relationship, and I couldn't have wished for anything better.

It took me two weeks before I went to bed with Kevan. He had a room of his own on the fringe of town along the river. One night we went to a party, and then back to his place afterwards. That was where I lost my virginity – willingly and happily. And as I did so I was thinking: 'This is the first time in my life I have ever known what passion means ... and it's wonderful!' It was two days before my nineteenth birthday, and what a lovely surprise present it was.

I've learned since that it's really quite exceptional. You don't find passion with everybody, even if you want to. Above all, you can't force it. I have had eleven lovers in my life, with varying degrees of passion both in and out of bed, but I consider myself a very loyal person. I give myself entirely to one man – but I give all of myself. I went out with Kevan for three years. And in my marriage, which would last seven years, I was never unfaithful, not once.

I went to America for four months to see the country before coming home to England – where I had applied for and won a place in Cambridge Medical School, close to the University, with no problem at all, to study the subject of my choice: radiography. They told me: 'It's because of your grades. You're a *very* bright girl. We would have taken you whatever subject you wanted to study.' The fact that Kevan would be back there to finish his own course was another good reason to choose Cambridge for the next three years.

I took to university life like a duck to water – in this case the placid waters of the beautiful River Cam, which winds through this university town like a gunmetal-grey ribbon. I was so lucky to have gone to Cambridge. My three years there were among the most formative of my life; they introduced me to creative, exciting people – and I dived headlong into the deep end of university life.

In my three years there I joined just about everything that was going – from the arts groups to the Port Society, where people sit around long tables quaffing port and changing the world. Kevan had come back from Switzerland and was in Jesus College, while I was in the Medical College attached to Addenbrooke's Hospital on the edge of the city.

The Port Society was one of *the* most cherished institutions – highly unofficial, but a must for any fresh-faced undergraduate anxious to make his mark and be accepted among his peers. It was also one of the hallowed male bastions of the University.

One good reason for this was that the entry ritual was somewhat daunting, and not many women had attempted it. If any. To get in, you had to drink half a pint of port in five seconds!

In my naivety I queried: 'Aren't there any women members?'

Kevan went quite pale. 'Absolutely not,' he said.

'Why not?'

'Because women can't do it, that's why not,' he said quite curtly.

'Wait a minute,' I said sweetly, looking as if butter, let alone port, wouldn't melt on my palate. 'Do you mean to say that if I can swallow half a pint of port in five seconds I'll be allowed in?'

'Dream on,' was his reply.

I called on Debbie, one of my girlfriends, for moral support. 'You've got to try it too,' I urged her.

The next meeting of the Port Society took place in the bar in the inner courtyard of Jesus College. Word had got around that two *girls* were going to attempt the unattainable: to muscle in on this stronghold of macho supremacy. The place was packed to the rafters, and the atmosphere was like one of those old noisy taverns you see in films about highwaymen or brigands. There were even two or three lecturers watching discreetly from the side – everyone knew about the Society, and the authorities turned a blind eye to its activities.

Two half-pint tankards were filled to the brim. We were both ordered to stand on a table. Someone handed me up my tankard. My girlfriend was panicking. 'How did you get me into this? I hate you! I'll hate you for the rest of my life ...'

I said: 'You can do it. I know you can. We've got to show this lot!'

The President, a young grandee named Donald, took out a stop-watch and consulted it. 'Five seconds, no spillage,' he announced loudly. 'Are you ready?'

We nodded. 'Then on your marks ... get set ... *go*!'

And I did it! I don't know how, but I took a huge breath, shut my eyes, and just poured it in! Everyone just gasped – and then broke out into a great volume of cheering which swamped me like a tidal wave.

Poor Debbie couldn't manage it. Port is very heavy and sweet, and to get half a pint down was just too much for her. But I was reluctantly accepted into the ranks as the first girl ever to sit at the long tables with the Port Society and be part of that very special body. In the months to come I learned that they certainly talked a lot, but whether they ever solved any of the world's problems remains highly questionable.

The upshot to that night was an unexpected confrontation with the Law, in the shape of an elderly policeman on the beat who saw me weaving unsteadily on my bicycle along the country lane that led to the medical college. I couldn't face any more port that night, but what I had downed was more than enough. In short, I was so smashed I was out of this world!

He grabbed the handlebars, and said sternly: 'Young lady, do you realize I can report you for being drunk in charge of a bicycle!'

I put my arms around his neck, and breathed heavily into his face. 'But, sweetie,' I squealed joyously, 'do you realize I have just joined the Port Society? Isn't it *wonderful*?'

He said: 'Look, I'll let you off this time. Just wheel your bike home, and don't try and get on it again tonight. All right?'

Next morning – ouch! It took me a day to get over the hangover.

The Port Society proved a lively place. One other gauntlet I saw flung down was the raw-egg-in-port challenge. 'It's a great pick-me-up in the morning for a hangover,' Angus, a law undergraduate with an accent that would baffle any jury, proclaimed on a winter's evening when we were lounging around our corner table in the long bar.

'What is?' someone inquired.

'The yoke of an egg in a glass of port. But the trick is – you've got to swallow it in one gulp, without breaking the yolk. It slips down as easy as quicksilver, I promise you. And within ten minutes, you feel better – as long as you keep it down!'

'It sounds awful,' I said. But the others were intrigued. Someone was despatched to the corner grocer's across the road and came back with a dozen eggs. Four of them agreed to try it. I abstained. I actually didn't like port all that much, though over three years at Cambridge I drank my share with the best of them.

Four eggs were broken, and the yolks were carefully poured into four glasses of port. 'Down in one!' ordered Angus crisply.

Gulp! Down they all went, into four eager gullets. There was a pause. Then: 'Umm ...' said one of them, his face already slightly flushed. 'Not bad. Let's try another ...'

And that's when the contest began. Cries of 'More port!' arose. Trays of glasses arrived. After three rounds the eggs ran out, and I was sent out for more supplies. I bought two dozen, just in case – and after the next dozen had gone down the hatch, so to speak, only two members were left who could face any more. Both of them were purple-faced and spluttering, and Angus's accent was so thick you could have stirred it. But he struggled on – and managed to swallow an eighth egg to be the outright winner.

How he kept them down, I'll never know. From that moment he was known as 'Eight Egg Angus', and treated with the respect he deserved. But I never saw him repeat that particular little ritual.

The kind of people I mingled with both at Cambridge and later in London were the self-styled 'intelligensia' – thinking, creative people. I never could stand air-heads! I would have to say I was on the lower end of being intellectual, so naturally those rather superior students attracted me like a magnet.

But it didn't stop me getting up to all sorts of pranks – I have a wicked sense of humour, and had plenty of opportunity to indulge it amid the hallowed walls and careering bicycles which between them are my abiding image of Cambridge.

We were silly, but never stupid. A little juvenile? Probably. We never threw bricks through windows or let tyres down – but we girls in the medical school did have a lot of fun at the expense of the boys. Now it can be told! I was the one who pinched their clothes when we all went skinny-dipping in the River Cam. Sorry, Bob! Sorry, Nick! It was me. Usually around the time of the May Ball, when everyone was letting their hair down and going slightly mad!

On a warm summer's evening we would be splashing around in the water in the nude. I would float gently and unobtrusively away from the others – and when no one was looking sneak out onto the bank and grab a pile of clothes from the grass. And the one next to it.

Off I would scamper into the bushes to hide them behind the rhododendrons or up a convenient tree. Then I would slip back to watch in mock horror when my fellow-dippers climbed out of the water – and started shouting for their clothes.

In my last year I hid them so well the poor lads had to walk back through the town with only a towel to hide their blushes! I pushed a note – unsigned – under their doors to say where the clothes were, and finally came clean a few days later when it was safe to admit it. By then they could see the funny side of it. Just about.

Another popular prank was to invite all the boys you didn't like to dinner in your rooms. 'The girls will do the cooking, just bring a bottle. And by the way, it's black tie. Goes well with the candlelight,' we would say coyly to all the known creeps who had been pestering us for most of the term. We would stay away, while half a dozen sweaty-handed great lovers turned up and milled around for an hour before they tumbled to it. Next day we pleaded wide-eyed innocence. 'No, *next* month ...' and, by next month, sorry, fellers, we had other dates.

But I would never knowingly hurt someone emotionally. Even when I was young, at the age when girls can be so cruel, I always tried to let a guy down lightly if he was genuine.

College days were as happy as my schooldays. I qualified without too many headaches – the work was fascinating, and deep down I felt I was doing something useful, if not earth-shattering, to help my fellow human beings. But all too soon the three years were up, and I had to face the big wide world and think about earning a living.

I would miss Cambridge. I would miss the camaraderie, the friendships that I hoped would endure for ever and never did, the laughter – oh, yes, above all, the laughs we had in college.

Medical students are notorious for practical jokes, and the mob I was in with were no exception. The funniest prank I was ever involved in had to be the time that John, one of our would-be doctors, was about to get married – to a radiology student named Christine.

On his stag night, actually the day before the big event, a group of friends took John out on the town and got him hopelessly drunk. We girls were out on a hen night with Christine. The boys carried John into Casualty and plastered both his legs, with a steel bar between them to keep them apart. Then they took him to the station, and put him on a fast train – to Glasgow! John woke up encased in plaster, wondering how he got there – and unable to move!

The poor chap persuaded a porter to wheel him on a luggage trolley to the first train back to Cambridge – he arrived at four in the morning, took a taxi to the hospital, and was cut free on a return trip to Casualty. And he managed to make the wedding.

Yes, I would miss Cambridge ...

But London proved to be just as lively. As a qualified radiographer, I was taken on in the Radiology Department of St Thomas's Hospital, that huge monolith on the South Bank of the Thames directly opposite the Houses of Parliament. The X-ray laboratories were on the first floor of the Lambeth Wing overlooking the river. In those heady, carefree days of the late seventies, working in one of the country's great hospitals, life opened out again for me.

I moved into digs in Swiss Cottage in north London with a girlfriend from Oxford University, another medical graduate, named Fran, and entered into the party-round with zest. We became part of the Chelsea Set – the King's Road was a hub of the social whirl, and a constant hive of activity. London was the place to be, and lots of my friends from the medical college had followed me to the capital. There was always somewhere to go, someone having a party, and never a dull moment for a bright young thing with no ties who was just out for fun.

It was all very casual. I went around in jeans and leathers and t-shirts, drank St Clements – orange juice and bitter lemon – and behaved like any other girl of my age, just twenty-one, having a good time. We would all gather at a pub in the King's Road we dubbed the 'Holy Fook'. Word of a good party would spread – and off we'd go.

The parties were lively and noisy, but for me never more than that. A lot of canoodling went on in dark corners or in empty rooms, and for the odd diversion we would hang people out of windows by their legs. But it was all pretty innocent, and we never let go of our victim – or lost a guest on the pavement below.

One silly practical joke that was a favourite of its day was 'doing the light bulb'. It was horrendously simple: when no one was looking, one of the young bloods would creep into an empty room, make sure the light was off, unscrew the bulb in the ceiling rose, insert a suitably sized coin, and screw the bulb back in. Then he would mingle with the rest of us.

When the next unsuspecting person walked into that room and flicked the switch – *poof!* All the lights in the building fused!

Very funny – unless you happened to be the host stuck in the dark yelling for candles.

Alcohol flowed in plenty, though I never drank that much. And without being prim about it – perish the thought! – I am quite proud that there were never drugs at any of my parties, even if the booze did flow in rivers. Fran and I acquired a reputation among the medical set for holding the best parties in town – even if they were more *Carry On, Doctor* than anything else.

We were tipsy and loud, yes. But I was never loose, or into drugs – not even cannabis, which seemed to be the taste of the times. For that, I can thank my mother. 'Value your body, don't abuse it,' she had hectored me on more than one occasion. 'Remember, it's the house you live in. It's all you've got.'

As for my moral outlook – whatever was to come later, more than once I had some drunken young doctor pawing at me in the kitchen before slurring: 'God, you're so straight-laced it's sickening!' and lurching back to the party in frustration.

The sort of circle I was spinning in had loads of raucous fun to keep it whirling. Many was the time I would find bodies draped over armchairs in the cold light of day – which was when the black coffee came out.

I must say I never saw myself as straight-laced, but neither was I promiscuous. I just didn't want to sleep around.

Then, or ever.

CHAPTER THREE

Business Affairs

The tall, dark-haired young man in the lemon-yellow leather jacket and track suit glanced at me, and gave me a half-smile as we passed in the street. I was on my way to buy a long mirror I had spotted in the Chelsea branch of Habitat, one that would be just right for my hallway. As I stepped into the shop, I couldn't help glancing back at him – and our eyes locked. He had stopped still on the pavement, and was staring after me.

I escaped into the shop, only to find that as I wandered around the store Mr Leather Jacket was trailing casually in my wake. Every time I looked directly at him he appeared to be deeply interested in some item of furniture. But he made no attempt to hide – and that yellow jacket stood out like a beacon.

Finally I heard someone clear his throat just behind me. 'Er – would you have coffee with me? And cakes?'

My mother had taught me not to speak to strange men, and definitely not to accept offers of coffee and cakes. This time he met my gaze with a quirky, if slightly nervous, grin.

'I'd like that,' I heard myself saying. 'Thank you.'

His name was Jim Player, and he was five years older than me. He did most of the talking during the next two hours, and by the end of it I knew he was a record producer who sang and wrote songs too, that he also owned an employment agency, and that I was in love with him.

I was twenty-one, and I was romantic and impetuous.

But it seemed to me that something special had happened in my life, and that I mustn't let it go. After two hours and enough coffee to keep us awake for a week, he invited me to walk with him to his car and listen to a soul record he had just made. We sat together in the car, and when I told him that his voice was somewhere between Michael Jackson and Stevie Wonder his reply was a rather stern 'It's my own voice, not someone's sound-alike!' But it was.

We were married a year later.

By then, in an amazingly short space of time, I had become a partner in my future husband's employment agency, and found myself rubbing shoulders with some of the most powerful businessmen in the City of London. The firm was a chauffeur and messenger agency, and had established itself in an unusual line: supplying chauffeurs to banks and business houses. Jim had cornered a lucrative market and, although it was early days when we met, the business was expanding by the week.

A staff of nine worked out of three rooms in ground-floor offices off Finsbury Circus. Jim was living in a small penthouse apartment in the Barbican, and had a music studio in West London where he went every day. 'I'll teach you everything I know about the chauffeur business, and then I'll leave it to you to run the show,' he declared, showing implicit faith in me from the outset; adding, somewhat less romantically, 'You start by making the tea!'

And I spent the first week doing just that – as well as getting to know what the agency was all about.

I caught on very quickly. I like to think I'm a bright spark, and organizing has always been one of my strongest points. Inside three months I was taking care of the day-to-day workings of the business, attending meetings in the City, drumming up accounts by going to the right receptions and making new contacts. It was fascinating, a challenge, and I loved every heady minute of it.

We had two books in the office: one for our regulars, experienced chauffeurs we could call on any time; the other for temporary drivers, men who perhaps had been made redundant from their last job and only wanted work until they could get something full-time elsewhere. Would-be chauffeurs would be given an intensive vetting: we asked them to complete a questionnaire and demanded two references, plus a clean licence and five years' professional experience behind the wheel.

Jim had decided to specialize rather than spread the work-load too thinly. The chairman's secretary would call up because their own chauffeur was on holiday or off sick, the bank would provide the car, and we would provide the driver. 'If you are being hired to drive someone's £40,000 Bentley, you can't be too careful,' Jim cautioned me, as he showed me the questionnaires. 'Remember that when you're interviewing them.'

All our chauffeurs wore smart grey suits and peaked caps, and our reputation for excellence soon spread over the Square Mile. At our peak we had numerous banks on our books, mainly in the City and the West End, and we could call on 5000 full-time chauffeurs, with a back-up of 150 'temps'.

It sounds extraordinary. But some banks had a whole fleet of limousines, and the chauffeurs to go with them – and a pecking order with a head chauffeur in charge. One corporation I recruited onto our books had no fewer than fifty drivers.

We also attracted celebrity status: our clients ranged

from Barbara Cartland and actresses like Jenny Seagrove to the chairman of MacDonald's. In my second year 'running the show', the thoughtful Barbara Cartland kindly sent over a huge box of vitamins for Jim, while my in-tray was constantly filled with vouchers for hamburgers!

At our height, the business was turning over two million pounds a year. Jim bought 'Gablecot', an elegant five-bedroom mock-Tudor mansion in Ham, a horse-ride from Richmond Park, complete with stone fireplace, an indoor swimming-pool, sauna, and a lovely garden. The house cost £450,000, and he spent a further £200,000 turning it into a veritable palace. At the top of the property boom in 1989 it was valued at £1.2 million.

We were married on 4 September 1982 in St Michael's Church, Highgate Village, the steeple of which is the highest point in London. I wore a dress of ivory silk taffeta which I designed myself, with puffed sleeves, a long train, and pearls sewn into every trimming. It was a picture-book wedding, and the only sadness for me was the absence of my father. He had last been heard of in Cornwall, with yet another wife, and I had lost touch with him.

Jim took me to America for our honeymoon – a week in Miami, then on to California to plough through the obligatory tourist sights of Disneyland and Universal City, and a final magic week in New York.

What a wonderful lifestyle we had! The agency was rich and running, and so were we. To sharpen my business acumen I enrolled for various courses such as Dale Carnegie ('Training Leaders'), the Landmark Education ('A Breakthrough in What Is Possible for People'), and

Werner Erhard's self-awareness EST ('Erhard Seminars Training'). Whether the New Age gurus did me any practical good is open to debate, but I found the management and leadership seminars stimulating enough to feel that I hadn't wasted my time.

Jim indulged himself in the luxury of a boat – a thirty-foot cabin cruiser called *Players Retreat* – which we moored at the bottom of the garden. 'Just a toy,' he would say casually, though his eyes lit up like a schoolboy's whenever we cast off for a spin in her. As for me, I had my own hobby – flying helicopters! I trained for it, and in 1989, after forty-two flying hours, I proudly got my licence.

Meantime our house became my personal palace, and I was proud to show it off to friends with dinner parties and social gatherings. Jim and I would go riding in Richmond Park. And, on my twenty-ninth birthday, Jim produced his trump card in surprises.

I woke up to find him standing by the bed with a bottle of champagne, fresh orange juice, and two glasses. 'I think it's time you had a business card,' he said. 'Take a look out of the window.'

I scrambled out of bed and went to the window – and could not restrain a yell of delight. There in the drive stood a Rolls-Royce, a gleaming black Silver Spur – with the final touch, a huge blue ribbon tied around it in a giant bow.

'Yours,' said Jim. 'Happy birthday!'

'Oh, Jim ...' I began. My knees actually felt weak with shock.

'You,' I said, kissing him, 'are a wicked man. And I love you so much.'

I did, too, and he knew it. I have always been a loyal person, and throughout our marriage I never looked at another man. I was proud of that, proud of the fact that if I committed myself to someone I would give that relationship everything that was in me to give. I would always be dressed nicely for Jim when he came back from the studio at the end of the day, and would often have a little surprise present to give him over dinner.

So where did it all go wrong?

The small cracks were there from the beginning, if only I had had eyes to see them. He was incredibly possessive, looking on me as his property, and was the first to admit it. I belonged to him, and only to him. Sometimes, when I stayed at home, he would phone me as often as ten times during the day to make sure I was there. I know I bring out the protective instinct in men – or so I've been told – but this was getting beyond a joke.

Jim looked on me as his 'little doll'. I could have lived with that, even if it did become stifling towards the end. But slowly, as the success of our business increased, so did the pressure. We both started to work longer and longer hours. We both put on weight, a stone in my case, mainly around the hips but also under my chin – the usual places. I was therefore able to commiserate with the Duchess of York when she later confided how desperately worried she was about her own weight problems, and her fury at being dubbed 'the Duchess of Pork'.

My husband put on two stone. We both began to drink. I realized that I was in a Catch 22 situation: stress causes many people to put on weight; you don't feel sexy any more, and you take refuge in more food or drink to compensate; sex goes out of the window; and that creates more stress in the marriage on this doleful, unending roundabout.

I also wanted children. Very badly. We tried for the first five years, but without success. I always wanted four, ideally two sets of twins – 'a twin set', I would joke, and Jim would respond with an exaggerated shudder. But he would have loved that, too. We even chose names for them: Pryce and Blake if they were boys, River and Storme for girls. It was actually predicted by three different clairvoyants over the space of twelve years that I would have two sets of twins, and the first would be boys ... but I'm still waiting, and praying.

Almost without realizing it we became more distant toward one another, as if suffering from a creeping emotional cancer. Days would go by, and we hardly spoke. Then came the sleeping-tablets – sleep is a great way to avoid the truth of what is going on in your life. Jim started staying nights at his studio, leaving me alone in my elegant, empty, five-bedroom ivory tower.

One terrible night, the fragile shell finally cracked. My mother had come to stay for the weekend, and the three of us went to a local Japanese restaurant in Richmond for dinner. Jim and I drank too much sake – it's the kind of drink that slides up on you when you're not looking – and shortly after we got home we became involved in the most ferocious argument in the hall. I had been getting ready for bed, and was in my dressing-gown – thankfully Mummy had gone upstairs to her own bedroom.

What that particular row was about I will never remember. But suddenly Jim was ripping the slim silver chain from my neck, and hurling it to the floor – and I was doing the same to him. Our lockets were strewn in pathetic bundles under our feet, before I turned and stumbled for the kitchen, grabbed a sharp steak knife from the dresser, and ran out into the night.

Jim had disappeared into the living-room. The first he knew of the drama was the sound of my Jeep roaring down the drive and out through the gates. I was at the wheel, tears streaming down my face, heading blindly for the City. As I drove I started sawing away at my wrists with the knife. I felt the flesh tear, and warm blood flow over my hands, but I drove on. Sometimes the blood stopped – and I would pull up and press the blade in until the veins were opened again.

I found myself outside the Barbican, where my brother Neil was living in the penthouse flat that had belonged to Jim before he moved. Upstairs, I rang his bell, hammered on the door – but there was no reply. I was dimly aware of a pool of blood spreading around my feet, before I staggered back into the lift and out into the street.

It was a strange night, and getting stranger. Automatically I drove to St Thomas's Hospital, parked outside the familiar Casualty entrance of the building I had known so well eight years earlier, and switched off the ignition. I sat numbly behind the wheel as Big Ben chimed the single stroke of 1 a.m., the sound carrying clearly across the river. My dressing-gown was soaked in dark blood, my hands were sticky, and my feet felt slippery by the pedals.

It was then that I heard the voice. It came from both outside and within me, deep and gentle, with a calm, almost hypnotic quality that transfixed me in my seat. Quite clearly, the voice said: 'You don't want to do this. I have a lot of things for you to do. We are not ready to have you – you're not ready to go yet. Calm down, turn the engine back on, and I'm going to get you home!'

I listened, and I obeyed. I drove from Westminster to Richmond, more than five miles, and all the way back someone was sitting beside me, talking me home through the night. We passed a number of police cars, but no one tried to stop the blood-stained woman behind the windscreen.

To this day I don't think it was me driving that Jeep. I was at the wheel, but someone else was in charge.

I know I'm in danger of being ridiculed, but that was the way it was. When I told Sarah Ferguson about it months later she listened open-mouthed, because she believes in these things too. 'I really believe I was touched by God that night,' I told her.

'I think so too,' she responded.

And when I finally walked through my front door, I knew with an overwhelming certainty that this night marked the end of my marriage. It would take me another year to walk out, but this was the moment it happened.

Jim was waiting for me in the hall, his face registering shock at the apparition stumbling in through the porch. All I wanted was for him to gather me into his arms and say: 'It'll be all right.' Instead, he uttered just three words: 'Oh my God!'

And he walked out into the night and got into his own car and drove away from me.

It was my mother who ran downstairs to help me. She grabbed hold of me to stop me fainting, took me into the kitchen, put my dressing-gown into the washing machine, mopped the blood off the floor of the Jeep, and managed to contact my brother to tell him to clean up the mess outside his front door before anyone saw it and started asking questions.

After that, things went from bad to worse. In a kind of eerie parallel, our business sank relentlessly with our marriage. As our personal troubles deepened, so did our debts. The cash flow seized up, our credit cards were close to the limit, and our huge mortgage still had to be paid every month. Jim sold our boat, then his car. My Rolls-Royce was my own, and I put it up for sale, but values had dropped so drastically that I took it off the market. In October 1989 the company went into liquidation – and the final humiliation came a year later when our lovely Gablecot was ordered to be repossessed.

In short, we lost everything.

I was a young woman with a Rolls-Royce to my name and precious little else! – though at least I had a roof over my head while I tried to stem the downward roller-coaster of my life.

My mother was brilliant. To end that dreadful year she took me to Scotland for Hogmanay to try to put the bad times behind me, and to drink in a New Year of hope. Unfortunately I was so low that drink is just what I did – I locked myself in my room at our Ballater country hotel with two bottles of red wine for company and refused to come out!

Next morning, with my head throbbing with a deserved hangover, Mummy sat me down and gave me a good old-fashioned talking-to.

'You've got debts of over £42,000, right?' I nodded. 'Well, the only way you're going to get out of it is to pick yourself up, dust yourself down – and start all over again!' She gave me the brightest smile she could muster. 'What I'm trying to tell you is that you've got to open up the agency again.'

Something in me came to life. It was as if I had been

in a maudlin stupor of self-pity for too long, and the words struck a forgotten chord. I was galvanized into action. Back in London, I started phoning people: the Corporation of London, the Department of Employment, HM Customs and Excise. Inside a week I had my old office premises back, had been granted a licence, had the printer's quotes for stationery, and had obtained the PAYE and VAT numbers I needed. The message I constantly drummed into myself, every morning in the mirror, was: 'I'm going for it!'

In the five weeks it took to set up the new company I was furniture-remover, interviewer, secretary, director – oh, and tea-maker. Very important, that. I was a one-woman operation, and I started up a whole new employment agency on my own, strictly 'temps' only. Anybody who wanted a more permanent job I would pass on to Jim, who was doing his best to start up his own agency, too. Despite the trauma of our split, we remained good friends.

In that frenetic period, as winter gave way to spring, I learned the meaning of the word 'workaholic'. I didn't go out. I didn't date anybody. I had no social life. I just worked. I grew to hate weekends, because the office was closed. I was up at 6 a.m. every day, and in the office by 7.30. Every night I would come home, make a sandwich, eat it in front of the TV with my two cats beside me on the sofa – then fall into an exhausted sleep.

And after three months I made my first tiny profit. When I saw the figures, I whooped out loud. It was modest – but now at least I could start paying off my debts, and pick up the threads of my life again.

It was that May that I saw the television programme that was to change everything. I was idly running through the channels during yet another evening alone at home, when I saw some ponies galloping around a field, their helmeted riders flailing away with mallets at an elusive white ball, and a lot of noisy whooping and hollering going on – mainly from those in the saddle.

Polo. I thought to myself: This looks interesting! I like horses. I need to come out of my self-imposed purdah and socialize once again. On the spur of the moment I picked up the phone and found the number of the Epsom Polo Club.

'I'd like to learn to play polo,' I said. 'Is there someone there who can teach me?'

CHAPTER FOUR

Saddling Up

'It's like golf,' said Bob, my instructor. He was tall and young and extremely good-looking. 'The same kind of swing, if you follow me.'

From the heights of my saddle on top of a blessedly docile pony, I nodded uncertainly. In my gloved hand the mallet, with its enormous handle, felt unwieldy, and I found it desperately hard to swing it at all, let alone emulate Arnold Palmer.

The green fields of Epsom Downs stretched away on either side of the ground as I was shown the rudiments of a sport that up to then had meant no more to me than a few glossy photographs in society magazines. But as I became more involved, I grew to understand the subtleties of the game. And ultimately I would find myself addicted to the almost feudal atmosphere, as well as to the sheer blood-lust excitement of the oldest equestrian sport in the world.

For now, I had to learn to ride a sturdy, short-legged polo pony fast, avoid hitting it on the flanks or tripping it up with my stick – as the mallet is called – and generally point it accurately in the direction in which I wanted it to go.

'Most of it is confidence,' said Bob encouragingly. 'When you swing, you can do it forwards and backwards, but be careful not to let the stick go in front of your mount. You'll find you ache above the elbows, but that will soon pass.

'Above all, protect the horse. That means no crossing

in front of the other riders at certain angles – that will cost you penalties, as well as being dangerous.' He smiled. 'Don't worry. You'll find the ponies know what they're doing!'

I learned polo dress-code: always wear brown boots, never black, white breeches, and a shirt in your team's colours.

In those early days I thought: You've got to be a little mad to play this game, and some of the characters I met later would serve to confirm this view. But it only took me one game on the field of battle to proclaim: Lead me to the asylum! I played at Back, the weakest player's position – and I loved every fantastic minute of it.

Bruises? I lost count. I fell off so many times I probably spent more time getting back onto my poor, patient pony than I did in the saddle. It didn't matter. When you're learning to ride you worry about falling off – but when you learn to play polo, all you worry about is hitting that small white ball.

There is another unwritten rule of polo lore: beware of the groupies or 'polo bimbettes' who follow the macho cowboys around the circuits, just as they do in tennis, motor racing, and other great sporting arenas. In this most élitist of sports the lure is the irresistible combination of looks and money, coupled with the royal stamp of approval.

Wasn't it Debbie Aldridge I recalled hearing in one episode of the long-running *Archers* radio soap: 'I thought polo players were either Prince Charles or sexy Argentinians with flaring nostrils ...' She and her scriptwriters aren't the only ones who think that way.

This notion does little to help the women who are trying to take the sport seriously, and who have had to overcome a patronizing attitude in what has always

been considered a strictly male domain. As Clare
Tomlinson, the highly respected captain of the English
women's team, put it: 'We are tolerated – just about.'

But the Epsom club members were friendly, and welcoming. In the clubhouse before my first lesson Bob
had explained some of the mysteries of the sport – the
rules, for a start. Up to then, all I knew about a chukka
was that it sounded like a game you found on a seaside
pier on a wet Bank holiday.

Bob made it as simple as possible. 'The game consists
of six chukkas lasting seven minutes each, okay? There
are four players in each team. One Forward (at number
one), two Midfield (numbers two and three), and a Back
at number four.' I had already noted the numbers on the
jerseys of the riders cantering around outside.

'Now comes the complicated bit.' Bob grinned, then
went on: 'Every player is rated according to his or her
ability, and given a handicap which is reassessed twice
a year by their club committee. These range from minus
two for a beginner to a maximum of plus ten for the top
players.

'We call it "high-goal polo", which means that the
total handicap of a team in a tournament must be
between seventeen and twenty-two in Britain. In the
States it's seventeen to twenty-six, but don't ask me
why. Are you with me so far?'

'I think so,' I said.

'You'll learn. Now, you also get "medium" and "low
goal" games. And that's about it – for now.'

By July I had played in three mixed friendly matches. In the clubhouse, quickly making new friends, I
realized I had entered another world. Perhaps my
Rolls-Royce helped – the Silver Spur always drew
admiring glances, and people were openly curious

about its owner. What had Jim said? 'Your business card.' How right he was!

In July I found I had enough money to fly to California for a holiday, and I was able to stay with friends in Beverly Hills. One of my new-found polo chums gave me some names to look up, in particular a circuit player affectionately known as Big Boy.

Big Boy turned out to be a gentle giant of a man, with an open nature and an instant invitation to spend Sunday at the Santa Barbara Polo Club, an hour's drive up the coast from Los Angeles. He and his girlfriend Liz collected me in a large white Buick, the kind you see in old Warner Bros gangster movies, and off we roared north up Highway One.

The polo club was like a miniature village, heavily guarded behind steel fencing, and ultra-exclusive. The July sun was like a blast-furnace, hot and dry, and I could hear the shrieks as we swung in through the gates, saluted by a uniformed guard. Girlish squeals filled the air, backed up by the rumble of hooves.

Big Boy had reserved a table for Sunday brunch, a barbecue which began at 11 a.m. on the clubhouse patio overlooking the greensward of the pitches. From our table, as we sipped dry white wine from the Napa Valley, I could see the surge of combat on the field – and I sat up sharply. It was an all-female game! The screams were coming as much from the field as from the dozens of spectators on the outfield, many of whom seemed to be husbands or boyfriends.

'What do you think?' Liz had seen the expression on my face. What a difference from the tight old-boy-network atmosphere back home!

'I'd love to meet some of those ladies,' I said.

'No problem. They'll be up here after the game.'

We chatted about polo. Big Boy said, 'You know, Sylvester Stallone comes here to play – he's hooked on the game. He usually reserves a table for twelve people every Sunday, whether or not he shows up. We don't get too many Britishers out here. But there's one guy in particular who drops by. Major Ron Ferguson. Do you know him?'

'Of course.' I'd heard of Prince Charles's polo manager. 'That is, I know *of* him. I've never met him.'

'He sure knows his polo,' said Big Boy. 'And he's very pro-American, and a great organizer.'

I had heard the Major's name mentioned more than once at Epsom, usually cropping up in connection with international or charity events. I was getting more than a hint of the power which the Duchess of York's father wielded in the polo world, a world that respected him probably more than any single individual for his knowledge and authority in a game to which he had devoted most of his life.

But for now, all I wanted to do was talk to these strong, athletic, outgoing women who were out there in the field like equestrian Amazons, putting everything they'd got into their game with such total commitment.

My chance came after brunch. Big Boy knew them all, and was only too happy to introduce me to the players as they relaxed on the patio after a gruelling match.

'Hey,' said Jessie, one of the captains. 'You want a game sometime?'

'I'm not sure I'm good enough,' I protested.

'Nonsense,' she said, with a smile that was dazzling-white against her all-year-round tan. 'We have all standards here. And we'll treat you gently, don't you worry!'

There was gentle laughter at my expense, but I didn't mind, not one bit. I felt at home among these ladies of the turf.

Soon we were discussing the all-male domain of polo, and one of them asked: 'Are we Americans very different from you guys over in Europe?' By guys, I presumed she meant women.

'There's a world of difference in your attitude,' I said, gesturing around at the menfolk who were busy stocking up at the barbecue with their families. 'But I reckon our ladies could give you a run for your money if you came over.'

'Why don't you organize it?' asked Jessie suddenly.

There was a silence, while I digested the thought. My mind darted around the possibilities like quicksilver.

Jessie was saying: 'The men's teams get sponsored. That's all you need. You've got to cover the cost of the ponies, hotels, travel, and maybe some spending money, expenses, for the teams. If you got twelve teams together from different countries, all you would need would be twelve sponsors. And I tell you – we'll be there!'

Yes, I thought. Why not? Aloud I said: 'I think it's a great idea. Leave it to me. I'll be in touch.'

CHAPTER FIVE

Major Ron

Why polo?

Good question. Why, indeed? I must have asked myself that question a thousand times as the weeks dragged on and I found myself getting nowhere in my efforts to launch the first ever International Ladies Polo Tournament.

In her steamy bestseller *Polo*, Jilly Cooper described the blood, sweat, tears and guts on the equine field of battle – as well as the intrigue off it – in a way that brought a hitherto little-known pastime into living-rooms across the land.

I had learned to ride from the age of three, when I was the kind of little girl you find in one of those Thelwell cartoons, riding a pony around the country lanes of Berkshire and later Surrey. But polo? Like so many people I had always seen it merely as a sport for an élitist enclave of the idle rich; a snob sport where breeding, both in human and horsey terms, counted for everything.

It has been called the 'sport of prestige and pleasure', and is probably still incomprehensible to most average citizens. I had had visions of a privileged few Hooray Henries galloping around a pitch waving those long-handled mallets at one another before repairing to the nearest tent to quaff champagne by the bucketful.

It isn't quite like that.

I played regularly throughout that long hot summer while I searched for sponsors, and tried to drum up interest in a project that was starting to look just too ambitious to get off the ground. And I learned the hard way that polo is no game for wimps. Any idea that it was a happy hunting-ground for chinless wonders would be quickly dispelled with the first thud of that hard white ball smacking into a horse's rump – and often its rider's too.

I obtained a list of all the polo clubs in the country, and wrote, phoned or faxed every one of them. No real joy. I thumbed through the pages of glossy magazines and noted the big advertisers, who surely had money to spend. Then I wrote off to them, too: Dunhill, Cartier, Porsche, BMW, Davidoff, Jack Barclay, Estee Lauder Cosmetics, British Petroleum. Result: nothing. My one success was an enthusiastic response from the Save the Children Fund, a worthy charity I had chosen as potential beneficiaries of the big event.

But everywhere I went, in clubhouses and polo grounds, one name was constantly mentioned.

Major Ronald Ferguson.

I became intrigued, and did a spot of homework. The Major had joined the Guards Polo Club in 1955 as a young soldier, and had risen through the ranks to become deputy chairman, a post he held for eight years. His awesome presence and knowledge of the game helped put polo on the public map. The Major's royal connections – as Prince Charles's polo manager for fifteen years, and as a former Commander of the Sovereign's Escort – turned the arid turf of what to many was a rather tedious sport into rich weekend pickings for thousands of royal-spotters.

The result was a queue of eager sponsors waving their wallets in the Major's direction, and a massive increase in spectators.

I also liked the Major's own attitude to the sport, an all-consuming enthusiasm like that of a religious zealot: 'It's the nearest thing to a cavalry charge,' he was to say to me later. 'And where else can you do that today?'

Here, without a doubt, was the best man to help me.

I had already written to the Royal County of Berkshire Polo Club, where he was Director of Sponsorships, doing everything to create the right impression – just as my courses in business psychology had taught me. Most of it was common sense anyway, but as Dale Carnegie put it: 'Dealing with people in everyday business is a fine art ...'

The stationery, folders and letter-heading had cost a small fortune, but I reckoned would be worth every penny. 'Your clients literally read *you* from your notepaper' was one injunction – but, even so, the overall response from around the country had been poor.

Now I picked up the phone and dialled the number to request a personal appointment. To my surprise, it was arranged on the spot. A woman's voice at the other end, pleasant and encouraging, suggested Friday, 9 November, at noon. Would that be convenient?

Wow – would it!

The least I could do to get along with Major Ferguson was to know something about the sport for which I was asking his help. I discovered that polo was far older than I could possibly have imagined: it dates back to 600 BC, and beyond, with its origins traced to Persia. A poet named Firdausi described a game played around that time between the Persians and the Turkomans – and in Iran today you can see the remains of two stone goalposts on a ground three hundred yards long, the same size as a polo pitch, at the historic site of Ispahan.

The game spread to Turkey, and on to Afghanistan, where a form of it was played, not with a ball, but with a decapitated human head in a sack, which had to be dropped in a bull's-eye circle in the centre of the pitch. That would bring in the crowds today, I thought, when I stumbled on this historical gem. On to Tibet, Kashmir and Bengal – which is where it got its British Raj image several centuries later, when it became the chief sport of the tea planters and, of course, the military.

Records show that in 1859 the Silchar Polo Club was founded at Cachar by cavalry officers and planters. Word went out, and three years later the famous Calcutta Polo Club was formed. The 10th Royal Hussars are credited with bringing the game to Britain after the Indian Mutiny at Lucknow – it seems that when they first heard about it they experimented by hitting a ball with walking-sticks.

Today's rules were drawn up by a Captain John Watson, an officer in the 13th Hussars, after a pitch was laid out in 1873 at Hurlingham in south-west London – a club today better known for its pre-Wimbledon tennis tournament. Captain Watson can take credit for changing the game from a wild, almost barbaric pastime into a scientific sport.

So much for the history lesson. Browsing around in my local library, I unearthed the invaluable information that if you want to go out and buy a polo pony – you'll need around £7,000 in your pocket – you should look for one that has been raised in Argentina, Ireland, Australia, America or New Zealand. Don't ask me why. Maybe it has something to do with the grass.

A yellowing sheet of paper warned: 'Great care should be taken that it has no hackney blood in it, that it does not bend its knees too much when trotting, that it has not a sour-looking head or a sunken eye, and that it is not too long in the back.'

Armed with these priceless facts, I felt better equipped to face the Major, whose reputation as an authority on the subject had crossed the Atlantic and the whole of America to the polo fields of California.

Quite frankly, and understandably, I was as nervous as – well, as a thoroughbred.

I had the Rolls polished until I could see my reflection in the door as I slipped in behind the wheel and drove out through the gates of Gablecot. I had tried to look as business-like as possible, with my dark hair tied back and very little make-up; skirt just above the knee; high heels – but not too high. I had decided on a smart Chanel suit in navy blue over a white silk blouse, giving what I hoped was an impression of elegance and efficiency. All my papers were folded into a smart Louis Vuitton leather briefcase with a combination lock.

I only had a rough idea of the Club's location, so I allowed myself plenty of time – too much, in fact, as I found myself at the imposing gates twenty minutes early. I drove on past, and spent the next quarter of an hour meandering slowly around the picturesque country lanes of Ascot, enjoying the autumn scenery and trying to control the butterflies fluttering around in my stomach.

Finally it was zero hour. 'Here we go, girl!' I muttered to myself. Taking a deep breath, I turned the Rolls in through the gates, and slid her smoothly under the curved wrought-iron insignia announcing RCBCP (Royal County of Berkshire Polo Club) in a huge half-moon above me, and up the drive to the clubhouse.

The tyres crunched on gravel past neat white-painted

fences. I took in clipped lawns, a long, low red-brick building, which looked like converted stables, with blue-painted doors and a sloping Spanish-tiled roof cloaked with lichen, and skylights that let the watery autumn sun shine through. And on the white-timbered façade above the main door, a clock with its hand pointing to the hour of noon.

I was spot on time, and I smiled quietly to myself as I noticed faces at the windows watching the great black Rolls strut her stuff in the drive! This was the same drive that Prince Charles must have used regularly on his jaunts to the polo field; the place where royalty rubbed shoulders with some of the richest men on earth; the inner sanctum of the privileged few.

And I was going to do my damnedest to become part of it!

'Just what can we do for you?' Major Ronald Ferguson took my hand in a firm but gentle grip. Then he sat his big frame down behind the untidy desk and smiled at me encouragingly.

My first impression was of a tall, kindly man, benign and balding, with thick gingery eyebrows that rose at the ends above eyes that were a commanding dark blue. He was casual yet impeccable in a light-blue La Coste cardigan and slacks, with a white shirt and a tie that looked a little out of place. Much later he would tell me that when he saw my Rolls-Royce approaching the windows he nipped out to a changing-room and put on the tie!

'Well, Major Ferguson,' I began, 'as I explained, I want to organize the very first international ladies' polo tournament next year ...'

He raised a hand. 'Yes, I know. But aren't you a little

premature at this stage? I mean, next season is a long way off.'

'That's the whole point. Nobody has done this before. I want it to work, and the more time I can concentrate on it, the better chance we've got to make it a success. If anything, I wish I had more time.'

He sat back and considered me, fingertips tilted together under his chin. I had to admit that at first sight Major Ronald Ferguson's presence was formidable, quite overpoweringly so, and I could sense a forceful personality that was almost palpable. If I could win this man over, I instinctively felt, the other barriers would go down like skittles.

He was saying: 'Have you ever done anything like this before? You know, it's a jolly difficult thing to stage a tournament. It takes an awful lot of thought, experience and expertise.'

I unlocked my briefcase and handed the blue folder across the desk. 'These are more detailed plans.' I eyed him directly, and found myself speaking louder than I intended in that quiet room.

'Look, Major Ferguson. This is going to work whether I hold it here or at the Guards ground. You know why I'm here. I *know* I've never done anything like this before. But we all have to start learning somewhere – just like you did once. I believe in this. It's my dream!'

My fists were clenched. All the frustration I had felt at being turned down so many times – by people who, as far as I was concerned, just didn't have my vision – started to boil over.

The Major put on a pair of spectacles and glanced down at my dossier. Then he looked up again, and regarded me judiciously – and not without a hint of amusement. 'Well, young lady' – his voice had lost some of its formality – 'I can see you mean business!

'Let me tell you, I'm impressed, very impressed, with your presentation and enthusiasm.

'I'm not sure if you are aware of it, but I was actually responsible for starting the Men's International Tournament – the Cartier – twenty-two years ago.' He paused, letting the words sink in. I hadn't known it, but the words were music to my ears. Already, I knew what he was about to say.

I was right. 'I can see this as an opportunity to start again! Something novel, something new.' Major Ferguson's eyes were positively glowing, and I found myself smiling with him. It was like seeing someone come alive in front of you.

I had no idea then, but for some time Ronald's life and career had been floating like the *Marie Celeste*, a dead ship without a rudder or a charted course, drifting through dark seas with no real aim ahead. Later he would take my hand and tell me: 'It was as though I had woken from a long sleep when you came into my life that day. I was given a brand-new life and another chance.'

For now, he stood up, took my hand with renewed vigour, shook it hard and said: 'I can tell you right now – I'm all for this. I need to talk to my chairman, but I'm right behind you and will recommend to him that we stage your tournament here.'

The chairman was Bryan Morrison, a millionaire music publisher who had made his own waves in the business as entrepreneur to former Wham! singer George Michael, to Pink Floyd and the Bee Gees. Bryan had met the Major fifteen years previously when he joined the Guards Polo Club, and still laughs when he tells the story of that first meeting. 'Ronnie looked me up and down and said: "Well, you can play chukkas, but I don't want you around at the weekends when there might by Royals about!'"

It seemed that Bryan, a self-made millionaire, fell out with the stuffy confines of the Guards, who were strictly 'old money' and felt that your breeding always meant more than your bank balance. He quit the club to open his own – and, in passing, to open up the game to people who would never have been accepted by the 'old guard', pointing out: 'Why play under someone else's harsh rules if you can form your own?' A sentiment with which, when I heard it, I entirely agreed.

I started to stutter my thanks, but the Major waved them away. As he escorted me to my car and looked on approvingly as I got behind the wheel, he said: 'I will call you, Miss Player, as soon as I have news. Then we must arrange for you to meet the Chairman.'

The very next day he phoned my office. 'Yes,' the gruff tones came down the phone, and I could hear the excitement in them, 'Bryan Morrison is very interested. When can you come up and meet him?'

The private boardroom at the 'Royal Berkshire', as the club is known in polo circles, is a compact room overlooking the stables, with paintings of ponies and riders dotted around the walls. The showpiece is a gigantic mural along one whole wall depicting the Major, Bryan Morrison and Prince Charles sitting on their ponies with the Number One Ground as backdrop.

Bryan sat at one end of the boardroom table, wreathed in cigar smoke, surprisingly casual in jeans and t-shirt. Every time I saw him he seemed to have a permanent halo of smoke around his head. He was a careful, compact, clever cockney in his late forties, whose quiet manner disguised a shrewdness that had taken him to the top of the notoriously unstable music business, and kept him there ever since.

I sat beside him, facing the Major. 'I've heard a lot about you, Lesley,' Bryan began. He shuffled my notes on the table in front of him. 'You've certainly impressed Ronnie. I've organized many tournaments in my time, and I can tell you exactly how you should do this one.'

He leaned forward and tapped an inch of grey ash into an ashtray. 'Now listen carefully. I'm going to break the rules for you! We usually take a fee, and do the organizing ourselves.

'But for the first time I am prepared to let you organize this on your own, and hold it here. Our reputation hinges on your making this work, you understand?' I nodded dumbly. The implications were only just starting to sink in. 'This is a very off-beat idea, but I get the feeling you can do it, and that you'll make a success of it.

'The part we'll play is to tell you how we would run things, and be here if you need help.'

I mumbled my thanks, but Bryan was already bending his mind to the details. This was the breakthrough I'd been longing for – and I owed it to the man sitting opposite me. My eyes must have been shining when I looked at him, because the Major grinned back at my delight and gave a little nod in return.

'You've got teams coming in from all over the world,' Bryan said. 'There's a recession on. You'll never be able to sponsor the whole thing. I suggest you sponsor each team individually to the tune of, say, £8,000. Offer them a complete package, including hotel, transport, hospitality – the works.'

I could see his mind racing, and popped in brightly: 'You mean £2,000 a player? Is that enough?'

'You'll find out,' said Bryan. 'It's a start, anyway.'

The charity involvement would help bring in the teams, and I hoped they would contribute their own generosity when it came to fees. I mentioned the Save the Children Fund.

The Chairman's face brightened. 'If they want to come in on it, that's marvellous.' All three of us knew that Save the Children meant the seal of approval from royalty, and probably Princess Anne. Bryan thought for a moment, then said: 'We haven't had them here yet. I think it's a terrific idea. Why don't you let them have the final day, with all proceeds that day going to them?'

Across the table Major Ferguson's big domed head was nodding its approval. It sounded fine to me. Bryan said finally: 'All I do know is that you should have this tournament stand on its own two feet as a commercial venture without relying on a charity as an umbrella.

'If it works as it should, it could become an on-going event. As a businesswoman, and I can see you are, you must make a profit from it. If not in the first year, then definitely in the second.'

God, I thought, this man is brilliant! He had grasped the whole concept immediately, and gone on down the yellow brick road to a fantasy castle of infinite possibilities. No wonder he had been so successful.

'You know,' he was saying, 'polo is the great leveller. It always has been. When I joined the Guards as a player' – he cast a sidelong glance at the Major, who acknowledged it with a grin – 'it was a hobby. But it took over my life.

'Off the field you might refer to rank, but on the field it's all down to who's best in the saddle. I beat many of my commanding officers, and they would be the first to congratulate me afterwards.'

He had made his own club unashamedly geared for the wealthy, from whatever class they hailed. An entry fee of £15,000 separated the financial men from the boys. But, he insisted, they came from 'across the board', with a whole new breed of young men looking for the thrill of a modern-day cavalry charge. 'It's the thrill of the game that gets you. Whether or not you rub shoulders with royalty doesn't concern you any more.'

He stood up and gave me his quiet, confident grin. 'Good luck, Lesley!'

If there was ground under my feet when I left, I didn't feel it. I was walking on air, and I just could not stop smiling. Major Ferguson once again escorted me to the Rolls, and stood in the drive to give me a farewell wave as I drove off.

Next day the first basket of flowers arrived.

CHAPTER SIX

Saying It with Flowers

They came out of the blue: two dozen beautiful red roses set in a green sponge oasis inside a wicker basket, the whole wrapped in cellophane and tied round with pink ribbon. It was delivered to my office off Finsbury Circus by special messenger. My secretary Sam brought the basket into my office, and laid it on my desk with a smile.

'Looks like you've got an admirer,' she said.

There was a card attached. 'Very best wishes for the exciting new project. I'm sure it will work. Love, Ronald.'

Well, well. 'Love, Ronald'? I raised a mental eyebrow at such early familiarity, particularly coming from an apparent scion of old-world courtesy and formality. But I would soon learn a thing or two about Ronald – as it was now obvious I should call him.

I rang him at once. 'Thank you so much for the flowers – er, Ronald. They're absolutely beautiful.'

'I'm glad you like them,' he responded.

'It was a very sweet thought,' I said.

There was the slightest of pauses. Then Ronald said: 'I have to fly to America very soon for a polo tournament. Before I go, I wonder if you'd care to join me for lunch at Claridge's so that we can discuss your own project? Also – it will give us a chance to get to know each other better, since we're going to be working together so closely.'

'I'd love to,' I said. I thought: what a warm person, so

welcoming, charming ... and harmless. It seemed like a splendid idea. Aloud, I said: 'Claridge's, did you say?'

'Yes,' he said. 'They know me there. I have my regular table. Go to the front desk and tell them who you are. Shall we say Friday at one o'clock?'

My mind was on the workload ahead, getting the tournament off the starting-block and into the race, and I gave Major Ferguson little further thought until Friday. I had never had to drum up sponsorship for anything in my life before, and I was facing a blank sheet – with, I must admit, an equally blank stare.

First step: how many teams do I want? It had to be a truly international event, and that meant teams from all the obvious polo-playing countries and maybe some from the lesser-known ones.

I counted them off: England, America, Argentina, Australia. What about Kenya or South Africa? Ronald's office sent me a list of every polo club in the world, and I wrote off to every single one of them to ask if they would be interested in entering a team of women players. I even gave them the date: Tuesday 13 August–Sunday 18 August 1991.

To my surprise and delight the replies started to come back thick and fast. My deepest apprehension, that I would never be able to amass an international field and would be left with a half-baked entry list, proved groundless. The in-tray started filling with enthusiastic inquiries and actual entries.

My next step was to form a committee. Well, everyone does when they're organizing anything, don't they?

More fool me – as I would eventually find out! With a handful of hard workers, I could have run the whole thing myself. As it was, the poison started to flow as the committee grew ever larger and more unwieldy, though fortunately there were enough genuine workers – rather than shirkers – who really gave their time and energies in abundance to make it work.

In the end we assembled twelve teams: from England, Scotland, France, Italy, Spain, Kenya, Australia, Pakistan, Argentina and, from America, California, Boston and Denver. I called them my 'angels on horse-back', though in the heat of battle – as I had seen with my own eyes in the dust of Santa Barbara – they could be right she-devils when roused!

Meantime, I had a date to keep with the Duchess of York's father.

On that mid-November Friday I hailed a taxi in Finsbury Circus. 'Claridge's, please!' I said, and felt quite grand. I didn't have to add the words 'Brook Street'. Every taxi driver in London knows it. Or, if they don't, they haven't done 'the knowledge'.

I stared out of the window at the bustling lunch-hour streets as the taxi took me through London Wall, Holborn, and on through the West End into Mayfair, until we pulled up outside the swing-doors of Claridge's. A top-hatted doorman opened the cab door for me, and wished me good-day. Under the twin flags of the Union Jack and the Stars and Stripes I entered for the first time the portals of one of the world's legendary hotels, a monument to tradition and impeccable service. It was just the sort of place, I reflected as I turned left inside the lobby and headed for the front desk, that Major Ferguson, the Compleat Englishman, would sure-ly choose.

I gave my name to the elderly concierge at the desk, and he replied at once: 'Ah, yes, Miss Player. This way. Major Ferguson is here already.' He hadn't even consulted a list or looked at a piece of paper. 'In the Causerie.'

The Causerie in Claridge's is located by the majestic curving staircase leading into the lobby lounge, and is less formal than the main restaurant. A cosy dining-area, with an intimate atmosphere, it makes an ideal meeting-place for people with a lot to talk about in relaxing sur-roundings – *causerie* being French for 'chat'.

Ronald Ferguson was waiting for me in a corner alcove. He rose, a towering figure immaculate in a navy blazer and dark-grey flannels which had the kind of crease you could cut your finger on. His smile lit up his craggy features, as he gestured for me to join him. 'Come in, come in, my dear! Do please sit down.'

His 'usual table' was discreet, with a view of the room that took in most of the diners but somehow precluded them from staring back. I looked around. 'You know, Sarah and I always have this table when we lunch here. It's help yourself to start with, but they'll do anything you want. And we almost always have a specially pre-pared dish when we come here – scampi. Do you like scampi?'

'Mmmm!' I nodded. I love food, and scampi was high on my list of favourites. He seemed pleased to hear it, and beamed approvingly. But first we got up and helped ourselves from a large smorgasbord table which is the Causerie's main feature. Anything from smoked eel to various pâtés seemed to be on offer, and as I returned to our table with my plate I found myself thinking: 'My God, here I am sitting in Claridge's with the father of the Queen's daughter-in-law!'

We started talking. But first Ronald called for the wine list, and chose a wonderful Pouilly Fuissé, crisp and dry and perfect with what we were eating. I read much later that he was supposed to be teetotal. Well, he may have been once – but not with me.

If he had been, I wonder if our affair would ever had happened.

We raised the first glass to each other, to the Tournament, and to the future. 'Lesley,' the Major said, 'you are a very unusual little lady. I must admit you do mystify me somewhat.'

'Really?' I said, trying not to sound coy.

'Yes,' he went on. 'I'm sorry if I'm embarrassing you, but I feel as if I've known you for years ...'

And all of a sudden he was talking about polo, and I sat riveted as the Major embarked on his most cherished subject with a passion and knowledge I had seldom heard from any man in my life. It kept me glued to my chair, virtually unaware of what I was eating or drinking – however delicious – or of time passing.

'I can never understand why so many people think we're a bunch of millionaire namby-pambies standing around swigging champagne or trotting around a field chasing a ball.' A grin took away the sting of the words. 'It's very dangerous, very rough – but, my God, it gets the adrenalin going. I think it's the most exciting sport on the planet.

'I love it all. The horses, the galloping, the "cavalry charges", the sheer thunder and guts of it. When you're out there you can forget all your worries ...' He paused ever so briefly. 'Well, *almost* forget them.

'You know, I've been playing for thirty-five years. I stumbled on it by accident – I'd joined the Life Guards and was sent to the Canal Zone in 1954. One day the CO said: "Right, Ferguson, you're playing polo tomorrow!" I had always liked ball games, and this was one sport that had it all: horses and a ball!'

'When did you first learn to ride?' I inquired.

'My parents put me on a pony when I was six months old, strapped into a basket! How about you? I gather you do ride?'

'Yes, but nowhere in your league,' I laughed. 'I was three.' I told him about the country lanes of Berkshire and Sussex, and the gymkhanas I had been put into as a little girl.

The Major chuckled gruffly. 'God. I remember those. I had a horrid little Shetland pony called Flying Flash – he used to stop dead at every jump.'

That first lunch went by in a flying flash. Before I knew it the time was three o'clock, and we seemed hardly to have started. I looked at my watch in disbelief. 'I've got to go! I never realized the time ...'

'Have you?' said Ronald regretfully. He shook his craggy head. 'Shame! But perhaps we can do this again?'

'I would like that,' I told him. 'I'd like that very much.'

'It's been wonderful to have someone to talk to,' he said. 'I must tell Sarah all about you.'

'Oh,' I said, slightly taken aback. 'That would be nice. I'd like to meet her.'

'You will,' said the Major. 'I'll make sure of that. I think you two will get along famously.' He leaned forward confidentially. 'We have a very close relationship. We're on the phone to one another practically every day.

'She tells me everything that happens in that household – and I tell her everything that happens to me. She's a very strong personality, you know. Andrew leans on her.'

'Really?' I raised an eyebrow at this open and unexpected revelation on a first meeting.

'Yes,' said Ronald. 'He's scared stiff of losing her. I put

that down to insecurity. Sarah often seems more like a mother to him, telling him to do this and do that. Sometimes I don't know how he stands for it. But he asked for it when he married her – she's a very free spirit. I think that's what he found so fascinating about her.'

That conversation at Claridge's was my first hint of the incredible vein of incaution that runs through the Ferguson bloodstream like fool's gold. I was about to witness it turn the very foundations of the House of York into shifting sands that would lead to ruin and despair.

'Don't mind my asking,' I said. 'But why did she marry him?'

'Well,' the Major answered, 'she's either in love with Andrew or in love with the Royal Family – and I think it's the latter.'

He stood up to make way for me, and once again I was struck by his old-world gallantry, the kind that sadly belongs to a lost era.

He was flying off to America, but we agreed to meet again immediately on his return the following week. 'Same place,' said Ronald, indicating his corner table.

'Definitely,' I agreed. 'I love it here.'

As we waited on the pavement under the fluttering flags while the doorman found us taxis, the Major turned to me. 'Lesley, would you consider it an inconvenience if I were to call you from America? Just to chat about work – or anything, really?'

'Of course not. I'd love to hear from you.'

A smile that was almost relief lit up his face. 'That's splendid. It's just that – well, I get quite lonely out there, and it would be nice to know there's someone I can talk to.'

'Of course,' I said again. 'I'll look forward to it.'

Major Ferguson gave me a polite peck on the cheek, handed me into the back of the cab, and waved farewell. I looked through the rear window to watch his tall figure dwindle into the distance as the taxi headed into New Bond Street and back towards the City.

It was only as I settled in my seat to stare unseeingly out at the busy pavements that the thought came to me: Hasn't he got anyone else to talk to when he's lonely? What about his wife?

The next time we met, I found out.

CHAPTER SEVEN

Tea and Sympathy

'Same place, same time?' Over the following weeks I got used to Major Ronald Ferguson ending his phone calls with those words, and I always felt my heart lift when I heard them. As with so many affairs, it is the first light-hearted, carefree weeks that are the best, before words like 'responsibility' and, worse, 'possessiveness' creep in and muddy the waters.

Of course, neither of us saw it at first. I failed to recognize the danger signals. Ronald seemed oblivious of what was happening to us, or the consequences. And in the end, when disaster struck, he hardly seemed to care – riding his own one-man cavalry charge into the valley to come to grief on the guns of gossip and scandal.

But in those first luncheon meetings, as we began to know and respect each other, our relationship deepened subtly, inexorably and irrevocably – until, too late, I realized what we had done to one another.

It was always scampi for him, while I rang the changes on the menu. And we talked.

How we talked.

I found myself unbending to this rugged, aristocratic Englishman whose veneer disguised an essentially solitary man beset by his own personal problems, who simply needed to talk to a sympathetic listener.

'I've got a lot of things on my mind,' he said. 'I'm worried about Sarah – she just isn't as happy as she should be. We normally speak on the phone two or three times a day, and I can't wait to hear from her. We're so very close. We tell each other everything.'

'Everything ...?' I interrupted.

He nodded. 'But I haven't heard from her for days. What I notice about the younger Royals is that they do things and take the consequences afterwards. Sarah can be like that. She's very headstrong. And she's so special that I hate it when she's unhappy.'

Suddenly Ronald was talking about his marriage – and the one before. I had heard of the break-up when his first wife Susan caused a huge scandal in horsey circles in 1974 by running off with Argentina's top polo player, Hector Barrantes, leaving Ronald alone after eighteen years' marriage to bring up their two daughters, Sarah and Jane. No wonder father and daughter were so close, I thought. For what it was worth, Ronald generously mentioned that in those days Hector had a handicap of eight while his was five, which presumably meant Hector was the better player!

I had also read a story that Susan had become fed up with her husband's alleged philandering, and that the last straw was when he had a fling with a colonel's daughter.

But oddly, I got the feeling now that Ronald still had a tender spot for Susan One. His second wife is also called Sue – she is the daughter of a wealthy Norfolk farmer – although he refers to her as 'Mrs F the second'. She is an attractive blonde, fifteen years his junior, whom he married three years after the shattering elopement.

Even on the day of their divorce, he revealed to me, he phoned her and pleaded: 'Please don't do it.' But she went ahead. And it was Ronald who became the single parent, looking after his two feisty teenagers in Dummer Down Farm, in the Domesday village of Dummer, located a few miles off the M3 in Hampshire, in the beautiful old farmhouse which had been his family home for more than half a century. Sister Jane is the polo-playing daughter – she married and went to Australia, and now, as Jane Makim, is good enough to play in the Aussie team.

I stayed silent as the floodgates of Ronald's memory opened, and the secret hopes, frustrations and longings of this intensely private man poured out.

'I was very much in love with her,' Ronald said. 'But I think I married too young. I was very inexperienced, and didn't know how to treat a woman. Of course, I do love my other children enormously; in fact they're keeping my marriage together.' The youngsters he was talking about were Andrew, who was eleven, Alice, nine, and little Eliza, aged five, from his second marriage.

I was starting to get goosebumps. The man sitting next to me had travelled the world, moved in the rarest circles of power and privilege, rubbed shoulders with kings, queens and princes – and here he was confessing his innermost thoughts to me after less than a handful of meetings. The fact that I knew so little about him obviously helped: we were like that stranger you meet on a plane – except that the journey was destined to last for months.

How could he be so lonely? 'It isn't that my wife doesn't understand me,' he said with a wry smile. 'If anything, she probably understands me too much! But Mrs F the second doesn't like travelling with me when I go on these polo jaunts. She doesn't even like polo.' I had the impression his marriage had become as dry as the autumn leaves blowing in the wind through Berkeley Square outside. I was right: Ronald would confirm it during our pillow-talk when our relationship had grown beyond friendship into something deeper – and more dangerous.

'It's just that I've always found it hard to find people to talk to,' he said at one point. 'And even though we hardly know each other, I feel already that I'm very close to you ...'

A faint flush spread over his features, and I could see it was uncomfortable for him to be talking about his feelings like this. It wasn't quite the same as meeting a stranger on a plane or train, revealing your innermost secrets to them, knowing that you'll never meet again. Ronald and I were more than two ships passing in the night – we were on a collision course!

I said gently: 'Ronald, let me tell you some things about myself and my background. It hasn't been all roses for me either. Perhaps you'll understand me better. You will also know things about me that are private – and maybe then you'll feel better about sharing some of your own life with me.

'I'm not about to make judgements on somebody else, I promise you!'

Carefully I went through the history of my own marriage, spelling out the pressure-points where it had gone sour, not sparing myself any of the gory details. Except for my suicide attempt – or gesture of despair, if that's what it was – which, for some reason, I did not reveal. I told him about the closure of the company, the torment I had endured watching seven years of hard work and hope simply disappear as if they had never happened. I even mentioned the boyfriends I had known.

At the end I sat back and looked at Ronald with a kind of wonder: I had told him far more than I had ever intended, yet in an exhausted way I felt uplifted. I was drained of a burden I had been carrying around like the sack of sand the old tramp carts around in Samuel Beckett's play *Waiting for Godot* – all he had to do was let go. And that long afternoon I had let go.

Immediately the atmosphere at the table lightened. We had been intense enough for one day. Ronald called for more wine, and now his features softened as he recalled the wedding-day in that summer of 1986 when he gave his daughter Sarah into matrimony with Prince Andrew in a ceremony at Westminster Abbey which was televised across the globe.

'What a wonderful day that was,' he reminisced. 'I sat next to the Queen in an open coach along the Mall, and I remember she wore ice-blue, with a beautiful string of pearls. The sun was out. People were cheering. It was unforgettable.'

He talked about being Polo Manager to Prince Charles. 'He has been a good friend, and very support-ive,' said Ronald. I took it he was referring to polo in general. But at our next meeting the Major would elab-orate on the unpleasantness at the Guards Club follow-ing that messy little business at a certain massage parlour.

But now he was snorting: 'How dare people suggest the PoW isn't aggressive!' The initials PoW for the Prince of Wales would become our shorthand as the plans for the Tournament progressed, and we approached Charles to ask him to write a personal message on the souvenir programme. 'I'm always having to warn him to steady up when he's charging in like a bat out of hell. Don't let anyone doubt that man's courage!'

'I have been asked more than once if I would go easy on him if we were on a head-on collision course, and I always give the same answer: it's every man for himself, and the only person I'd be thinking about would be me!

'One of my riders pointed out that he didn't want to make a name for himself by killing the heir to the throne. But when you're out there at full pelt, that isn't usually the first thing that comes to mind!

'One time I saw him playing, and a rival shouted: "Take the man!" to a team-mate. Next thing Charles had been barged clean out of his saddle onto the grass.'

Remembering how the future monarch had broken his arm in a bad polo fall, I couldn't help asking: 'How often have you been hurt?'

'Too often!' retorted the Major, not without some pride. 'One paper even called me a walking miracle. They printed a picture of me with little arrows pointing to the fractures!' He jabbed a knobbly finger at various parts of his anatomy.

'My nose has been broken twice by the ball, likewise a fractured jaw. I lost my front teeth the same way, even wearing a grid-mask, and they're now screwed into my gums. Three cracked ribs. All my fingers have been broken at some time – and a few toes crushed by the brutes trampling on me!'

He was fifty-nine, he told me, but had no plans to dismount from the saddle and leave competitive playing. 'Even if I'm stiffening up a little and don't go bulldozing in like I used to, it can still be pretty hairy. The worst moment for me was when I broke my neck in a bad fall in 1970. I actually landed on my head! I was paralysed on my left side for two months, and they told me I'd never ride again. But I came through. They can't keep an old warhorse down!'

In that first month we met several times at Claridge's, finally varying between lunch and afternoon tea served in the lounge. We would find a quiet corner, and sink into armchairs as if we were in some London club – and still we talked.

Ronald told me he already looked upon me as his protegée. 'They've assigned me to you,' he said. 'And I'm delighted. When you came into my life it was like a breath of fresh air. I had been a bit low, what with one thing and another, but you've given me a new lease of life.'

The one thing turned out to have been the embarrassing exposé in a Sunday tabloid of Major Ferguson, father of the Queen's daughter-in-law, visiting a dubious West End massage parlour. The Wigmore Club in Marylebone, it appeared, was nothing more or less than a high-class brothel.

The other was that this lapse resulted in the Major being dehorsed from his £28,000-a-year post as deputy chairman of the Guards Polo Club, with all the attendant public humiliation that ensued.

Anecdotes of 'sexual frolics' with a redhead named Julia and a couple of 'bubbly blondes' called Lorraine and Kim titillated readers over their breakfast cornflakes, backed by grainy photos of Major Ron furtively leaving the club.

I remember reading about it at the time, and vaguely wondering what effect it would have on the Palace. A *Sun* cartoon by Franklin summed it up, showing the Queen in a Digger's outfit shortly before her Australian tour, with a pair of crocodiles salivating at her feet, ordering a footman: 'Tell Major Massage I'd like a chat with him!'

Some commentators surmised it was the end of Ronald's chances of a knighthood – though judging from the ennoblement of our politicians who have been caught *in flagrante delicto*, I could see no justice in that draconian suggestion. The Major was also in the running to be the Queen's Crown's Equerry, a post that would have made him responsible for the day-to-day running of the horses, carriages and limousines in the Royal Mews.

But the Wigmore Club would be a subject I would raise with Ronald in more intimate and suitable surroundings than the tea lounge of Claridge's.

He was still hopping mad at what he regarded as a far more heinous verdict on his private activities and a slur on his personal reputation: being stripped of his Guards Club title after the thirty-three years he had been a stalwart of Smith's Lawn, earning himself the nickname of 'Mr Polo'.

The official reason, after a lot of to-ing and fro-ing, had been his lack of business flair in handling the Club's annual £750,000 budget. But, Ronald insisted as he stirred two spoonfuls of sugar into his tea with more than customary vigour: 'I was stabbed in the back, Lesley, I really was. That was a year ago and I still haven't really got over it.'

At least he could see the funny side as he recalled a quote from a fellow member: 'If you eat with sharks, you must expect to get bitten!' We both laughed. And Bryan Morrison had come to his rescue to offer him the job at the Royal Berkshire. 'And that's brought us together, which is something to be thankful for,' he added.

Ronald Ferguson was a full twenty-five years older than me, and we were separated not only by the gulf of age, but also by our upbringing: he the traditionalist, me the Modern Miss. Yet I found I could talk to him as if he were an equal in so many things. Vulnerable as I was, those early weeks drew us together and made us open our hearts, each finding in the other comfort and solace for the bruising knocks that life had thrown at us.

The stiff-upper-lip mentality ingrained into so many of his class and background was there – but beneath the outer shell I found a sensitivity that was irresistible. The Major was as tough as old riding-boots on the outside – but he was a softie at heart.

Here was a man who could weep openly when Sarah valiantly stood by him at the leaving ceremony at the Guards Polo Club, presenting her father with an inscribed polo stick; a man who would shed further genuine tears when he was forced to break the news to loyal retainers at his seven-hundred-acre Dummer estate that he was having to lay a number of them off.

It had dawned on me early on that here was simply a lonely man, someone who seemed so natural and, yes, sweet. And he was becoming so protective that I already felt he was like the father I had never really known.

One afternoon in the tea lounge, with the early Christmas shoppers thronging the expensive shops of Bond Street a stone's throw away, Ronald leaned across in his armchair, took my hand in his, and said earnestly: 'Don't ever underestimate yourself, young lady. There is something special and different about you that is very rare.

'Many people say I'm not the most intelligent of men, and perhaps that's true. But I'm loyal and trusting, and I have been hurt so many times – perhaps because I'm naive in many ways.'

He paused, and took a deep breath. Then he said: 'I want you to know I care about you, and I only wish things could be different. If only I were twenty years younger and circumstances were different, then perhaps I could have what I wanted.'

There was a hunger in him and an intensity in his voice which disturbed me. His face suddenly looked almost haunted.

I didn't answer him, and we finished our tea in silence.

Two days later he got what he wanted.

CHAPTER EIGHT

The Galloping Major

The first time Major Ronald Ferguson and I made love was in the guest bedroom of my beautiful home close to Ham in Surrey. It was an imposing eight-bedroom mansion with a wonderful view of the river meandering past the lawn. But that late-November afternoon the view was the last thing Ronald and I thought about. We only had eyes for one another.

Gablecot, on Lower Ham Road, has been described as 'one of the finest character houses on the Thames', and it lived up to its description. It was Ronald's first sight of the house, and even for a man used to vast properties he was impressed.

He had been due to fly to America again to discuss sponsorship for an upcoming event, and I was pottering about the house when the phone rang around mid-morning.

Ronald said: 'Lesley, will you have tea with me this afternoon? The trip's off, and I'm feeling really fed up. I need some cheerful company.'

'Of course,' I said. 'I'm here all day. Come any time.'

The phone rang again after lunch. 'I'm on my way,' he said. There was a slight pause. 'Er – do you have any food in the house? I'm rather hungry ...'

I laughed out loud. 'Of course I've got food,' I chided him. 'No one goes hungry here!'

'What I really would like,' he said, 'is tomato soup. But it's got to be a tin of Heinz!'

'Any variety you want,' I said. 'It'll be waiting.'

I hurried into the kitchen and rummaged around in the larder. Sure enough, one tin of Heinz tomato soup was on the shelf. I heated up some rolls, and laid the table by the window in the kitchen with our lovely bone-china plates and best silver. I checked the fridge: yes, plenty of white wine there – my favourite Sancerre with its unique gunmetal taste. And behind the large wooden chopping-board, half a dozen red Mouton Cadet bottles in a rack.

In the panelled living-room I turned up the gas log fire behind the brass grate. A warm glow filled the room. With its oak-timbered ceiling hung with chandeliers, its panelled walls and large picture windows, the drawing-room was both spacious and cosy. The carpet was a thick-pile pale blue, cheerful without being intrusive. The sofas were soft brown leather.

Don't ask me why, but as I busied myself preparing for him I found myself humming my own version of the David Bowie song: 'Ground control to Major Ron ...' It was a catchy lyric, and I couldn't shake it off.

I heard the sound of wheels on gravel, and saw Ronald's BMW estate car parking beside my Rolls-Royce outside. It was burgundy – the same colour as his polo helmets. You couldn't miss the Jack Russell insignia on his bonnet – or the distinctive number plate, ROW 500.

It was to be the first of many visits to my house in Ham, and as our affair deepened I couldn't help wondering at the risk he was taking. Anyone who knew Ronald knew that car – and the internationally famous Ham polo ground was just down the road. But as he became more besotted with me, he seemed to throw caution to the winds. Whenever I mentioned my fears, he just shrugged those big shoulders of his and said: 'Don't worry so much. It'll be all right.'

But that wintry afternoon, with the leaden skies gathering over the Thames and the last of the golden leaves scattered across the paths, I was more surprised than concerned about any future that might be unfolding for us. When I opened the front door to him, how could I know that I was opening a new, critical chapter in my life which would affect both of us for ever?

Ronald's tall, distinguished figure, immaculate in navy-blue blazer with the buttons glinting silver in the late sunlight, stood smiling at me. 'Hello, my dear. I'm so glad you're here.'

He turned and stared out across the clipped lawn to the river, where clusters of small cruisers bumped gently at their moorings on the far bank beside their owners' bungalows. He nodded his grizzled head. 'Very nice, very nice.'

'Please come in ...' But all of a sudden he had turned back and swept me in his arms in a huge bear-hug. 'Very nice,' he said again, only more gently.

Taken aback, and slightly breathless – Ronald had a very strong grip – I led him into the kitchen, and pointed proudly at a saucepan on the stove. 'Tomato soup!' I did a mock curtsey. 'Just as sir required.'

He laughed, and relaxed visibly. 'Will you show me around?' he asked, gesturing at the house.

'Of course.' I was only too delighted. I was proud of my lovely Gablecot, even if it was so huge and somehow hollow with all those empty bedrooms that should have been filled with laughter and voices. I took him through the dining-room, with its stripped wood floor and antique carved stone fireplace, and on to the three communicating rooms – the reception area, breakfast room, and back to the kitchen.

Several of the rooms were over twenty feet long, and high-ceilinged, so that Ronald's own large frame seemed completely at home. I led the way up the oak-panelled staircase to the landing, and waved casually along it. 'Bedrooms,' I said, 'loads of them. This one's mine ...'

Immediately Ronald popped his head into my bedroom and took in the big double bed and the marble-tiled bathroom beyond.

'Oh,' I said, suddenly remembering. 'This you must see!' He followed me through to the bathroom, and I gestured grandly at my pride and joy: the circular double whirlpool bath at the far end.

Ronald's bushy eyebrows went up. 'Umm,' he said. 'Plenty of room in there ...'

Downstairs I threw open the doors to the indoor swimming-pool, more than fifty feet long, with french windows and sloping glass roof-panels running the length of the tiled surrounds, and the sauna and small gymnasium nearby. Through the windows we could see the neat guest lodge beyond the rockery. Ronald took my arm and we strolled across the mosaic tiles to the window, where for a few nostalgic moments I stared out at the landscaped garden with its yew trees and honey-suckle, which for so many years had been my shelter from the world.

He caught my gaze. 'What's the matter?' His deep voice was full of concern.

'I was just thinking: I'm about to lose all this ...'

'Yes,' he nodded. 'It seems such a dreadful shame.'

'Come on,' I said, shaking off the shadows. 'Lunch is served!'

I poured out the soup. 'Can I take it by the fire?' Ronald nodded towards the living-room. I had taken a lot of trouble to make the table look attractive – but so what! It was only a bowl of soup.

'Of course.' I picked up a tray.

'And – er – have you any wine?'

'Only the best for m'sieur!'

His eyes widened approvingly when he saw the Sancerre from the fridge, and positively glazed at the sight of the Mouton Cadet labels in the wooden rack. Major Ferguson knows his wines like he knows his ponies, and in all the months I knew him we never had an inferior glass.

He chose the Mouton Cadet. We sat on the brown leather sofa by the fire, and just talked. Outside, the winter afternoon drew in, and lights flickered on across the river, stretching away like fireflies into the gathering dusk. I was reminded of lines I had learned once from a poem by Sir Walter Scott:

> November's sky is chill and drear,
> November's leaf is red and sear ...

'Sear?' said Ronald, puzzled.

'Dried up, withered,' I said, with an arch look at him. We were on our second bottle of wine, and because I hardly drank the effects were beginning to tell.

'I hope you're not looking at me!' he said dryly, and we both laughed.

The two bottles were empty. Ronald asked where the cloakroom was, and I said: 'Me too. Use the downstairs loo. I'll go upstairs.'

I weaved my way up the big staircase to my bedroom, and into the *en suite* bathroom. A few minutes later I came out to the landing – and there was Ronald, standing right outside my door.

'I wondered where you'd got to,' he said, a trifle lamely.

'Here I am,' I said, with that artificial brightness born of a glass too far. Vaguely I saw his hand reach out and take mine in its large, firm grip. He motioned me towards my bedroom, but I shook my head. 'No – not there.' For some reason I could never bring myself to make love to another man in the conjugal bed, whatever had happened to my marriage. Not then. Not ever.

Ronald understood. Without another word he tugged me gently along the corridor to the first guest bedroom, a beautiful room almost forty feet in length with mirrored doors and pale-green flocked wallpaper. I called it the 'Green Room' – and I have to say that no colour could have been more appropriate to Ronald's lovemaking. When it came to sex, he was desperately inexperienced.

The king-size bed awaited us. Nothing had been planned. It just happened. In my whole life I had never been to bed with a man so much older than me.

We undressed separately, without speaking, without even looking at one another. I was in a slight haze, but part of me was fully aware of what was about to happen – and didn't care. Some unseen force had drawn us together. I sensed Ronald's loneliness; he sensed mine. I was lost, unsettled, needing not just a shoulder to cry on, but a rock of support. I was very vulnerable. In short, I needed a hug!

If one quality of romance is surprise, then this had to be one of the most romantic nights of my life – because something was plucked out of nowhere, totally unheralded, and in that hour two people became special to each other.

We made love that first time entirely without speaking. Ronald had a body that was fit but a little on the flabby side. I couldn't help noticing how thin his legs were – I expected iron-man thighs from someone who rode as often and as brilliantly as he did.

We laughed a lot, Ronald and I, in those early days. Inevitably I called him 'my galloping Major' – and even that first time, which in terms of sheer physical satisfaction left me stimulated but not gratified, I was able to laugh with him.

He was not, I have to say, terribly well endowed. And on that initial occasion there was very little foreplay. Most of it came from me before Ronald heaved himself on top of me, grunting and gasping, for the final furlong. Then it was all over, and he rolled off me with a deep sigh and lay beside me, our fingers entwined, staring up at the ceiling.

He looked across the pillows at me, and his voice was suddenly quiet and serious. 'Do you realize this is the first time I have made love outside my marriage?'

I hadn't. But even allowing for my befuddled brain, something didn't sound quite right, though I couldn't work out what it was. I let it pass.

Ronald went on: 'I haven't made love since my last child was born. Eliza. There's been nothing physical in my marriage since then.'

'How old is Eliza?' I found myself asking mechanically.

'She's six years old,' said the Major.

Physically speaking, that was the way it would be in the future — myself doing almost all of the caressing and arousal, finding my enjoyment from Ronald's pleasure and my own contentment from his hunger for me. Eventually it would turn into an unhealthy obsession. For now, it was fine.

Our sex – apart from one memorable occasion when we slept together at the Duke and Duchess of York's home, Sunninghill Park – was very 'normal'. If it lacked adventure, there was enough warmth and affection to recompense me.

I drifted off into a doze – and an hour later woke with a start to find myself in Ronald's arms, his craggy face on the pillow beside me smiling into mine.

My first words were hardly those of someone impaled by Cupid's arrow. 'Oh, my God, what's happened?' I exclaimed.

Ronald was kind enough not to point out the obvious. Instead he hugged me more tightly and said: 'I have to tell you that I have never, ever made love like that in my life.' There was a tone of wonder in his voice, like a little boy wide-eyed at a new discovery, and I couldn't help smiling back at him. It was nice to see someone so happy.

He went on: 'I've never really been comfortable like this, where it all seems so natural.' There was a pause. Then he said: 'You know, I haven't had sex for a long time. But that was beautiful. I actually made love to you!' It was as if he couldn't believe it had happened.

But it had. And now we embarked on an affair that would ultimately become more powerful than either of us – and come close to destroying us both.

But in that cheerful green bedroom, where the colours seemed to be heightened in vivid contrast to the dark winter afternoon outside the window, we were cocooned in the magic of our togetherness. Curled up in Ronald's arms, I felt safe and curiously at peace. In our love-making I had been the dominant one, and always would be. But now, in the aftermath, he became the protector, perhaps even the father I had never really had.

Ronald left. He left in a hurry, without even taking a shower. One minute he was lying beside me, cradling me in his arms; the next he had slipped his arm from under me and was out of bed and reaching for his clothes, which were folded with military precision across an armchair.

'I've got to get back to the Club,' he said. 'They're expecting me. I'm late ...'

I closed my eyes. The room was spinning a little, and so were my thoughts and emotions. I felt a kiss on my forehead. That was all.

Then he was gone.

I lay in a daze, trying to gather myself and calm the shock-waves that were building up. Delayed reaction, I thought. Come on, girl, pull yourself together. It's no big deal.

But it *was* a big deal – the whole pack. And somewhere in there was the King of Hearts – and the Joker, laughing at us for our weaknesses and the ease with which we give in to temptation.

My mind was starting to become fragmented, soaring like a starburst in all sorts of directions at once, as I lay on one side of that big bed and felt the warm sheet where he had lain grow cold under my fingertips.

Then the phone by the bed rang, making me jump. It was Ronald, from his car phone. Much later I was to feel a sense of relief that no retired bank manager or radio ham had nothing better to do on that evening than scour the airwaves.

His first words were: 'I'm so sorry ...'

Mechanically I answered: 'I'm sorry too.' But in our hearts, I knew that neither of us really believed it or meant it.

There was an awkward silence. I lay with my head on

the green pillow, the phone pressed to my ear. My head had started to throb with the first signs of a hangover, and I was lost for words – a rare state for me.

Then suddenly his words were gushing out in a torrent. 'I'm so happy. It wasn't planned, I know. But I'm just so happy. You're the best thing that has ever come into my life. Lesley, I think I'm falling in love with you...'

'Hey!' I said. 'Hold on.' It was all getting too much, too soon, too sudden. Inside, I thought: *Wow!* Is this really happening? Aloud, I began: 'Ronald ...'

But he interrupted. 'No, wait ... Lesley, I want to know: do you regret it ... what we did ...?'

'No,' I said softly. 'No, I don't.' Then, more urgently: 'But it wasn't meant to happen, and I don't want anything to jeopardize the tournament or your marriage. I think this is wrong ...'

'It won't,' he promised. 'It's so right. It's so right! But all right – I'm sorry I'm talking like this.'

We agreed to speak again in the next few days and arrange to meet somewhere, preferably, I felt, on neutral ground. Ronald became his old brisk self, and with a final goodbye the phone went dead.

I felt better. Right then I felt very dearly about him in a caring way, but I didn't want him doing anything stupid or coming on heavy with me.

I took the phone off the hook, drifted off again, and slept like a baby. The last thing I remember that fateful November evening was the dim echo of this words.

'Lesley, I think I'm falling in love with you ...'

CHAPTER NINE

Tomato Soup

'Tomato Soup!' said Ronald. 'That's our codeword.' He grinned boyishly. 'If we're going to keep our secret, we may as well do it properly.'

In the days that followed our first love-making, I tried to analyse my feelings about Major Ronald Ferguson. I was thirty-two, he was fifty-nine. He could have been my father, and it would be quite likely that anyone seeing us together would jump to that conclusion.

The phone calls had started again the very next day. And messages on my answerphone. 'Lesley, my darling, once again thank you for those wonderful, precious moments. Take care, my little one. I cherish your reciprocated love as I have never cherished anything before.' I had tried to appear demure, off-hand, cool, sophisticated – you name it. But I was both flattered and excited by having had such an obvious effect on a man who was a recognized and respected figure in the twin worlds of royalty and extreme riches – worlds that remain only a pipe-dream, a receding horizon, a fantasy land for most of us.

For me, fantasy was about to become fact.

Comfort and closeness, that was what I wanted from Ronald. He filled a void at a time when I was terribly vulnerable – with my marriage in turmoil, business worries, and our lovely home about to be repossessed, it was a time of dreadful uncertainty and anxiety.

I realized that these were the key factors as we became more enmeshed in the web we had spun for ourselves, and I felt myself drawn towards him in a bond of genuine affection as I grew to know him better. Ronald gave me what I wanted, comforting me, hugging me, cosseting me, loving me.

But another voice inside me, small but insistent, kept saying: 'This is stupid. This is not going to work. This is a married man you're tangling with.' I had always been against people having affairs outside their marriage, and had steered well clear of ever getting myself involved in that way.

But now here I was, being courted by one of the best-known married men in the whole of Britain, a man instantly recognizable in America and across the world...

For the next two weeks we met on a couple of occasions for lunch in Knightsbridge, but we didn't sleep together again immediately. I was being torn in all sorts of ways, confused about getting into something that might prove too deep – yet not wanting to lose somebody special, either.

We had long talks on the phone. The conversations usually began with discussions about the projected polo tournament, then moved into other fields – and into the first unhealthy signs of the obsession that would grow to envelop and haunt me. 'I have found my soul mate,' Ronald declared. 'But what on earth can I do about it? I can never be natural in public.'

And, again, more messages left for me. 'Can you have any idea just how much I want to hug you – to put my arms around you and feel your comfort?' I was due to go to Palm Beach in Florida for Christmas, and then on to Colorado for some skiing in the haute-couture resort of Aspen. Some friends I had met on a previous trip to America had a chalet there, and it would not be wildly expensive.

I love skiing, and the Rockies have wonderful wide, easy slopes that go on for ever – unlike Switzerland, which is far more challenging with its narrower runs. What was it that Noel Coward once said? 'The trouble with Switzerland, my dears, is that it is so *perpendicular!*'

Ronald was not at all happy about my going away. Already, by that winter of 1990, he had given me the first of what would eventually turn out to be an avalanche of presents – including, believe it or not, a polo pony that had once belonged to Prince Charles.

But for now it was an early Christmas present of a bottle of Cartier perfume that he handed across the table at the end of a lunch in a chic restaurant behind Harrods. He took my hand and said earnestly: 'Above all else, Lesley, I don't want you to feel uncomfortable about what happened between us. If you do, it will never happen again, I promise.'

'Thank you,' I told him quietly. Our eyes met in a long look, and he got the message – the lady wasn't saying yes, but she wasn't saying no.

I fished in my handbag. 'This is for you.' It was a silver tie-pin from the gift shop at the Victoria and Albert Museum; it had a silver house on it with silver smoke curling up from the chimney. I had written on a card: 'This is a little house for you to put your heart in when you feel really lonely.'

Ronald stared down at it in silence. When he looked up again, I saw that his eyes had misted over. All he could do was shake his head. It was the first real glimpse I had of the depth of the emotions he kept so securely hidden from the world.

In that moment I thought to myself: I'm starting to

fall in love with this man ...

Before we left, he said: 'All right, Tomato Soup, will you give me your number in Palm Beach so I can ring you on Christmas Day? I'll have Jane with me, but I can escape to the study and no one will hear.'

The call duly came through, from wintry Basingstoke to sunny Florida. 'God, I envy you,' Ronald said, but without any rancour. 'I just wish I was there.'

I thought a lot about my galloping Major while I was lazing away the hours in the sun. Christmas Day in the Sunshine State is a curious anomaly: picnics on the beach, or for other families it can be a traditional turkey for lunch – except that the bird is barbecued on the patio and the kids are splashing noisily about in the pool. It is all very odd if you have been brought up hoping to find the snow piled up outside the window when you wake up on Christmas morning.

I was the guest at a house rented out for polo-playing friends by the Mexican ace Memo Gracida, so I did not wish to appear ungrateful. But behind the smiles and the endless 'Have a nice day!' wherever I set foot, I longed for the really traditional taste of Christmas: the walk to the local pub through snowy lanes encrusted with frost; the long, lazy Christmas lunch with crackers and the funny hats I remembered from my childhood.

And the Queen's Speech at 3.00 p.m., when all we could manage was to sit like stuffed penguins around the fire and listen to Her Majesty's dulcet tones wishing us health and happiness in the year ahead.

When Ronald came on the line it was late afternoon in Hampshire, morning in Florida. 'We'll be having lunch later,' he said. 'Are you enjoying yourself?'

'The people are very nice,' I said non-committally. 'I

think I'd rather be home.' All of a sudden I thought I would bring him some Christmas cheer. 'Did I ever tell you the silliest joke I ever got out of a cracker?'

'No. Let's hear it.'

It had stuck with me ever since I was fifteen.

BILLY: What's that dog you've got?

BOBBY: It's my new bloodhound. Come here, Pongo!

BILLY: That doesn't look much like a bloodhound to me ...

BOBBY: Bleed for the man, Pongo!

Ronald's gruff chuckle came three thousand miles down the line. 'I'll try to remember that one,' he said, as courteous as ever. But somehow I doubted if he would ever tell it to his family around the table. I could almost hear him thinking: Oh, no, not another Lesley joke!

I returned to London in mid-January, to a country full of doom and gloom, accentuated by the ever-growing threat of the Gulf War. For weeks America had been tense under the gathering thunder-clouds; they had even affected the hedonistic sidewalks of Aspen. There the skiing jetsetters were treated to a daily diet of war preparations on TV, which even gave the idle rich pause for thought.

But then I came home – and within twenty-four hours of returning I was in bed with him again. And this time, how different it was.

Ronald called me as I was unpacking my single case in my bedroom at Gablecot. The house was on the market, and I was fighting a losing battle with the bank, who were after repossession. But for the moment I was able to remain there, though sometimes I felt like a tightrope walker watching the wire fraying under my feet – with no safety net to break my fall.

'Lunch tomorrow,' he said firmly. 'Usual place, usual table. Usual time. Can you make it?' That meant one o'clock at Claridge's.

For some reason I felt a surge of excitement. 'I can make it,' I said.

We sat together in the familiar corner table of the Causerie. Scampi arrived for him and Dover sole for me, along with a crisp Chablis. But now I felt an extra warmth between us, a new umbilical cord linking us in our mutual longing. I noticed the silver tie-pin with its little silver house on his red and blue striped Household Cavalry tie, and felt pleased that he had worn it for me.

First, Ronald had to get something off his chest. 'It's Sarah,' he said without preamble. 'Things just aren't right at home. Can you guess what she told me last night? That she and Diana have some sort of pact about their marriages. Both of them have decided they aren't in love with their husbands – and they're going to leave them together and support each other¦ I told her: "Don't be so ridiculous!" But you never know with that girl ...'

He was less forceful this time, less pressing in his attentions, and as a result I relaxed and felt I could be myself.

We talked about life, and about love. 'People always say that when you're in love you become who you really are,' I told him, expounding on a subject I always loved to discuss – as long as it was with the right person. 'You don't have to pretend. You can be yourself.

'I go one stage further. I believe that when you are truly, deeply in love, you become the person you *always wanted to be* in your dreams. Does that sound very silly?'

Ronald shook his head and smiled at me. 'No, Lesley, it doesn't sound silly at all.'

He drove me to Ham in his burgundy BMW estate, and this time it was as if we were two different people: caring, passionate, selfless in our love-making, each wanting to give fully to the other. I took the initiative again, but this time his response equalled mine, and we were two kindred spirits locked in one another's arms, living only for the moment in that pastel-green room, with the dark January night outside the window another world away.

When it was over, even though I had not actually experienced total fulfilment, I lay back amid the rumpled cream sheets and thought: This is heaven!

I took Ronald's hand and led him back to my bedroom, and into the bathroom where I ran the jacuzzi. While he lounged back in the swirling whirlpool, happily naked, I wrapped a towel around myself and padded barefoot downstairs to rummage around for half a dozen candles. I also collected a bottle of Bollinger champagne from the fridge and a couple of glasses on my way back. Then I went back for six empty wine bottles in the scullery.

I have a 'thing' about candlelight. It is surely the most romantic light in all the world. The jacuzzi was big enough for four people, but we weren't expecting any more guests that night as I placed the candles in the bottles and arranged them round the jacuzzi against the wall.

Our faces were lit by the glow of the candles as I sank down into the warm, foaming water. Ronald poured the champagne, and in the flickering light we toasted each other.

'To us,' he said.

'To the future,' I responded.

From that moment our affair began in earnest.

CHAPTER TEN

Steven Wyatt

Then the letters began. First it was flowers, a dozen red roses once a week, with a little one-line message on the accompanying card in Ronald's own handwriting. 'Love – R.' Then the phone calls, as regular as clockwork every morning, promptly at 8 a.m., from the Royal Berkshire clubhouse or from his car phone. Then the letters.

I started to feel the pressure mount, and knew that I had to tamp down the emotions of this volatile, excitable man. 'I never want to lose you as a friend. You are the only one I can ever talk to. Please don't run away ...' His voice was pleading, cajoling, querulous, yearning, as mercurial as his moods.

Or he would relay his feelings about his wives, present and past. 'There comes a time when you need to share, to talk, to give yourself body and soul to someone that you live for. I have never ever in either of my marriages been able to talk and discuss everything.'

It ran in the family – an incredible vein of incaution flowing through the bloodstream of the Fergusons like fool's gold. I would discover a similar uncontrolled streak in Sarah – impetuous passions bubbling to the surface, spilling over, bringing the headstrong Duchess of York headlong into conflict with those who would try to call her to heel on the Establishment leash.

I was in the throes of organizing the Tournament, meeting confirmed sponsors and potential backers, and fielding the daily calls from Ronald, when I accepted a dinner invitation from a girlfriend called Jacqueline.

And that was when, out of the blue, I met Steven Wyatt.

Was it lust at first sight? Who can tell? All I know is that I fell for this Texan Romeo during a night of passion that helped me unite with my own sexuality again after months of torment, self-doubt and frustration.

A woman can be as sexy as she wants in her own mind, and in her fantasies. But it takes a special man to bring out the full depths of her sensuality – so that all at once she seems like a priceless diamond, but alive, with the whole world witnessing the myriad aspects of her radiance.

Steven Wyatt was such a man.

Neither Sarah nor I ever called him Steve, though the Press seemed to conclude that it was the right kind of macho name for a celebrated lady-killer, the rogue who set the cat among the royal pigeons with the discovery of those first controversial photographs in his London apartment.

Jacqueline's dinner party took place in the early spring of 1991, at an elegant town-house in Chelsea.

I arrived at nine o'clock, late and a little flustered because I had been running around town all day, going to meetings and attending to a hundred and one things that needed sorting out, little things that never mattered afterwards but seemed vital at the time.

It was one of those days when there just weren't enough hours to go around. I drove up in my Rolls-Royce, managed to find a parking-place that was not 'residents only' and where I wouldn't get towed away or, worse, clamped, and rang the bell.

I'd had no time to change, and was casually dressed in black slacks and a crimson hunting-jacket. The moment I was shown into the living-room by a maid, I realized that I would probably get the prize for the least well-groomed woman on show. As I looked around at the bevy of chic cocktail dresses, puffed sleeves and high heels, I mentally erased the word 'probably' and substituted 'certainly'.

It was a buffet dinner, with a table groaning with food set out in the middle of the dining-room, the guests circling around like a bunch of toreadors cautiously approaching a bull. Pride of place in the display went to a huge pink salmon trout nestling in a bed of green lettuce – though by the time I walked in the creature was in a sorry state, looking as if the vultures had been at it.

Jacqueline pressed a glass of white wine into my unresisting hand and said: 'Come and meet Steven. He's from Texas.' She dropped her voice. 'He's in oil. Stinking rich! But he's lovely – and he's just right for you!'

She led me across the room to where a stocky man stood holding court in the centre of a rapt group of women. I could see that they were hanging on to his every word as if they were in the presence of the Second Coming. Steven was in his late thirties, around five foot eight, with a thatch of brown hair and soft blue eyes like a puppy. With his permanent tan and easy charm he reminded me of the American actor George Segal, and radiated a similar boyish appeal.

Jacqueline managed to exert her authority as hostess and find a gap in the gaggle. 'Steven, meet Lesley. She's just arrived. Lesley – this is Steven.'

'How are you?' The voice was low, rich, confident. He couldn't shake hands because he had a plate in one and a glass in the other. But his smile was enough – the sort of wicked smile a girl should be warned about in the same way she's warned about taking sweets from strangers.

I had never heard of Steven Wyatt, and therefore knew nothing about his reputation. But suddenly the room seemed to belong only to the two of us. Other voices faded into a murmur as he expertly backed me into a corner and started firing questions at me – not unpleasantly, like a cross-examination, but as if they came from a genuine interest in me.

'Have you ever been to the States?' – Yes, twice.

'I hear you play polo?' – Well, I said, I can stay on a pony, just about! I told him how I practised at various polo grounds like Ham, Cowdray Park, the Royal Berkshire – but taking care to omit the name of Major Ronald Ferguson.

'How did you learn?' It seemed as if he really wanted to know. I told him about my trip to California, about the forthcoming tournament, and his eyes danced with enthusiasm. 'That is just great,' he said. 'It's going to be terrific, I know it is.

'Do you have any boyfriends?' The question was so direct it took me aback. 'Of course,' I said, smiling. 'Hundreds of them. You'll find them queueing outside!'

He liked that, and we laughed together. It was highly flattering, and I readily succumbed to his obvious flirtation. Here was a ladies' man, I could tell – but somehow I wasn't offended by the very unsubtle approach. Charm is everything! Other women came and went. Steven contrived politely to take them into his aura for a few minutes, and just as charmingly get rid of them. But he monopolized me throughout the evening.

At 10.30 p.m. he looked at his watch. 'I've got to go,' he said. Then he looked directly at me. 'I'll call you.' He didn't even add: 'Okay?'

'You don't know my number,' I said.

'I'll get it,' he responded. I sensed that he was reluctant to see other people watching him take my number. Yet he ostentatiously made a point of taking other women's numbers as he circled the room saying goodbye to them. Why was I so special *not* to be asked?

It was only when I was driving home an hour later that I realized that I didn't even know his surname.

The phone rang next day as I was at my desk going through my diary for the week.

'Hi, this is Steven. I told you I'd call.' His voice was quietly pleased with itself.

'How did you get my number?'

'Jacqueline gave it to me. I hope you don't mind?'

'No,' I said. 'I don't mind.'

'Good.' He sounded relieved. 'Perhaps I should explain that I didn't want to embarrass you by taking your number down in front of everyone.'

'That didn't stop you taking the others,' I said, trying not to sound tart.

He chuckled. 'They don't count,' he said softly. 'You do.' There was a pause. 'Will you have dinner with me?'

'Why not? When had you in mind?'

'Tonight.' Christ, I thought, he moves fast.

I consulted my diary. That night I had to attend a reception at the Mansion House, an important function for me because it would be an opportunity to meet some top City businessmen and bankers.

'Sorry,' I said. 'The earliest I can do is Thursday.'

Thursday was two days away.

'Okay, Thursday it is,' he said without hesitating. 'I'll call you in the morning to confirm when and where.' The phone clicked off.

Prompt at ten o'clock on Thursday morning he came through again. 'Hi,' he said without preamble. 'We're not going out for dinner tonight.'

'We're not?' The man had called to tell me our date was off?

'No. I'm going to cook you dinner in my apartment.'

He sounded as if he were doing me a favour.

'Oh.' I couldn't think of anything else to say.

'Listen,' he said. 'I want to tell you that you are a *very* privileged lady, because I *never* cook dinner for one person in my apartment. Well, maybe once. But I can't wait to meet you again. And I also want to tell you that I am really taken with your energy and your enthusiasm about the way you live your life. I want to know a lot more about you ...'

It went on in the same vein for several minutes, but the upshot was that I finally said yes, though with a few misgivings. I remembered that smile ...

Later I found that the other lucky recipient of Steven Wyatt's culinary – and associated – arts was Sarah.

But now Steven's voice was coming down the phone with the friendly persuasiveness of a politician telling us we had never had it so good – or were about to, anyway.

He gave me the address, and made me repeat it to make sure I had got it right. No. 34 Cadogan Square, an elegant, high-class area where Chelsea meets Knightsbridge, and where the wealthy and famous have their London homes. Film stars, millionaire businessmen and socialites rub shoulders as they head off to the rarefied shopping precincts of Harrods, Habitat and sundry other top-bracket establishments within walking distance. Restaurants for celebrity-seekers, such as the San Lorenzo in Beauchamp Place, or for discerning palates, such as the English House in Milner Street, are just around the corner. Steven had chosen his London pad well.

His directions were explicit, almost overly so. He sounded quite anxious on the phone that I should know exactly where to go, and what to do when I got there. It was as if he didn't want me hanging around on the pavement asking directions of anyone. 'Press button 3, and it will be the door marked "F" on the second floor,' he instructed. 'Got it?'

'I've got it,' I told him, scribbling it down. 'Button 3, second floor, door F.'

'Seven o'clock,' he said. 'I'll be waiting.'

He was, too. I had dressed casually but elegantly, in a white silk blouse and black evening skirt, with black tights and Polo Ralph Lauren black shoes with heels that were high without being obvious. Over my shoulder I had draped a Max Mara woollen sweater. I had no idea or intention of sleeping with Steven Wyatt that night, and I dressed more for comfort than effect.

How could I know that four hours after I walked into his apartment I would be in bed with this guy – after breaking the rule of a lifetime and sleeping with a man on our first date?

I pressed the buzzer marked '3'. Instead of the door opening, there was Steven's stocky figure hustling down the stairs to answer the main door himself. He escorted me up the two red-carpeted flights to his flat.

Inside, a large hallway opened out on to a spacious lounge that doubled as a dining-room. I noticed a telephone on a cane table just inside the reinforced door – 'It's burglar-proof,' Steven mentioned casually. The sitting-room was a vast expanse large enough to swing an elephant in, let alone your average cat. Beige wallpaper, matching curtains; three bay windows looking down on to the leafy square. I caught a glimpse of half a dozen architectural prints neatly arranged on the far wall before Steven waved me towards the kitchen.

Through the open door my nostrils caught a delicious aroma of something cooking in a saucepan on the stove. 'Umm,' I sniffed appreciatively. 'Pheasant?'

'Right!' Steven looked pleased. 'In a casserole. And a few other things too.'

The few other things turned out to be a duck pâté, a tossed salad to go with the casserole, and cheesecake as the dessert. A table in the dining-area by the windows had been meticulously laid for two, with place-mats, silver cutlery, cut glass for two different wines and water – and candles. Black candles.

'Come and talk to me in the kitchen,' Steven said, leading the way. He had welcomed me into the flat with a courteous peck on the cheek, nothing more. I looked around the small, modern kitchen with its red motif tiles: there were plates and dishes everywhere, a bowl of half-prepared salad beside a chopping-board with green peppers and onions on it. And in the corner I couldn't help noticing a bundle of empty Harrods bags.

I felt the first faint flutter of excitement – Steven really had gone to the most enormous trouble.

'A glass of wine?'

'I'd love one.'

He produced a bottle of chilled Mersault from the fridge – delicious! And in the corner, with its cork out to allow it to breathe – a bottle of red Château Lafite Rothschild, *very* expensive.

There were no chairs, so I hoisted myself onto one of the cupboards and sat watching him as he busied himself chopping onions. Steven was very easy to talk to; it was as if we had known each other for years instead of days. He had that gift of making a girl relax almost in the first breath. I found myself telling him about my background, my upbringing, and regaling him with stories about university life that had him hooting with laughter.

Then he started talking about himself. There was no ice to break, but if there had been it would have been dispelled immediately with his discovery that I really had not the slightest notion who he was. He kept asking: 'Do you know who I am? *Do you know who I am?* – and I didn't! It was a bit weird, because he was almost paranoid about that one area. But he soon calmed down, and the evening got back on course.

Finally he stared at me for a long moment, then said: 'You really don't know who I am, do you?'

I said: 'No. Why? Are you somebody special?'

'No,' he said hastily. 'No, I'm not. But ...' He hesitated. 'But I do want you to get to know me first, before anyone else tells you about me.'

I thought he was referring to the jolly little circle whose phone numbers he had snapped up at Jacqueline's party a week ago. I could just imagine the poison tongues at work if they found out I was having a gourmet dinner cooked for me by the man they had all been hungering after.

We went into the living-room, passing by two mustard-coloured sofas and a low antique coffee table to get to the dining-area. I caught my reflection in a large mirror above the open slate fireplace, and then Steven was holding a chair for me to sit down. What a gentleman, I thought!

I had no idea then, but this was the table, this was the room, this was the flat that Sarah had visited – to create a furore in the world's Press, and cause two-inch head-lines like 'DANGEROUS LIAISONS' to scream out their message to a scandal-hungry public. Nor did I know then that it was here, in this apartment, which he owned – and which would cost £575 a week to rent – that the damning photographs of Sarah and Steven had been found, photographs that whipped the speculation into a fever that would start the boat really rocking for the Yorks' already fragile marriage.

No, I had no idea as I sat down that evening to din-ner that the speculation was at its height, and that the tabloids were speaking openly of 'the intensity of Fergie's friendship with Texan oil tycoon Steve Wyatt ...'

How on earth could I have missed it all? Don't ask me – but I did!

The casserole was excellent. Tender and succulent, it was worthy of a top restaurant. 'One star in the *Michelin Guide*,' I said approvingly.

Steven looked pleased. 'I'm glad you appreciate good cooking,' he said, in that half-joking, half-serious way of his.

That first evening, with the flickering candles carving laughter-lines across his handsome features – and he *was* good-looking, this Texan they called a cross between Bobby Ewing and the Incredible Hulk – we spanned the universe together. And beyond, because Steve was inter-ested in spiritualism and, like me, in self-improvement and creating greater awareness of the mind.

I even told him of my own ideas of God and the here-after – something I never, ever did with an almost total stranger.

So we talked – how we talked. Of this and that and anything and everything. But somehow nothing mun-dane. Small talk was for the birds that night. But despite the intensity of our discussions, there was a whole heap of humour, too.

The strange thing is that Steven didn't shoot a great line to get me between the sheets. He wasn't 'coming on' to me at all. And that's the biggest come-on for a woman – the fact that he wasn't making suggestive overtures, or trying to rush me into bed. Women like to be chased, even in this 'enlightened' day and age! I started to wonder: Why not? What's wrong with this guy?

He had talked to me, he'd cooked for me, we'd drunk wine by candlelight and sweet music – and then, nothing!

But Steven was an artist with women. He knew how to make them feel special. He had a rare gift – he knew that if women are pushed away, they'll come back! They are fascinated by men like that, because it's a subtle challenge to their femininity, to their emotions, to their own physical needs. If only other men could learn that!

Around eleven, I said: 'I think I'd better go.'

He gave me a small smile, and poured more Château Lafite into my glass. He kept his arm around my shoulder – then suddenly bent and turned my face gently up to his and kissed me softly on the lips.

'You need a hug,' he said. 'You're a person who needs to be hugged.'

He lifted me slowly from the chair, and we embraced by the table. The next thing I knew Steven had swept me up in his arms and was carrying me into the bedroom! Talk about romance.

I suppressed a squeal: on the bed half a dozen teddy bears stared up at me from the pillows! Memories of my recurring dream came flooding back – but I pushed them firmly aside. Instead I dramatically swept the toys off onto the floor. This was one picnic where teddy bears were definitely *not* welcome.

Steven looked surprised and amused, but made no comment.

He must have slipped out at some point earlier to arrange it: music was being piped through from the record-player, and the exquisite strains of Vivaldi filled the room as he laid me gently on the huge double bed, with its bedspread of dark burgundy.

I realized that I was being expertly seduced – but I didn't care. I was literally swept off my feet!

The bedroom itself was very ethnic, with carvings on the bureau and colourful paintings on the walls.

Steven put a finger to his lips. 'Ssh! Don't move or say anything!' he said.

Then he started to undress me.

As a lover, Steven was wild! As he undressed me he talked quietly, soothingly, in that rich, hypnotic voice, and his hands were gentle and caressing as his finger-tips softly located my erogenous zones with the touch of an expert.

I swiftly forgot my guilty feelings about it being the first time on a first date, and found myself completely relaxing under the touch of an erotic master.

He started with my high-heeled shoes, then my dress, then the rest. When he had taken all my clothes off, and I lay stretched out like a sacrifice on the altar of passion, he slipped quickly out of his own things.

Steven was very gentle, very tender, very caring – and, as our caresses grew more intense, very passionate. In terms of sheer sensuality he gave me everything that Ronald could not or would not give me.

As we explored each other's bodies, the only draw-back I could find was that Steven was even hairier than Ronald! It is a physical feature that has never appealed to me in men. It didn't really matter. I had noticed it, but it had no effect on my feelings for him. We laughed a lot, and talked a lot. Steven knew how to make a woman happy, and that night I was delirious, ecstatic, lost in the kind of haze they normally write about in Mills and Boon novels.

Significantly, neither of us had been drinking much – both those beautiful bottles of wine were still half-full on the table in the next room, and the cork stayed in the champagne bottle by the bed. There was no tipsy 'rolling around in the hay', nor would there ever be between us. There was no need for it, and we both instinctively knew that the act of love was too precious to abuse.

When it was all over he wrapped his arms around me and we slept together like two children.

I didn't stay the night. Around two o'clock I awoke, and tickled his nose with one finger to tease him awake. 'I'm sorry,' I whispered. 'But I've got to go.'

'Must you?' he said drowsily. 'Stay the night – please.'

'I can't,' I said. 'I'm a working girl, remember? I've got to be in the City in the morning.'

'Go straight from here,' he argued. 'I'll bring you breakfast in bed – champagne and hot croissants!'

Oh, sweet temptation! But I steeled myself, and said firmly: 'No! I'd love to – but no.'

'Maybe next time,' he said.

'Maybe,' I said, slipping out of his arms. Before heading for the bathroom, I bent over and kissed his cheek. 'I'm glad there'll be a next time.'

And in all those intimate hours we had spent together, not once had the name of Sarah – or her father – been mentioned.

Not yet.

CHAPTER ELEVEN

In Love Again

Steven phoned me the next day on my private line at the office. We talked for an hour. 'Is anyone listening in?' His voice sounded anxious.

'No,' I said, laughing. 'And the phone isn't bugged, either!' This was a whole year before it became fashionable to pry on royal conversations.

'Last night was wonderful,' he said.

'Wasn't it just?' I could still feel the afterglow, like a sky still ablaze long after the sun has slipped out of sight over a dark horizon. 'I have to tell you that I feel terrific.'

'Me too,' he said. Then, after a pause: 'You do know you're really special, don't you, Lesley? I want to get to know you better, and I want you to know just who I am.'

I thought: He's right. In truth, at that point I really didn't know much about Steven Wyatt, his background, or his business. Our long talk the previous night had been about other things, in more esoteric, more profound areas. Somehow we just hadn't bothered with: 'Who are you, what do you do, and where do you come from?'

Obviously I had not been reading the right papers, or I would have seen his name bandied about as the new Playboy of the Western World.

'I'm flying out to the States tomorrow,' he said. 'I've got to see my mother. But I'll only be gone a few days. Will you have dinner with me the moment I get back?'

'Of course I will,' I said.

'Promise?'

'Promise!' And I meant it.

'I'll hold you to that,' Steven said. 'And I'll call you when I get there.'

He was as good as his word. Two days later the phone rang. It was Steven, calling from America.

'Where exactly are you?' I asked.

'Home,' he said casually. And we went on to talk of other things for more than an hour, while the clock ticked up the bill and the phone stayed glued to my ear while that rich drawl came down the line from the wide open spaces four thousand miles away in Texas.

I had no idea then that 'home' was the sprawling 20,000-acre ranch near the Rio Grande where the Duchess of York had been a house guest in November 1989, when she was five months pregnant with Princess Eugenie. Her hostess was Lynn Wyatt, the glamorous wife of oil billionaire Oscar Wyatt, and it was then that Sarah met Lynn's two sons by her former marriage: Douglas – and Steven.

Sarah was guest of honour on an official visit to the British Festival at the Houston Grand Opera. In the Dallas lifestyle of the mega-rich, getting a British Royal to stay under your roof was the choicest social plum anyone could pick, and the Wyatts were not slow to capitalize on their incredible stroke of good fortune.

After the opera, the guests had trooped off to a huge ball, where Steven monopolized Sarah for the rest of the evening. And the following day they had flown in the family helicopter to the huge Wyatt spread – with Sarah, who is a licensed pilot, taking the controls for one stretch over the vast rolling scrubland of the Old West.

In all, her trip lasted six days. It was long enough for her to fall under the spell of the handsome Texan who had been so attentive to her every need and who was so unlike the husband she had left behind in England. The two men could hardly have been more different. As I saw for myself, where Andrew is the rugger-playing type who likes the camaraderie of his friends in the services — he was a Lieutenant-Commander in the Royal Navy at this time – Steven is a non-violent son of the 'flower power' generation who believes in peace, not war, and is in his element in the company of women.

'Friends of Andrew and Fergie were able to pinpoint this as the time that their marriage started to come unstuck', remarked one shrewd observer of the scene.

I had no idea of the drama behind the scenes, or that Sarah and Steven were still seeing each other as I waited impatiently for my new lover to return from America. Nor had I heard of his curious business dealings with Saddam Hussein's government through his father, a legendary figure in the oil world, who, despite global opinion, was reportedly still trading with Iraq: dealings that would culminate in the autumn of 1990 with Steven asking Sarah to host a dinner for him and the Iraqi oil minister in her second-floor apartment in Buckingham Palace.

This turned into a night that was pure, undiluted fodder for the gossip columnists; particularly when the jovial threesome went on to Le Gavroche, the Michelin three-star restaurant in Chelsea which charges the kind of prices that would cost most of us a second mortgage.

A top-drawer reception was in full swing, hosted by the Tory party Treasurer Lord McAlpine. Sarah had been invited for dinner along with Andrew, but had declined.

He was somewhere on the high seas, and Sarah indicated instead that she would arrive by herself after the dinner was over. When she turned up with two extra guests, both of them uninvited, one can only imagine the consternation at the top table!

I learned later how McAlpine's wife Romilly tried to save the day by seating Sarah between her husband and another VIP – only for Steven brashly to grab Sarah's hand, sit himself firmly down in the next chair, and inform the world loudly: 'Mah woman and I sit together!'

This story circulated in house parties from Belgravia to Boston for weeks to come, and probably reached Her Majesty's ears before the guests were reaching for their hats and coats. The next day, so Ronald told me, Sarah received 'a snorting letter' from the Queen's private secretary, Sir Robert Fellowes, roundly ticking her off for being stupid enough to hobnob with the Iraqi oil merchant. Sarah merely responded: 'Oh dear, I've upset Bellows again', and threw the letter into the nearest bin.

Steven would ride any minor storm like that with ease. As I grew to know him, I found him to be a mass of contradictions, a split personality redolent of Jekyll and Hyde – though without any evil intent. He just wanted to be famous.

One side of him, the side I grew to love, was utterly genuine: disarmingly open, spiritual, deep-thinking. This was a man who drank herbal tea, believed in mind control and, like me, had followed the teachings of Dale Carnegie's 'know thyself' philosophy and Werner Erhard's EST training, which subsequently became known as Centre Network. He, too, was fascinated by the unknown, and wanted to explore the cosmic mysteries that govern so much of our daily lives.

If Steven did indeed become a Svengali to Sarah, then I can believe that too. She was impressionable – and the man's magnetism was almost tangible.

Yet I still find it hard to accept that Steven set out or intended to spark off the disastrous train of events that culminated in the royal scandal of the decade.

Decade? Discounting poor Princess Margaret's desperate love for Group Captain Peter Townsend, there had been nothing like it for more than half a century, since Edward and Mrs Simpson in the thirties.

But Steven was a victim of his own ego. The other side of him, the side I found distasteful and rather pathetic, was that of a man striving for celebrity status. He was rich and running – but he wanted to be running with royalty and to relish all the trappings that went with it.

On only our second date, he would say to me: 'I want to climb mountains, Lesley. I want to walk across continents. I want to get to the top of the highest mountains in the world ...' Indeed, he was planning some crazy walk across Peru, and said he was trying to get permission from their government to allow him through.

At least, as a social climber, Steven Wyatt could say that he made it beyond the foothills – thanks to Sarah. By the time we met he had been invited to a number of royal events, and even found himself seated next to the Queen at a dinner at Windsor Castle. Through Sarah, he had won entry into the inner sanctum of the royal lifestyle, if not the whole-hearted approval of some of the 'old school' advisers who found his manner too brash for comfort.

He had also been at the christening party for Princess Eugenie in December. I remembered the lovely official portrait of the Royal Family (minus Steven) taken by

Terry O'Neill at Sandringham, where the nine-month-old baby bawled her little lungs out – a taste of things to come which I would later see with my own eyes!

In those heady days Steven was riding high. His downfall would come more than a year later with those embarrassing holiday snaps found by a cleaner four months after he had left the Cadogan Square flat – an amazing oversight on his part, I must say. They revived all the ghosts of scandal and gossip which haunted Sarah for so much of her marriage, even if much of it was due to her own headstrong thoughtlessness.

The 120 photographs had been taken when Sarah slipped out of Britain with baby Princess Beatrice aboard the Wyatt family plane and jetted off with Steven into the sunshine of Morocco. With them in the party were other friends of his, among them American actress Priscilla Phillips. But it was the pictures of Steven and Sarah sitting cosily together in a swing-chair which set the tongues wagging – he had his arm around her shoulder, and she had hers around his back.

The result for Steven was the modern-day equivalent of being sent to the Tower – an order from on high to 'chill' Steven out from Sarah's inner circle of intimates.

But when he was part of the circus, Steven could certainly put on a show. At a glittering 1990 December ball at Buckingham Palace to celebrate a clutch of royal birthdays, he proved he could rival Gene Kelly on the dance floor. He was there in the ballroom with Sarah and Andrew to toast the Queen Mother, who was an indestructible ninety, Princess Margaret, sixty, Princess Anne, forty – and Andrew himself, who was thirty.

Not bad for the son of a man who was once charged with murder! No, not Oscar – but Steven's real father.

For now, I was just glad when the phone rang and his

familiar drawl came down the line. 'I'm back,' he said. 'Do we have a dinner date?'

'We do,' I said. 'But this time you're *my* guest.'

He protested – but I insisted. And that really blew his mind!

'Lesley,' he said, genuinely impressed, as we walked through the door of the exquisitely furnished English House restaurant a short stroll from his flat, 'I have never, but never, had this happen to me before.'

'You must know the wrong women,' I said, giving him a sidelong smile. 'Does it worry your macho instincts?'

He grinned and squeezed my arm as the maitre d' found us the table I had requested in a raised alcove at the rear, discreetly away from curious eyes.

'Not any more,' he said, responding to my bantering tone. 'If it's inevitable I'm just going to sit back and enjoy it!'

The English House is exactly what it says it is – a small, intimate restaurant where you feel you are a personal guest stepping into someone's welcoming front room.

Despite his best efforts to remain nonchalant, Steven was still perplexed. Obviously girls didn't behave this way in Texas. 'I still can't believe you're doing this,' he said, shaking his head as I ordered the first glass of champagne.

The meal that night came to over a hundred pounds, but I didn't begrudge a penny of it. As we dined on Dover sole and Chablis, Steven unburdened himself – and I found the true man behind the mask he presented to the world. Perhaps it was the man Sarah had found too – though even then her name was not mentioned that night.

He talked about his stepfather for the first time: Oscar, the oil tycoon whose Coastal Corporation company was reputed to own five per cent of America's oil reserves. 'I never really knew my real father,' he said. 'My mother separated when I was six, and I have no idea where he is now.'

What Steven didn't tell me, although I found out much later, was the skeleton in the family cupboard. His real father was a New York property investor named Robert Lipman, who had married Lynn Sakowitz, an heiress whose family owned Houston's largest store, but they separated in the late fifties. In 1968 Lipman was charged in London with the murder of an eighteen-year-old model in Chelsea during what was called 'an LSD trip to hell'. At the Old Bailey he was found guilty of manslaughter and sentenced to six years in jail.

Meantime, Lynn had met and married mega-bucks Oscar, the main stockholder in the eight-billion-dollar conglomerate Coastal Corporation. Oscar adopted Steven and his brother and in 1963 changed their name from Lipman to Wyatt. 'He taught me all about the oil business,' Steven said, elaborating on his work with the eagerness of someone talking about a favourite hobby. His blue puppy eyes were alight with enthusiasm.

He worked for Delaney Petroleum. 'My office is in St James's, and I broker oil deals for Oscar,' he said, and went on to explain the intricacies of big business in the multi-billion-pound oil industry. 'It makes the world go round,' he said.

My affair with Steven Wyatt lasted just five weeks: five rapturous, carefree, ecstatic weeks when I walked on air and my world was the way I always dreamed it should be. My business was going well. The tournament was shaping up into something that would become one of the most talked-about polo events of the year.

And I was in love.

I opened my heart to this easy-talking, easy-listening Texan, who could have been the inspiration for the song 'How to Handle a Woman'. Eventually, in return, he talked openly of past women he had escorted in his life – names like Pamella Bordes, Robert Maxwell's daughter Ghislaine and the American actress Priscilla Phillips. There was one notable exception. My Texan oilman was the soul of discretion when it came to Sarah, and her name never came into our conversation.

Which is why I had no idea that they were having their fling until the day her father told me ...

Many times we went out for dinner to small, intimate restaurants in an area where you are spoiled for choice – such as Toto's, near Beauchamp Place, where Steven had taken Sarah for their first London date after they met in Texas, or the sophisticated 190 Queen's Gate, where the food was so good that it was the late-night haunt of the capital's top chefs after they had closed up their own kitchens.

Steven had always asked me to keep our affair quiet. 'It's our secret – for now,' he said. 'Let's be discreet.'

But there was one nasty moment when a mutual girlfriend – I'll call her Annie – said to Steven: 'I hear you and Lesley have been to bed together.'

He was shocked. 'Who told you that?' he demanded.

'Lesley did,' Annie said. What a bitch! I had never even hinted at it in front of her.

Steven was furious. He rang me up and began raving: 'How dare you talk about us to your friends ...'

'Hold on!' I stopped him in mid-flow. 'Wait a minute. I haven't breathed a word to anybody. Who says I have?'

He told me the name. 'Oh, Annie's just jealous, and trying to stir things up,' I assured him. 'She did ask me about you, and I denied outright that anything was going on between us, just as you told me to. Don't believe anything that stupid girl says.' As far as I was concerned, that was the end for Annie.

What I didn't tell Steven was that a few days after our first meeting at the Chelsea party, Annie – who had been there and had witnessed the obvious chemistry between us – had rung me and confided: 'Darling, that guy you were talking to – Steve? You do realize he's a one-man walking stud farm, don't you!'

I didn't let on then. But, yes, *now* I knew ...

Normally, at our dinners, Steven paid. But even though I was being escorted by a man reportedly worth £250 million – though I never suspected it then – I insisted on paying on a second occasion when we went back to the English House. 'My treat!'

It was on that night that I revealed to him how I had slashed my wrists and driven through London in my blood-soaked night-dress. Steven listened, his face intent. At the end of the sorry saga he lifted my chin with his fingertips, and looked into my eyes with a fierce intensity that was almost hypnotic.

'Lesley, don't you ever do that again,' he said. 'I'll protect you from anything like that ever happening to you. And just remember this: no one man is ever worth it.'

Then, as if to show that he too had been through a similar trauma, he went on to tell me about the first love of his own life, a girl named Dorice Risso, who had been his Arizona college sweetheart. They were together for more than four years, and in the spring of 1989 he asked her to marry him.

'She was my very first sweetheart,' he recalled nostalgically. 'I took her home to meet the folks, and thank God that Ma liked her very much. It's important to me – she has to like every girl I bring home! Ma can be a real mother hen when it comes to my love life.

'Finally I proposed to Dorice – and she said yes! I was deeply in love with her, and I couldn't believe how happy I was. Life looked so sweet. All the arrangements were made for us to be married in Dallas. We fixed a date. The church was booked. The reception was fixed.

'My job was taking me all over the place, and we didn't see each other for a few weeks. When the wedding was just a month away she came out to London to see me for a few days. We were discussing all the details, and when I saw her off back to Dallas everything was fine.

'And you know what happened ...' His voice thickened suddenly, and there was a long silence.

'No, tell me,' I encouraged gently.

Steven took a deep breath. 'She sat next to a guy on the plane – and by the time they got to Dallas she decided she didn't want to marry me. She called me from the airport and told me it was all off! Then she went off with this other man – and I never saw her again.'

I reached across the table and took his hand. 'Oh, Steven. I'm so sorry.'

'Yeah ...' His head bowed briefly. 'I'm still not sure I'm really over it.'

I wondered aloud if that was why he seemed to be playing the field so avidly – to compensate, but without getting burned again? He nodded seriously.

'I don't think I'm trying to prove anything. Sure, I've been with a lot of women, but no one in particular. That's why when you see stories about me and other women I want you to take no notice of them, you understand?'

I had to admire his frankness. Part of Steven's attraction for me was his openness, and the fact that – like it or not – at least you knew where you stood with him. I called for the bill – and pushed his hand away when he produced his gold credit card and tried to reach for it. 'My treat!' I said firmly. 'Remember?'

'Okay,' he laughed. 'I must say that you are a very unusual young lady. At least let me buy you a glass of champagne – at my place!'

We held hands as we strolled back through the quiet streets – but I couldn't help noticing that Steven let go of mine as we approached his entrance, and kept looking around. But there was no one about, and he quickly produced his key and ushered me through.

That was the start of another sensual night of loving. It was all the better because I had seen something of the real Steven Wyatt behind the dashing playboy image, and the more I saw, the more it felt right to be with him.

One thing struck me as unusual, and it happened every time we were together. Shortly after midnight Steven would leave the bed with an apologetic 'Don't be angry – I've just got to make a quick phone call.'

Sometimes the quick phone call would last close to half an hour, but I was too drowsy to care. Eventually I would come to realize it had to be Sarah he was calling with such regularity, always around the same time.

But that night, once again, I left in the early hours. We both had work to do the next day, and he would be travelling again later that week.

'I'll call you,' he promised.

'I can't wait.' My heart was light and carefree, and I

found myself singing all the way home as I drove the Rolls through the dark streets of London.

It was the next day that I made my first mistake with Steven Wyatt.

I told the Major about him.

CHAPTER TWELVE

Cat and Mouse

I thought about it long and hard. Sitting on a stool in the kitchen over a cup of coffee, I stared through the window down into the huge courtyard of the Barbican, where I was now in the small penthouse flat my agency had rented. Fountains were playing, couples were strolling arm in arm, and spring crocuses were popping their yellow heads up in flower-boxes all around the square. It was going to be a wonderful summer.

But first ...

First I had to get my life sorted out. There were two good reasons why I should tell Major Ronald Ferguson about Steven Wyatt, and what was happening between us.

I knew I was falling in love with this handsome, charming Texan – and not just because he was handsome and charming; or because he could give me such physical pleasure between the sheets.

Steven Wyatt had produced a magic feeling inside me – and, in turn, I had made him feel he was with a woman unlike any he had met before. Or so he told me, and I wasn't about to argue with that.

The second reason was that it was a natural way to cool Ronald's ardour, and to stop the Major sinking ever more deeply and uncontrollably into the dark waters of his obsession. Still his messages poured in. If he didn't hear my voice, there would be up to half a dozen on the answerphone. 'I have gone through total agonies. I have placed you on my pedestal, and every day I just wait for the next telephone call or a brief glimpse of your porcelain face ...'

This was getting far deeper than I had ever imagined or intended. They say that sometimes it is better to be cruel to be kind, and I felt that surely now was one of those times.

I reached for the phone – and sat for a full minute with my hand poised over it before picking up the receiver, then I dialled the familiar number.

Eventually he answered. The gruffness lifted from his voice as soon as I asked him if he could spare the time to come round, preferably that day.

'How about teatime?' he asked.

We sat on the soft, black leather chairs in the lounge, with the tray on a low table in front of us. I was careful to sit a little away from him, on one of the other sofas. I suddenly realized that this was going to be more difficult than I'd thought.

I poured him out a cup of his favourite Earl Grey. Two sugars. He sat back and studied me.

'You're looking well,' he said.

I managed to keep from blushing, but I felt so good inside that it must have shown.

Somewhat hesitantly I began: 'Ronald, I've got something to tell you ...'

'Yes? What is it?'

'I think you should know that I've started seeing someone ... a man ... his name's Steven Wyatt, and ...'

But Ronald's face had paled, and he almost choked on his tea. '*What!*' he rasped. '*Who* did you say?'

'His name's Steven Wyatt,' I repeated. Then, lamely: 'Do you know him?'

'Yes, I know him,' said the Major flatly. 'I know him

very well indeed. But you obviously don't know much about him.'

'Yes I do,' I said defensively. 'He has told me all about himself.'

'Has he?' said the Major. 'Well, I would most strongly advise you not to see him any more.'

'But why on earth not?' I was totally bewildered. I had been prepared for Ronald to be angry, jealous, upset – but this cold hostility seemed to be directed elsewhere, and not to be motivated by hurt or emotion.

Major Ferguson stared at the carpet for a long moment. Then he looked up. 'He has been linked to Sarah,' he said. 'Didn't he tell you?'

'No!' I said, truthfully. 'I had no idea ...'

'Well, he has. Have you told him you've been working closely with me?'

'No! Yes – oh, I don't know.' I really couldn't remember. Somehow I didn't think Ronald's name had ever come into our long talks, just as Steven certainly hadn't mentioned Sarah. 'No, I don't think so.'

'Well, I suggest that you tell him immediately.' Ronald's thick brows were drawn together, and in that moment he looked as fierce as I had ever seen him. His voice hardened. 'Have you been intimate with him? What does he feel for you?'

'Wait a minute,' I cried. 'What is all this about?' Suddenly I had a blinding flash of perception. 'Are Steven and Sarah having an affair?'

There was a pause. Then Ronald shook his head.

'No,' he said.

It was one week later that he admitted that this was the first time he had ever lied to me, and that it would be the last.

'All right,' I said. 'When I see Steven again I'll tell him

about us. But I won't say how close we've been.''

'You do that,' said Ronald. He left without finishing his tea.

Steven was away for several days. While he was gone, something very upsetting happened. My mother phoned me. I had told her about this Texan jet-setter who had come into my life, though without going into any intimate details.

But Mummy's instincts were as sharp as ever. 'I think you should take a look at the *ES Magazine*,' she said. 'And buy the *Daily Mail*, too.' *ES Magazine* was a glossy supplement to the *London Evening Standard* which came out on the first Thursday of every month.

'Why?' I inquired. 'What's in it?'

'Your Texan friend,' said my mother. 'Just buy them!'

That was when I shed my first tears over Steven. I bought the papers from my local newsagent, and took them back to the car. The first article, in the *Mail*, featured a picture of Steven smiling out of the page with a lovely young girl next to him whose sunny smile equalled his own. Her name was Fiona Feeley, and it didn't require much imagination to realize that they were what is known in gossip columns as 'an item'.

I was so shocked that I just burst out crying, and sat behind the wheel weeping bitter tears and tasting the salt that ran into my mouth. If there were any passers-by I didn't notice them – but they would surely have wondered at the bizarre sight of a poor little rich girl crying her eyes out in a Rolls-Royce ...

The other article made it worse. The magazine had gone to town on Steven, probing his past, his present – and his possible future as a suitor for Sarah. Suddenly I realized why my Texan oilman had been so cagey at being seen with me near his apartment.

It all started to make sense – except that no one was actually saying that he and the Duchess of York were more than just very good friends.

My own senses were reeling, as if I were trapped in a Hampton Court maze of blind alleys. In just forty-eight hours my world had turned completely upside down, and emotionally I felt as if I had been mugged with a blunt instrument.

I had tried to tell Ronald I was in love with another man. Instead he had flashed the first warning-light indicating that I might be caught up in something way beyond my comprehension. The lover I thought was so open and frank was involved with another woman. Worse, he was exerting some kind of influence over a member of the royal family whose own father was besotted with me ...

It was the sort of nightmare scenario that had all the makings of a Hollywood soap series – except that it was real, and it was happening to me.

That night Steven phoned from New York. My eyes were dry by now, and so was my voice when I read the first paragraphs of the *Daily Mail* story out to him.

'Well,' I said, throwing the paper down. 'How about that? Isn't that something?'

His voice came back without a hint of hesitation. If anything, he sounded angry. 'Didn't I tell you?' he said vehemently. 'What did I say about stories of me and other women? I said: *Don't believe them!*

'I know,' I said. 'I can't help it. I just saw it today ...'

'I've been out with a lot of people. Fiona is just one of them. And I'm not seeing her any more – believe me!'

'I'd like to,' I said, weakening.

'Good girl. I'll be back at the weekend. I really think

it's time I told you everything about myself, and then you'll understand. It's important that you do. Okay, trust me?'

'Okay,' I said.

What I meant was that I'd try.

Steven had said once: 'I want you to know *me* for *me*! And I want to know *you* for *you*. Don't let the rest of the world cloud us. They don't know – they can't know. What we've got between us is too special to lose.'

It was a great line, and I fell for it – happily, willingly, even with that small warning voice inside me saying insistently: Be careful, be very careful! Even though neither of us had ever used the word 'love' aloud to each other, even in the most euphoric moments of rapture, it was getting mighty close.

We had gone a long way down that famous bumpy road that Frank Sinatra sang about, and got to the stage where we were telling each other: 'It's important to me that you know who I am. It's important to me that you know the real me. It's important to me that you trust me. It's important to me that you care about me ...'

Two nights after his return from the States, Steven and I were back in the English House, at our own favourite table in the alcove. There had been some intriguing cloak and dagger stuff right out of James Bond before we got there, and from then on I knew that I was getting in deep.

Steven had called me the day he got back to fix our date, and somehow his voice was different. It sounded tense. 'Tomorrow night? Why don't you come round here first, and we can go on together.'

'Fine,' I said. 'I'm looking forward to it. We've got a lot to talk about.'

'We have,' said Steven. He hesitated. 'Er – you'll find a different name on the door. Take no notice – it's still me in there.'

'Why?' I asked.

'Precautions,' was all he said. 'Call me at three o'clock tomorrow afternoon and we'll fix a place to go.'

Next day I rang from my office in the City. Each time his line was busy. I tried for a full thirty minutes before I got through.

A voice, a strange American voice, answered in a muffled American accent: 'Yeah?'

'Er – may I speak to Mr Steven Wyatt?'

'Mr Wyatt has gone away for a few days,' the voice said. It sounded as if it was speaking through cotton wool – or a handkerchief.

'Oh!' I was taken aback. 'But ... Well – Mr Wyatt asked me to call to confirm a dinner we were due to have tonight ...'

'Lesley?' It had been Steven all the time.

'Steven! What on earth is going on?'

'More precautions,' he said again. 'I'm sorry. I'll explain tonight.' We agreed to go back to the English House, and I confirmed I would be with him at seven.

'Be careful!' he said, and hung up, leaving me looking at the receiver in bewilderment. Careful of what?

That night I found out.

As I walked up to the entrance of No. 34 Cadogan Square, I noticed a movement from the next doorway. A man in a raincoat was hovering in the shadows. I noticed that he had a camera slung around his neck. He watched me approach the entrance, but made no move to intercept me or to take a picture.

I felt his eyes on me as I selected the buzzer. Sure

enough, there was a different name opposite No. 3. For some reason I flattened my hand over the whole intercom so that he couldn't see which bell I pushed. Steven's voice came through, muffled and disguised once again.

'Yeah?'

'Me!' I said.

The buzzer sounded, and I slipped through. Upstairs, he was waiting for me with the door open.

'There's a man outside with a camera,' I told him.

'Only one?' he asked sardonically. 'They call it doorstepping.' In the living-room he poured me a glass of champagne. At least his style hadn't changed. We raised a glass to each other. 'To happy times!' Steven said.

'Happy times!' I echoed.

He seemed to come to a decision. 'To hell with them,' he said. 'I've booked the English House. We'll still go out – and we'll go out together!'

We finished our glass, and took the red-carpeted stairs down to the street. As we walked out, Steven took me firmly by the hand as we passed the next doorway.

It was empty.

Now, heads bent together across the white tablecloth, the meal of tender roast rack of lamb over, a glass of champagne in front of us, it was time for the truth game.

'I really hoped we would have more time to get to know each other before you saw all this,' he said. 'All this' referred to the scores of reports chronicling the 'dangerous liaison' of his relationship with Sarah, coupled with emotive headlines like 'Palace Rocked by Depth of Fergie's Friendship' … 'Jet-setter Who Broke the Rules of Royalty' … 'Queen Ordered Fergie to Ditch Texan Wyatt as her Friend'. With – how about this one?

– 'Wyatt, a Drugs Party and Silk Stockings' by way of a bonus.

That last choice titbit, I should add, came from a 'blonde actress' named Margo Schwab, who revealed how she and Wyatt went to a party where cannabis was taken – adding: 'Other people were sniffing the smoke, but Steve and I didn't.' Big deal – so where was the story?

And this was the man sitting opposite me who had apparently hypnotized the Duchess of York into such a state that, according to another report, she had even changed her hairstyle, 'which showed how sad she had been'.

Was he really one of the 'highly socially visible group of young Americans who have relentlessly partied, charmed and cheque-booked their way into London Society'? I realized at last why Steven had been so paranoid about the Press, and the reasons for the furtive way we would approach his apartment. When you are hounded by the paparazzi, it would make anyone behave like a fugitive.

He looked across the table at me. 'What's wrong?' His face registered concern, as if he could read my thoughts. 'Is it the papers, and what they're saying about me?'

'Not just that,' I said.

He burst out: 'When I got back my answer-phone had almost run out with messages, and all about the same thing. Once the tabloids get their teeth into you, they never let go.'

He reached across and took my hand. The soft blue eyes were almost pleading. 'It's started to happen, hasn't it? I wanted to protect you from the Press and having your photograph appearing everywhere, which could happen. That's why I may have seemed to be behaving strangely.

'I wanted our relationship to be based on positiveness – but it's too late now. They're linking me with Sarah – the Duchess of York – and I really think I should start telling you everything ...'

'I think so, too,' I said. 'But before you say anything about Sarah, there's something I have to tell you as well.'

'Oh?'

'I'm organizing this polo tournament ...'

'I know that ...'

'But do you know that I'm working very closely with Major Ronald Ferguson?'

If anything, Steven went an even whiter shade of pale than Ronald.

'Oh, Christ!' he said. 'You don't mean it ...'

'I do,' I said.

'Jesus!' He looked stunned. Then: 'Do you know Sarah?'

'No,' I said. 'But I'm due to meet her shortly.'

'Oh,' Steven said. He took a slow sip of his drink. His next question caught me off guard. 'How close are you to Ronald?'

'Exceptionally close,' I said. 'Actually – too close ...'

Steven was too much of a gentleman to ask me outright if I was having an affair with Major Ferguson, but I knew he didn't need to.

We talked until past midnight, but somehow I didn't feel I knew him any better than the Steven I knew already. I sensed that there was something he was holding back, but I knew better than to press him. It would come out in its own good time.

Arm in arm, we walked slowly back along Milner

Street with its façade of small, elegant terraced houses, and turned into Cadogan Square. Neither of us spoke, and I listened mechanically to the hollow clicking of our footsteps on the cold pavement.

Why did I feel a sudden chill inside me? I have always worked on instinct, sometimes bordering on the psychic, and I can pick up impressions that defy logic. Now I was getting vibes from Steven which unsettled me. I put it down to the trauma of finding out how we had both become players, unwitting or otherwise, in the drama of deceit and duplicity that even now was growing more intense by the hour. And spreading – to encompass not only Sarah and her father but Prince Andrew also, and ultimately to affect the very Monarchy itself. Dangerous liaisons indeed! I put the doubts away and clung to Steven's arm.

But now he suddenly eased my hand away. 'I'll go ahead in case there are any photographers around,' he muttered. I felt that chill again, and now I knew why. The earlier bravado had completely evaporated. Steven couldn't announce to the world that he had a new girl-friend because Sarah would read it in the papers. We didn't have a hope ...

There was no one around to spy on us. Steven left the front door on the latch and I slipped in and followed him up the stairs. Inside, I drank more champagne, and I ended up in his arms again.

For once my instincts let me down. They didn't give me even a hint that it was the last night of loving that Steven and I would enjoy together.

After it was over, and I lay in his arms contentedly gazing up at the ceiling, he suddenly asked: 'Lesley, is there anyone in your life?'

I turned my face to his on the pillow, and smiled. 'You!' I said.

He looked away.

'Why do you ask that?'

He kept his gaze averted. 'It's just that, well, I think it's only fair you know that there is someone I'm very fond of – she's in New York. You're here, and she's there ...' The words came out in a rush. 'I want to see what happens with her before I get too involved with you.'

I could only stare at his profile, turned away from me in guilt and perhaps even embarrassment. I knew what Steven was saying – he didn't want to see me again.

We hardly spoke again after that. Any words that came to me stuck in my throat and I was physically unable to utter them. I was literally choked – but I also knew that anything I said would be useless. Worse, I might lose any shreds of dignity that remained between us.

Steven was saying: 'I'm flying back to America at the weekend, and I'll be in Washington for a while. I'll call you, of course.'

He would phone me twice from Washington. Each time he said he missed me, asked how I was, said nothing of any importance or value. Then the calls stopped.

That last night in Cadogan Square I said nothing. All I knew was that I wanted to remember Steven Wyatt, my Texan lover, for the happy times.

The tears came later.

CHAPTER THIRTEEN

Love Letters

Other tears were being shed too, as Major Ferguson's overtures became ever more pressing. We would argue on the phone, and as often as not the row would end with Ronald slamming the receiver down with a crash that shook my eardrums. And, as sure as day follows night, flowers would arrive by special messenger next morning with the message: 'I'm sorry. Love – R.'

If I was away for a weekend, I would come back to the Barbican flat to find the answerphone overwhelmed with messages from him. One Monday morning in July 1991 which I will always remember – however hard I try not to – was spent in virtually call after call, with one or other of us slamming the phone down until it became close to farce.

'Ronald,' I told him when I rang back on the first call. 'We can't go on like this. I want us to be friends, but it's obvious that you want more – and I am not prepared to give it to you. I just want to call it a day. Forget the Tournament! Forget everything!' *Slam* went the phone – his end.

My turn next, when he called back. 'Lesley, don't you have any idea how your coming into my life has given me fresh hope? How you've woken me from a long sleep?'

'What do you mean?'

His voice was thick with a kind of desperation. 'I don't think I can live without you – you're too important to me now. But as long as I know I've got you and that you care about me, then I know I can survive.'

I felt a cold hand of apprehension touch me suddenly. What had I done? I hadn't given him any false promises, or raised his hopes for a future with anything deeper than friendship – surely not?

I tried to keep my voice even. 'Ronald, this tournament is important to me. You know it is. But if you think I have used you or wooed you into a false sense of believing something – then you are so wrong. I do care for you, and you're one of the best friends I have. Let's not spoil that.'

His voice came back, muted. 'Sorry, sorry. Please forget what I've said.' A pause. Then, a low growl: 'Will you be there for me if I leave Susan?'

'*No I will not!*' And *slam*! My end this time.

The next call came at two o'clock in the morning. The bell shrilled in the silent flat, jerking me from sleep, unsure for a moment where I was. I groped for the phone. 'Hello? Who is it ...?' But I knew.

Ronald, quiet and intense.

'I'm so upset, so lonely. I hope you don't mind my calling. If you think I'm being rude, just tell me and I'll go. I can't sleep, and I wanted to say hello, and just hear your voice.'

For some reason I wasn't angry. 'That's all right. I'm here, and I'm not going anywhere. Go back to sleep. Goodnight, Ronald.'

There was no other man in my life. If there had been, perhaps that would have solved the problem. I could never forget that I, too, had been lonely, lost and unsettled when I met Ronald; needing comfort, needing someone to be close to, someone in whom I could confide.

But now this had taken on an alarming new dimension. It had become an obsession that was dangerously close to paranoia.

The first letter had arrived a few weeks after our initial meeting. It was almost a mirror-image of the words he had so often spoken to me, or the messages left on my answerphone. As were the others which followed relentlessly, week after week, an avalanche of desire, frustration and anguish throughout that extraordinary summer.

Sometimes Ronald was incautious enough to fax me messages of love from the Royal Berkshire clubhouse – into my own office! Luckily my staff were the souls of discretion – until some months later, when one letter did find its way into a Sunday tabloid to change our lives irrevocably.

Ronald, I thought in exasperation when the first romantic fax rolled out of the machine in May 1991, when will you ever learn? Why don't you just announce our engagement, and be done with it!

And still the constant emotional bombardment on my answerphone: 'When we are together in our ultimate intimate moments, it is absolutely sensational. I know that comparisons are odious – but truthfully I have never encountered anything like it, ever.'

Meantime, in the tight, closed world of polo, doors magically opened. I met the world's top players: names like Carlos and Memo Gracida from Mexico, Alex Olmos from Argentina, the Heguy brothers, Alfonso and Gonzales Pieres; names that were written in legend in clubhouses across the globe wherever the drumming of ponies' hooves was heard on the hard turf of a polo pitch.

As the big date neared, things were moving well, with potential sponsors starting to make themselves known.

A major literary event during that season was the publication of Jilly Cooper's new blockbuster novel *Polo*, and the launch party, held at the Hyde Park Barracks, was described in polo circles as the "hottest ticket in town'. Ronald had not wanted me to attend – because his wife would be there.

All week he did his best to discourage me. 'You don't have to come, you know.'

'But I want to,' I protested. 'It's important for the Tournament. All the top people will be there.'

'I'm really worried about you meeting Susan.'

'Does she know about us?' I asked.

'No, certainly not!'

'Well, that's all right, then. I'm certainly not going to tell her.'

Anxiously he said: 'You won't make a scene, will you?'

'Ronald,' I said, 'surely you know me better than that by now.'

I was adamant, and invited one of my committee members to keep me company. We took a glass of champagne from the tray at the entrance and wandered into the reception hall, chatting casually and indulging in a game of 'spot the celebrity' in the animated throng of players, polo wives and uniformed officers. Voices rose from all sides. It can be quite illuminating, the things you overhear in a snatch of conversation in a crowd like this.

One female scribe for a glossy magazine was breathlessly excited to discover 'all the innuendoes in polospeak'. Thus: 'Getting mounted in order to score with sticks and balls, riding people off – it's a bonkbuster writer's fantasy!'

To each her own, I thought, moving on.

They were a varied bunch, and some I would not have expected to be associated with the game: Lord Patrick Lichfield, 'Bungalow' Bill Wiggins, one-time escort of Joan Collins, Sandy Gall, Esther Rantzen, Derek Nimmo. The authoress herself was in white polo breeches, dazzling everyone with that famous gap-toothed smile and saying 'Super!' a lot.

I spotted Ronald across the room. He was in a small group that included a very tall, very blonde woman I recognized as Sue Ferguson, and Patricia Hipwood, heiress-wife of the England captain, Julian Hipwood. Julian was one of our top players, with an eight-goal handicap, who spent his polo life commuting between Palm Beach in Florida and Midhurst in Sussex.

I saw Ronald looking increasingly agitated as we approached. 'Come and meet Major Ferguson,' I said to my friend. 'I'm sure you've heard of him.'

In turn Ronald introduced me to Sue. I said at once: 'I want to thank you, because your husband has been such a big help with the Tournament.'

Strangely, I felt no twinge of guilt, even though I was standing talking to the woman whose husband wanted to abandon her for me. Instead I found myself liking her from the outset, and wanting her to like me. Was there a hidden guilt somewhere after all? Sue was saying: 'It sounds fantastic. I wish you every success. Tell me all about it ...'

The Major was hovering around us like an anxious watchdog, and Sue turned and waved him away with a light laugh. 'Go on, Ronald, we want to talk.' It was obvious that she had no idea about our affair.

Poor Ronald retreated to a corner where he hung around, not once taking his eyes off his wife and his mistress. But he was quite safe. And I found myself warming to this rather shy woman who preferred to talk about designer clothes than about polo.

The champagne flowed, the noise grew louder. Then came the speeches. But just as Jilly was starting to thank her publisher, Mark Barty-King, for his support and faith in her, there was an almighty crash from the corner – and there was Ronald on the floor! He was stone-cold sober, too. The Major would go for long periods without touching a drop, and this was one of them. But a trestle table on which he was leaning had given way under his weight, and down he went in a welter of glass and plates.

I was first over to him to shield him from any photographers who might try to snatch an unfair picture the kind that would be fodder to the gossip pages and allow people to draw their own conclusions. But no one pointed a hostile camera in our direction and Ronald unhurt, scrambled to his feet and whispered his thanks It had been a trying evening for him, as he was at pains to point out during his 8 a.m. call next morning.

I would meet Sue Ferguson again several weeks later when she attended my Tournament, and she was just as affable – and just as unsuspecting.

Later that following morning Ronald reinforced his feelings in the way he knew best: with flowers. A bouquet of twelve red roses arrived on my desk. And a card with two words on it. 'Thanks – love, R.'

CHAPTER FOURTEEN

Sarah

Outside the windows of Major Ronald Ferguson's office the March winds were sending black clouds scudding across a lowering sky. Beyond the lines of oak trees standing by the No. 1 polo ground like bedraggled sentinels, the great bulk of Windsor Castle rose in the distance like a grey fortress. Rain spattered against the glass, at first light, then heavy, until it sounded like a military tattoo.

Ronald had called to ask me over to the Club to tie up a few loose ends concerning the glittering ball we planned which would be the icing on the Tournament's cake, and to sign some letters. He had greeted me by the door with a bear-hug and a hearty 'Hello, Lesley, I'm delighted you're here.'

He took my hand and led me towards the office, looking as happy as I'd ever seen him. With a big grin he looked down at me and said: 'I've got my two grand-daughters here today, and you must meet them.'

It didn't quite register with me at that moment who the granddaughters would be. And when I entered the cosy warmth of Ronald's office, I took in only a large pram in the middle of the room – and a small toddler, as pretty as a picture and with the cheekiest little face you ever saw, sitting on granddaddy's desk in a sou'wester with small yellow Wellingtons stuck out in front of her like Paddington Bear.

The little mite was pulling all Ronald's pens from his holder and solemnly laying them out on his blotter.

'Now just what do you think you're doing, young lady?' Ronald beamed. He obviously doted on her. 'Eugenie, say hello to Lesley!'

Then the door opened, and there was Sarah.

When she came in out of the rain I had to look twice before I recognized her. Even then, I wasn't sure. Droplets clung to her headband as she took it off and shook her red hair so that the water cascaded around the office like a shower bath.

'Sarah,' said the Major, 'this is Lesley. I told you about her – the one organizing the Tournament.'

'Oh, yes,' said the Duchess. She smiled, and extended a damp hand. 'I've heard all about you.'

Not *all*, I found myself hoping, as I took her strong grip and smiled back at her. She was absolutely drenched, in a mud-stained grey track suit and trainers. Another tiny wet bundle of energy in a matching yellow sou'wester and Wellingtons raced in, and I recognized Princess Beatrice.

It didn't seem quite the thing to curtsey, so I contented myself with a cheery 'Hi, how are you? You look jolly wet, I must say!'

I liked Sarah on sight. Was it because we shared a common bond – as well as the love of her father? Later she would tell me the feeling was mutual, and agreed that much of it was because we were both commoners – but both had realized we could achieve things in our lives which others only dream about.

She had assured her father that she was ready to take on all that being the Duchess of York entailed. But as I watched the House of York tottering on its crumbling foundations, I was forced into the belief that Sarah had very little conception of the responsibilities attached to being the Queen's daughter-in-law.

Too much of her world was fantasy come true: the trips, the gifts, the freebies, the fun, the fawning and genuflection wherever she set foot, the fair-weather friends ... what a difference from that memorable night when I had seen Prince Charles giving a lecture in the Round Church in Cambridge when I was a medical student.

A young undergraduate had asked him: 'Are you proud to be the Prince of Wales?'

Charles replied: 'It is my duty to serve the people.'

The student pressed him further. 'What would you rather do if you had the choice?'

I would never forget his reply. 'I would rather be a person on the land simply farming and being a normal commoner. But I can't do that because I was born to serve the people.' He knew it and he meant it; he understood his position, and there were tears in my eyes when I heard him say that.

Sarah would never be like that. But it didn't stop me liking her for what she was, and I was truly happy when she became an 'instant friend', the kind you confide in from the time of your first meeting. Moreover, we found we could count other curious parallel threads running through our lives.

We had both had deep relationships with older men – hers with Paddy McNally, which she would tell me about much later; mine with her father, virtually every detail of which Sarah knew and approved, from the first day he kissed me. We also shared an independent streak that would get us into all sorts of trouble – but how can you fight your nature?

Beyond our obvious love of horses, and savouring the thrills and spills of life in the fast saddle, lay a deeper common bond: an insatiable curiosity about life – and death – that took us into the avenues of the mystical and the unknown.

At least we balanced all that with a sense of fun and the ability to see the ridiculous side to everything. 'That,' Sarah would tell me, 'has been my downfall on more than one occasion when I was supposed to be serious. It isn't always easy to keep a straight face, and when I get the giggles – I'm lost!'

I also sensed in Sarah that same earthy energy that is immediately obvious in both her children – particularly little Bea – together with an electric personality, and above all a hunger for experience that, tragically, would eventually contribute to her downfall and disgrace.

Sarah had once been described by a (female) newspaper columnist as looking like 'an unbrushed red setter struggling to get out of a hand-knitted potato sack'. The lady added generously: 'She also looks great fun, powerfully sexy, tremendously boisterous and thrilling to men.' Yes, I would say Sarah is all these things.

But, right then, all I knew was that I was in the presence of this bright, cheerful girl with the flame-red hair and wide, blue-grey eyes – who was sympathizing with me over the enormous amount of sheer, grinding hard work which her father and I were putting into the Tournament and the ball.

'Dads has told me all about it. I must say it sounds like a nightmare,' she said.

'It's all rather exciting, really,' I said. 'At least, that's what I tell myself every morning when I wake up.'

'The big thing is not to panic,' said the Duchess firmly.

Little Beatrice was tugging at my sleeve. 'Look at my boots,' she cried shrilly. 'They're all wet!'

'I think she's taken a liking to you,' said Ronald, smiling. I wasn't sure whether he was talking about Sarah or Bea, but I detected a look of relief on his craggy features.

Someone had taken a liking to me, because only two days later I received my first invitation to Sunninghill Park House. From Sarah herself.

'We must get together' had been her parting words as she gathered up her children and left her father's office. 'You'll come to dinner, won't you?'

Ronald was delighted. I had to go home soon after that, but in my Jeep the car phone rang almost as soon as I turned out of the Club gates. 'Sarah really likes you; she thinks you're terribly sweet. She really does want to see you again.'

'Great,' I said. 'I liked her too.' Obviously it meant a great deal to Ronald, and if it made him happy then I was happy for him too. But however much he had talked of his daughter in the past weeks, I had only sensed the strength of the bond between them. There were clues, but nothing tangible, to the depth of the dark waters I would be treading as I became inextricably drawn into the destiny of the House of York.

It was two days later that the phone rang in my office. My secretary, Samantha Clarke, took the call. 'Can I speak to Lesley?' The voice, Sam told me later, was crisp and cool.

'Who is calling, please?'

There was a brief pause. 'Tell her it's Jane.'

'What can I do for you, Jane?' In the background, the office switchboard was in overdrive, its lights blinking like Times Square.

Sam was under orders to field all calls, and for days now had valiantly been doing her Canute act against a sea of enquiries from the media, potential advertisers, and would-be gate-crashers who had sniffed out a lucrative venture and wanted to get a slice of the action. The momentum was increasing, and already I was getting down to the fine print of ordering flowers for the main marquee and working out transport and accommodation details for the teams.

'Can I take a message?' Sam was saying patiently. 'Lesley is rather tied up at the moment.'

She put a hand over the mouthpiece and called through the door to me. 'Someone called Jane. She says she can only speak to you, and that she knows you.'

'Look,' I said impatiently, 'I don't know anyone called Jane. Ask her to leave a message and I'll call her back.'

Sam relayed this, listened for a moment, then called through again. 'Lesley, she says she can't give me her number, and this is to do with her father.' She paused. 'Um – Lesley, she has an incredibly posh voice ...'

I took the call. Sarah's voice came down the line. Yes, I hadn't noticed it, but on the phone she did have an incredibly posh voice!

'It's me, Sarah,' she said. 'Jane Ambler is my secretary. I hope you don't mind?'

'No, not at all. But my people here are very discreet...'

'I'm sure they are,' she said hastily. It would be the first of many games that Sarah would play with nicknames.

'I rang to say how much I enjoyed meeting you,' Sarah said. 'Dads has told me so much about you ...' She paused. Then: 'I know how much you mean to him. He really does care for you, you know.'

There was an uncomfortable silence. For once I was lost for words. What was I supposed to say to the Duchess of York about her father, who was quite liter-

Me, aged 2½ – and the smile that had won first prize in a baby show

Wedding day. The autumn bride, September 1982

Above: 'Gablecot', my £1.2-million home, and a lifestyle to match

Left: Rich and running, with my beautiful black Rolls Royce Silver Spur – she brought faces to the windows at the polo club

Below: Welcome to the Club!

Above: The indoor pool

... and (below) the kitchen where the Major invented our code name *Tomato soup!*

Major Ferguson the ladies' man.

Ronald … with his second wife at a book launch

… his first wife Sue, who ran off with an Argentinian polo star

… and with Stefanie Powers and me at a polo launch

... with a model on a
promotion launch

Above: Sunninghill Park – or 'South York' to the media

Below: All smiles for family gathering: Ronald and Sarah and little Beatrice, with me on the end

A message from the Major

More gifts. The nameplate of the polo pony which once belonged to Prince Charles – and which Major Ron bestowed on me. The whistle and clock were family heirlooms

On show together:
Ronald and I launching
the ladies' tournament

My dashing Texan lover Steve Wyatt. But behind my back he was playing a double game – with the Duchess of York

Steve and Sarah in Texan high society

Inside Wyatt's flat in
Chelsea

Above: The dining room: dinner for
two, and black candles

Below: Steve's bedroom – teddy bears
and Vivaldi

James Hewitt – The polo player who made the Major feel jealous

Tally ho! The ladies in action

John Bryan – balding, but what a charmer!

Catherine Lœwe – Bryan wanted a threesome in bed

The Duchess with John Bryan

John Bryan's penthouse flat in Chelsea

Lakeside frolics with Sarah in Geneva

Sarah's birthday card to me

Before the fall. Happier
days for the Duke and
Duchess of York

Above: Glamorous company at Ascot, that's me with Jane Seymour (left) and Stefanie Powers

Below: Growing space between us. The tension mounts on our royal trip to Florida

ally besotted with me?

I cleared my throat. 'Um – I know. And I'm very fond of him, too.'

Her voice took on a sudden warmth. 'Lesley, I'm really glad to hear you say that. I hope we're going to see a lot more of each other.'

Over the next weeks the phone rang many times. Sarah and Ronald gave me a nickname – 'Freda'. Why, I never knew; except that Steven Wyatt was 'Fred'. But we talked for long hours, Freda and Jane, our conversations ranging over topics from the mystical to the mundane as we got to know and like each other, and to find much in common. It was always Sarah who called me at that time, never the other way round. And it would be Sarah who insisted that I accompany her on two royal trips – acting as her lady-in-waiting – because it made her Dads so happy. In one way it was wonderful to be asked. But each time I would find myself put in the same room as the Major, something I could well have done without. The emotional pressures on me were building remorselessly, but I still thought I could handle them.

And all the time, unknown to me, the foibles and follies that would ultimately cause the fall of the House of York were gathering relentlessly in the wings.

CHAPTER FIFTEEN

The Truth Game

It was on a cool, showery day in mid-April that Ronald dropped his bombshell. He had called to see me at my flat in the Barbican, on a day when I was looking forward to hearing progress reports from a committee meeting I had called for that evening. The various strands were knitting together nicely to create what would surely be an outstanding event.

The doorbell rang just after lunch. Ronald strode in, gave me a rather perfunctory greeting, and started pacing up and down as he always does when he has something on his mind, rubbing a hand over his head as if to polish up his thoughts.

At last he said: 'I've got to tell you something, and I don't know how to do it.' He stopped almost sheepishly, like a small boy caught pinching sweets from the corner shop.

'Go on,' I said, humouring him. Ronald tended to take some things a little too seriously at times. 'Try!'

'I have never in my life told you a lie before, Lesley – but I did the other day, and I can't live with it.' By then, he knew I had broken up with Steven.

I asked: 'What's the lie?'

The Major said flatly: 'Sarah is unhappy, and I am going through hell with her. I told you she wasn't having an affair with Steve Wyatt. Well, she is – and she doesn't want to be with Andrew any more.'

I stared at him across the small living-room. 'What ...?'

'It's true.' Ronald looked at me. 'I'm sorry.'

'How long has it been going on between them?' I demanded.

'Several months. I really am so very sorry ...'

But I hardly heard him. It meant that all the time Steven had been saying those beautiful things to me, creating my trust, building my hopes, he had been two-timing me – and indeed Sarah too, no doubt whispering the same words of romance and intimacy into her ear as they lay in that same room and that same bed.

At least, I thought stupidly for no reason, the teddy bears probably got a laugh out of it! I was going to have to see someone about that dream ...

It all made sense now – how Steven had ditched me so abruptly and cruelly the moment he heard I was working with Major Ferguson, making the lame excuse: 'Have you got a boyfriend? Because I've got a girlfriend in New York ...'

And one in Buckingham Palace too! I felt a surge of anger rise in me like bile. What a fool I'd been – a silly, romantic, idiotic, trusting *fool*! The more I thought of it, the more furious and upset I became – and the more certain that Steven's girl in New York did not even exist.

Ronald was looking at me anxiously. I found words at last. 'Tell me more ...'

'Sarah asked me to have lunch with the fellow, I didn't want to – but she was so insistent that in the end I agreed. He phoned me, and it was the oddest thing: he kept saying how wonderful I was, and how much he had heard about me. He was being very open about his love for Sarah, and talking to me as if I was a future father-in-law! I wanted to be angry, but I couldn't.'

'Did you see him?' I asked numbly.

'Yes, at Claridge's two days ago. He told me how he

was going to build up his business and was going to
be very wealthy. It was as if he was telling me how
well he could support my daughter! It was all very
strange. I know it's wrong, but I'm powerless to stop
the affair.'

'Why is Sarah unhappy?'

'Wyatt has told her about some other women he is
seeing in Washington. I don't know the details, but she
is very disturbed. It's all so confusing.' He stepped over
and took me in his arms, and this time I did not try to
pull away.

We finished off a bottle of white wine, and Ronald's
own pent-up feelings poured out, as if triggered by
Sarah's problems.

'I'm going through absolute purgatory at home. I've
got incredible financial problems. Jane [Sarah's sister] is
having family trouble in Australia. And I feel I've lost
you – and that's what hurts most.'

His voice broke, and he sounded so distressed that I
heard myself saying gently: 'You haven't lost me,
Ronald. I'll always be your friend.'

And the next thing we were in my bedroom, and
together on my bed, and the afternoon was passing in a
hazy cloud as we clung to one another. We shared our
tears, too, and the pillow was wet with them – but we
cried for different reasons.

It was the last time I would make love with Ronald
Ferguson, and I would live to regret that rainy April
afternoon in the Barbican for the rest of my life.

Six weeks later I found that I was pregnant.

The first hint I had was when I started putting on
weight. My breasts became heavier, too. I had missed
a period. We had a saying in our family to describe

'the curse': 'Auntie's come!' – only this month she didn't. But it was when I woke up feeling sick that the awful, unbelievable thought struck me: Gosh, no, it can't be! But it was. I had been suffering from violent stomach trouble, probably food poisoning, at the crucial time, and my doctor later explained that this can affect the proper working of the Pill.

But it was. I hurried out to my nearest Boots, and bought a pregnancy test-kit. First thing next morning I tested my urine sample with the small impregnated plastic barometer – one line on the scale meant negative, but two ...

I stared dumbfounded as the tell-tale two lines slowly stole across the plastic face.

Unsteadily, I sank down onto the bed, buried my face in my hands, and wept bitter salt tears. The savage irony of the blow that fate had dealt me was overwhelming. The number of times I had taken that same test when I was with Jim, yearning for my own children, over five long years. The tiny clothes I had actually bought and stacked quietly away in a suitcase, a full baby wardrobe – twin sets of romper suits and bootees in white and yellow. I was going to have twins, wasn't I, if it was written in the stars, as those three clairvoyants had unanimously forecast?

But not this way. No, dear God, not this way ...

My first thought was: I want to keep it. My second was: It's going to be Sarah's step-brother, or sister.

I saw my doctor in Wimpole Street, and he confirmed it. He had been our family doctor for years, and knew my history, knew that the one thing I had always wanted had happened – and the dilemma I was in. I did not mention the father's name, not to him, nor to the only other person I told: my mother.

'Isn't it ironic?' the doctor said, his voice full of sympathy. Then, briskly: 'Now listen carefully. I want you to think about it for the next week, then let me know how you feel. Live with it for a few days, live with the idea that you're pregnant, but don't make any hasty decisions.'

'I'll try,' I said.

The worst part was seeing the other families in the parks – children playing together while their mothers and fathers looked on, smiling. I agonized for five days, blindly walking the streets without really knowing where I was going or even where I was. The world became grey and colourless, and I felt curiously detached from reality. The concrete courtyard of the Barbican became like a prison exercise yard as I circled it incessantly, watched by inquisitive cleaners as I passed them time after time. I remember walking through Covent Garden, seeing the happy faces around me, until they blurred through the tears streaming from my eyes.

People looked at me curiously, but made no attempt to reach out to me. Why would they want to get involved with a weeping woman, anyway? I went into pubs on my own, something I had never previously done, and drank too many glasses of wine.

And I cried every day.

I didn't want the baby to grow up without a father. But I could imagine the headlines: 'FERGUSON BASTARD BORN!' I thought: This baby won't forgive me if I bring it into the world with such a lifelong stigma.

I am not a passionate anti-abortionist, though I have never believed in taking an unborn life. But you should be able to choose, and circumstances dictate everything. And if a thing is not right for you, you *know*.

Ronald had told me enough times that he wanted me

to have his children. More than once he had said: 'I want you to get pregnant.'

I knew it was a hook to snare me for the rest of my life. It would also be his excuse to leave his wife and family. The whole Ferguson family would suffer, just as the baby would be made to suffer when it was older.

'Ronald,' I had told him, 'it's quite out of the question. I'm not having children with you. You're married; you've got three children at home. I'm not doing that.'

He would accept it with a shrug and a sigh and drop the topic – until the next time.

Meantime something inside me was growing bigger by the day. I could practically chart its progress, because I had kept all the baby books I had bought during my marriage. I found them tucked away on a shelf, and took them down and dusted them. For the next five nights I sat up in bed with just the reading-lamp switched on, turning the pages, looking at the diagrams that showed the size of the tiny mite inside me and told me how my own body was changing. How big was it? Half an inch? Three-quarters? An inch? I would switch off the light and cry myself to sleep until the next grey day dawned.

It was Ronald who unwittingly made me come to my decision, and to my senses. I had given up work for the week, and when he could not reach me there he phoned the Barbican incessantly. I left the answerphone switched on. My mind was in such turmoil I couldn't bear to talk to anyone except my mother.

Click! I would hear his voice pleading, cajoling, panicking. 'Please pick up the phone, Lesley ... I know you're there ... What's wrong? ... I love you so much, I can't bear it ... Will you talk to me, please ... I just want to hear your voice ...'

On the Thursday of that week, I came to my decision. The answerphone recorded no fewer than eight messages in the afternoon. And I thought: If he's like this now, what will he be like if I have his baby?

The advice centre were efficient, informative, uncritical and swift in their counsel. 'There's no way I'm going to have this baby,' I told them firmly. 'I haven't got a partner, and I don't want it.'

'Say no more,' said the lady in the white coat, pushing a piece of paper over the table. 'Just sign on the dotted line! You can take this form to the clinic, and hand it in when you are admitted. They will take good care of you.' It cost me £300, and I paid by credit card.

Mummy came to pick me up at 3 p.m. in her old Fiesta, joining around twenty other relatives or friends of the other girls who arrived during the afternoon to take their loved ones home.

She had said to me: 'If you want to keep the baby, I'm here for you. If you don't – I'm still here.' What more could a daughter in distress ask?

Back in my flat she wrapped me in a dressing-gown, put me to bed, and made me some soup. Then she gave me a cuddle. 'Sleep tight, darling,' she said quietly, and switched out the light.

I hadn't cried at all that day, nor did I ever again over the baby I never had. My only thought before I fell asleep was how lucky I was to have such a wonderful mother.

It was a full year before I told Ronald. We had lunch in a private upstairs room at the Royal Berkshire Hotel, just the two of us alone, and at the end of the meal I said: 'Ronald, there's something I've got to tell you.'

I recalled the pact we had that we would never lie to

one another. Now I said: 'I did lie to you once – last year. There was a time when you were trying desperately to get hold of me. You remember I told you I hadn't been myself or feeling too well?'

'Yes,' he said instantly. 'In July ...'

'That's right. Well – I was in hospital.'

He slapped a hand on his knee. 'I knew it! I knew something was wrong ...'

'You're not going to like what I have to tell you ...' My heart was going at a hundred miles an hour. This was proving to be one of the hardest things I had ever had to do in my life. Ronald was out of his seat and pacing the floor.

'Go on. What is it?'

I told him then. I told him everything. 'It was my decision. It was the only way ...'

He sat down, his face grey with anguish. 'For God's sake, why didn't you tell me? Why did you do it?'

I took both his hands in mine and leaned forward intently, gazing into his face. 'Because you would have wanted me to keep it. And you would have used it as an excuse to leave Susan. Be honest. Wouldn't you?'

After a long moment he nodded his grizzled head. 'You're right. I wanted you to have my baby – that was the one thing in the world I wanted. I would have changed my life, left my wife and family for you – yes, you were right not to tell me.'

We left the hotel separately, as we always did now that the story of our association had become public property. Ronald went first. Before he did so, he gave me a hug, kissed me, and said with the old humorous glint in his eye: 'You know, I do miss being with you. In every way. Maybe one day ...'

Then he turned and strode from the room.

CHAPTER SIXTEEN

Welcome to Sunninghill Park

'Freda?' I recognized her voice, playing games again. 'It's Jane! I rang to invite you to supper.'

'Oh,' I said. 'Sarah, that's lovely!' I was genuinely thrilled.

'Friday night,' she said. 'It'll be late. You'll stay the night.' It sounded like a royal command, and I had said yes before I even thought about it.

I added: 'What can I bring – a bottle of wine? Or a dessert?'

'Lesley,' said the voice on the phone gently. 'I'm the Duchess of York. You don't bring things like that to my house!'

I did anyway – a bottle of champagne, vintage Bollinger, her favourite, as I ascertained an hour later from Ronald when I rang to tell him the news.

But he knew already.

My first impression when I walked through the great oak front doors of Sunninghill Park House was that I had blundered onto a film set. Not *Dallas* – the comparison that so many people tried to make with the Queen's five-million-pound wedding gift to her favourite son and his bride – but something far more spectacular.

The Press had dubbed Sarah's new home 'South York', and in the months to come I would sometimes hear her refer to it in those words with a wry smile. But for my money it left *Dallas*, South Fork and

J. R. in the shade.

I had taken the Rolls. The bottle of Bollinger was nestled in a wicker basket in the boot – '85 vintage, a good year, or so my local off-licence had assured me. My small overnight bag was next to it. I couldn't help but feel a mounting sense of excitement as I turned left off the main A30 Bagshot–Staines road and steered the sleek black Silver Spur between two open faded white gates which, in the early evening, looked decidedly in need of a fresh coat of paint.

I found myself bumping down an uneven driveway until a pair of heavy wooden gates set into a high brick wall loomed up ahead. I could see the roofs of various outhouses, and the sloping pink tiles of Sunninghill Park itself, and I knew I had reached the inner complex of the five-acre estate. There was a small guard-house by the gate, and inside I glimpsed a uniformed policeman peering out. He appeared at the door, and I wound down the window to call out my name.

The officer consulted a sheet of paper. 'Thank you, miss.' He noted the number of my car and pressed a button. The polite but firm ritual over, the gates swung open, and I was into the inner sanctum of the Duke and Duchess of York's official residence.

A short driveway led through a group of outhouses to a neat courtyard, and I turned right under a stone archway to reach the main entrance. A young man with a fresh face and a matching smile, wearing a black jacket and pinstriped trousers, was already waiting for me on the steps: Terry Holdforth, the butler. I would get to see a lot of Terry in the weeks to come, and he never, ever put a foot wrong.

'Miss Player! Welcome to Sunninghill.' The guard at

the gate must have alerted him. Everything was so smooth, quiet and efficient (the Establishment moving on well-oiled wheels) that I felt the welcome mat had been unobtrusively laid out before I even stepped from the car.

Terry opened the oak doors wide, and stepped back as I stood, stunned, on the threshold. From the outside, Sunninghill Park House was large, sprawling, but somehow bland. Its red-brick façade and sloping hacienda roof with bright pink tiles was smart and elegant, but lacking in character. Perhaps it was the newness – after all, it was less than six months since Sarah and Andrew had held their famous £60,000 'Bunfight at the Yorkie Corral' house-warming.

Guests like Michael Caine, Elton John, David Frost, Billy Connolly and Pamela Stephenson had tucked into Beluga caviar and champagne – and, presumably, been left open-mouthed like me when they stood on the natural stone floor inside the entrance hall, staring up at the medieval minstrels' gallery and the huge glass domed ceiling that let the sun's rays pour in to flood the white-painted walls with light.

There seemed to be flowers everywhere, the Kew Gardens effect heightened by two tall ornamental trees on either side of a wide square arch leading to the lounge and dining-room.

I found my voice. 'My suitcase is in the boot. It's unlocked. And a present ...'

'We'll take care of everything. This way, please, Miss Player.' Terry led me across the hall and under the arch to the first doorway. Inside, Ronald's tall figure rose to greet me.

'Lesley! Welcome aboard!' His booming voice filled the room, and was itself filled with pleasure. He kissed me on both cheeks. 'Come in! Come in!'

The living-room was vast, and suddenly I felt very small. It was as if I had walked into an austere French château somehow combined with a homely farmhouse. My first impression was of a huge fireplace flanked by comfortable chairs, chintzy curtains that matched the two sofas, tartan drapes down the entire length of peach-coloured walls, and a grand piano packed with family portraits. Silver-framed photos of Sarah, Andrew and the princesses smiling out at the world overflowed onto the mantelpiece above the fireplace, and clustered on several small antique tables round the walls.

And teddy bears! I couldn't believe it. Was I being haunted by them? Buried deep in the armchairs and sofas were the innocent brown faces of half a dozen teddies – all of them, it would turn out, belonging to Sarah. Was this the stuff of dreams – or some kind of portent?

But then Ronald was taking my arm, and was guiding me out through the french windows onto the patio. The evening sun had turned the sky purple, and was casting long shadows on the lawn beyond the terrace. 'Champagne,' he said. 'We're celebrating.'

'Celebrating what?'

'You ... me ... everything,' said Ronald. The rugged face was alight, and he was looking as happy as I had ever seen him. 'The Tournament's going great guns. Sarah's a little tense, but she'll get over it. Above all, you're here ...'

Terry had appeared like a black-garbed wraith, holding a tray with a long-stemmed champagne glass, the bubbles still freshly fizzing.

I smiled at Ronald's enthusiasm, sharing his mood, and raised my glass. 'To us,' I said. And, after a pause:

'Where's Sarah?'

'Oh, on the phone,' said the Major. 'She'll be with us in a minute. Andrew's away, so it's just the three of us tonight.'

Even as he spoke there was a flurry of movement from inside the room, and Sarah came hurrying out, dressed in jeans and a pink sweater, her red hair tied back into a short pony-tail. I myself was wearing a blue dress that was smart but not overly so, which could double for a house party or a cosy supper for three.

'Lesley!' Sarah took both my hands in hers and gave me a light kiss. She had a high colour on her cheeks, and I couldn't help noticing that she seemed to be flustered. I wondered if it had anything to do with the phone call. 'I'm so glad you could come.' There was no doubt that she meant it. She took a glass for herself, then added: 'And thank you for the champagne. There was no need to, you know. But thank you for a lovely thought.'

Suddenly, out on that terrace with the twilight stealing over the fields, surrounded as she was by all her wealth and the respect her position commanded, Sarah seemed curiously vulnerable. I remembered a statement one of her friends had made about her: 'The thing that people misunderstand about Fergie is that she is basically desperately insecure. If anyone likes her, she will automatically like them.'

I liked her. But in that moment I felt a sudden premonition, the first sense of something wrong in that house, like a chill finger inexplicably touching my spine. It sent an involuntary shiver through me before I pushed it aside.

Sarah noticed it. 'Are you cold?' she inquired anxious-

ly. 'Let's go inside.' She could be like that, I would discover: caring and thoughtful – about people that mattered to her.

What I would soon realize was that I mattered to her
because I was important to her father's happiness and
peace of mind. And headstrong Sarah, loyal as only a
loving daughter could be, would do anything to ensure
their continuance.

For now, we enjoyed ourselves. 'Let's have dinner,
then I'll give you the guided tour!' she said, sounding
more like her vivacious self. Sarah's moods would blow
as hot as a furnace and as chill as a glacier, and I would
soon see how volatile her emotional barometer could
become.

'Where's – er, Prince Andrew?' I asked, instinctively
using his Christian name while trying to retain some
degree of respect. Despite the opulence of the sur-
roundings, informality seemed to be the keynote. In all
my visits to Sunninghill Park, I never saw Sarah in anything other than blue jeans and sweater – this usually in
her favourite pink.

'He's away,' she said shortly. 'At sea somewhere.'

Ronald said quickly: 'Well, let's see what he's
missing!'

I couldn't help staring around as the Major ushered
me into the dining-room. A polished oak table took up
most of the space, large enough to accommodate the
twenty-four replica Chippendale chairs that had been
specially made for them by Dorsetshire craftsmen.

But the most striking feature had to be the huge, glittering chandelier suspended above it, and I stared up,
momentarily mesmerized by its beauty and the myriad
lights flashing off the crystal tear-drops like a kaleido-
scope.

Sarah laughed at my expression. 'Lovely, isn't it? We got it in Venice when we were on a trip. Somehow we got it back in one piece!'

I recalled that the Queen had reportedly spent £250,000 on the interior of this magnificent mansion. Wherever I looked, the evidence stared back at me. All right, the purists had lambasted the interior of the 'Dallas Palace', calling it 'a cross between a supermarket and the J. R. Ewing ranch'. But, really, what business was it of anyone but Andrew and Sarah? It was their home, after all.

I had read about the fifty rooms, the twelve bedrooms, and other extravagances – and I must admit that a loo seat that plays *The Star-Spangled Banner* has a lot to answer for. That had been another of Sarah's lighthearted acquisitions to liven the place up, the result of a day out in Disneyland.

But the lounge had been criticized by one designer, Sandra Wicks, for being 'totally unco-ordinated'. She complained: 'It looks as if Fergie has gone into a shop and said: "I'll have that ... and that ... and that ..." without giving much thought to what it would actually look like when she got it home.'

To me it sounded more like a jibe against fellow designer Nina Campbell, whose colourful eye had been responsible for the final fabrics and furnishings. Nina was the darling of the jet set, a visionary who designed homes for people like Rod Stewart and Adnan Khashoggi. She had reportedly been given the run of the Buckingham Palace cellars, as well as those of Windsor Castle, to rummage around for suitable pictures and furniture. The result, as one observer scathingly remarked, was 'A mix of chintz country house and high-tech modernism'.

You can't please everyone. For me, there was a lot that was good and precious little that was bad about the contents and the colours of Sunninghill Park House. But what struck me immediately, and would remain with me throughout all my visits, was the lack of warmth about the place. It wasn't so much a home, more a museum stacked with wondrous objects, or a hotel. The word that came to me was *temporary*. And that surprised me. Because if anyone had been brought up in a real home, in that Domesday farmhouse in Dummer which had been the family's base for more than half a century, that person was Sarah Ferguson.

But that first evening, I didn't bother to question the whys or wherefores. Terry had left supper for us on the sideboard – a help-yourself buffet of chicken legs, cold cuts and salad, and had laid out a smaller, more intimate table for us in an alcove by the window which had seating for four. For dessert Sarah and Ronald always had the 'Ferguson special' – Welsh rarebit. She would pick up a small hand-bell from the table and ring it when she wanted service. Welsh rarebit was a family tradition, while the rest of the guests would normally settle for an ordinary sweet, or cheese and biscuits from a splendid cheeseboard.

'And your daughters?' I asked. 'Where are they?'

'In bed,' said Sarah. She smiled. 'They wanted to see you, but I pack them off to bed early. They'll be here at breakfast.'

So we sat, just the three of us, in that quiet alcove, and talked far into the night, with Terry occasionally appearing like a shadow to refill our glasses or take our plates away.

In those first intimate hours I got to know Sarah, and to realize the depth of her devotion to her father and his own fierce love for her – and his dependence on her. On that first night there was very little small-talk, apart from the revelation that we were both qualified helicopter pilots! Almost immediately I found we were delving into far deeper waters, and the conversation drifted quite naturally into matters of the heart and soul. We covered the spectrum from herbal teas to spiritualism!

I found that Sarah was fascinated by the esoteric and the unknown. Like me, she had tried to fathom the oldest mysteries of all. 'I've often wondered why we're here on this earth, and whether there's a purpose to life,' she said. 'I'm always asking questions, but I don't seem to get too many answers!'

We had touched common ground immediately. 'I know the feeling,' I told her.

As we tucked into delicious cold ham and cheese, with a refreshing white wine – 'We've got a wonderful cellar here, Lesley, just you wait and see!' – Sarah's mood changed completely. 'Andrew doesn't drink, but that won't stop us, will it?'

'Certainly not,' said her father, and we laughed and raised our glasses to a future that seemed to be growing rosier by the hour.

Andrew's name was not mentioned again that night.

CHAPTER SEVENTEEN

Sinninghill ...

Supper over, we moved into the lounge for coffee and liqueurs – champagne for Sarah. Relaxing on sofas around the large fireplace, the talk turned inevitably to the forthcoming Tournament, now coming up on me fast.

Ronald said: 'The dates are all confirmed. It should be a great weekend.'

'Provided the weather's right,' Sarah cautioned. 'You know what August can be like.'

'I'll keep my fingers crossed,' I said. 'As long as we don't have a cloudburst, we'll be fine.'

'You'll be finer with this news,' said Ronald. He looked like a man who had rubbed the magic lamp and was waiting for the genie to appear as he paused for effect. Then: 'Prince Charles and Princess Anne are going to write us a joint foreword – one page each for the souvenir programme!'

I couldn't restrain a gasp. 'Oh! But – that's incredible!' I cried. 'That's going to clinch the whole thing. It's *got* to be a success now.' Up to now I had only dimly realized just how much this whole Tournament meant to me, with all the months of hard slogging, the uphill climb from nowhere and no one to achieving now the peak of royal acclaim as the seal of approval for all my efforts.

Sarah laughed at my excitement, and Ronald joined in. All of a sudden Sarah jumped to her feet. 'Come on, I'll show you your room.'

We left her father by the fireplace nursing a brandy

while she led me down the corridor to the guest wing. My room was one of two adjoining guest bedrooms on the ground floor, each with an imposing four-poster bed and its own *en suite* bathroom. The wallpaper was in a cheerful country pastel shade, there was crisp white linen on the bed, and when Sarah took me into the bathroom I saw pale-blue towels with 'S & A' monograms embroidered on the corners. They were huge – big enough to cover a bed!

On one wall of the bathroom was an amazing *trompe l'oeil*, a three-dimensional optical illusion of a monkey reaching into a bowl. My eyes widened still further at the range of toiletries by the basin: shampoos, fragrant soaps, bottles of Hildon mineral water.

'Gosh!' I exclaimed. 'This is incredible!'

Sarah laughed again at my expression. 'I've got masses more,' she said. 'The companies send them to me. You should see our store-room – it's piled to the ceiling! I'll take you there; I call it our Aladdin's Cave.'

I was well aware of how Sarah had been criticized for all the 'freebies' she had been gathering like a magpie since she had been given the keys to the kingdom of her marriage – in particular that infamous trip when she brought back fifty pieces of luggage loaded with gifts from America.

That brilliant stroke of public relations probably did the Duchess of York more harm than anything else – until those pictures of her cavorting with John Bryan by the pool in the South of France a year later. The British public can forgive virtually anything. They cannot forgive greed.

But now was hardly the time to mention such discordant matters. I just gaped around at the opulence of my first night under the roof of Sunninghill Park, and nodded dumbly.

'Come back when you're ready,' said Sarah, as she left the room. 'Make yourself at home. This place is yours now.'

My overnight case had been left beside one of the chintz-covered armchairs. I had very little in it except fresh clothes for the morning, but I took out a pair of slacks and a blouse, opened the wardrobe – and stopped dead in my tracks. There on a set of hangers were a blazer, a suit, trousers ... I recognized them at once by their size.

My mind went into overdrive. It was no accident. I had deliberately been put in the same room as Ronald. It meant that Sarah not only knew all about us, but was conniving in her father's deceit in his marriage – and under her own roof, too. And Andrew? I doubted it. In all the times I was at Sunninghill, I am convinced he viewed Ronald as simply a friend, and had no knowledge that we had ever shared a room in the Queen's house.

Faced with that wardrobe, I thought: This is all I need. I was also having my period, and not feeling particularly at my brightest and best. I walked slowly out of the room and back along the carpeted corridor to the lounge, suddenly plagued with mixed feelings about the rest of the night.

Strangely, nobody except me seemed to think anything was amiss. Sarah lounged back in a deep armchair, one leg dangling over the side, sipping champagne. Her father chatted about the princesses, asking how Beatrice and Eugenie were getting on at school. It was like any family gathering. But for me, quite bizarre – because I had suddenly realized that it was taken for granted in that great house that I was

Ronald's mistress, and I was presumably expected to behave as such.

I looked across at Ronald, and caught the gaze of the man who had helped to make all my dreams of the past year become reality. Beneath the bushy ginger brows, his eyes were laughing back at me. Whatever his faults, I owed this man so much. I felt a warm glow of gratitude seep unheralded through me – and something else, too.

All right, so we were sharing a room!

Around midnight, Sarah yawned and said: 'I'm off to bed.' I caught a glance at her father. 'See you both in the morning.'

'Right you are, my dear,' said Ronald. 'Goodnight.'

The door closed behind her. Ronald and I chatted desultorily for another ten minutes. Then he looked pointedly at his watch, looked across at me, and raised one eyebrow. Bedtime, said that gesture, loud and clear. I nodded, rose from the sofa and made for the door. Ronald opened it for me – then took my arm and led me firmly off down the passage to the guest bedrooms.

The house was quiet, but I sensed that there were people awake: perhaps Terry and Heather, his wife; certainly those who never sleep – the security guards, the special armed royal protection squad from the Thames Valley police, constantly vigilant.

Outside the bedroom we both stopped. Then Ronald opened the door, and with a courtly bow extended a hand for me to enter. We had drunk enough wine by now to loosen our inhibitions, but still I could not hold down a feeling of indignation –righteous or not – that somehow Sarah and her father had planned all this at my expense.

Ronald started to unpeel his canary sweater, but I

raised a hand. 'Just a minute,' I said, pushing him down firmly onto the bed. He succumbed willingly. 'Listen, I want to get one thing straight: Sarah knows, doesn't she? About us.'

'That's right,' Ronald agreed amiably. 'We tell each other everything. But old G.B. won't talk. She's a great girl.'

'G.B.?' I said, puzzled. 'What do you mean?'

'My pet name for her. G.B. Stands for Ginger Bush. It's our little family secret. Andrew doesn't like me calling her that in front of him, let alone anyone else, so I try not to. She even has a necklace with G.B. on it, but very few people know what it means.'

Ginger Bush! Christ, I thought – what a family! I wondered if the Queen knew.

Ronald looked directly at me. 'Lesley, do you really mind?'

'Well – no,' I said doubtfully. I felt trapped, but there was nowhere to run. I was still confused – about my emotions, about my feelings for this feckless, foolish, ultimately lonely man who was so desperately trying to take over my life and make me fall in love with him. I would never feel more for him than I felt that night, and it wasn't enough. That I knew.

But still, I owed him.

Aloud I said: 'I thought you'd be the one who should be worried.' I gestured at the wardrobe, where his clothes had been neatly stacked. 'I mean, we don't want half the world knowing, do we?'

'They don't,' he assured me. 'And they won't. Now – get undressed and come to bed!'

'I'm sorry,' I said. I wanted this euphoric evening to be nice for him too. But ... 'I can't do it tonight. I've got my period.' The stark truth was that I was bleeding, but from the after-effects of the abortion, and not Auntie's visit.

Ronald was stretched out on the bed. I remembered something that had been nagging at the back of my mind ever since our first afternoon of love-making.

'One thing I kept meaning to ask you ...'

'What?'

'When we were first together that day, remember you told me it was the only time you had ever made love outside your marriages?'

'Yes – and it's true.'

'But what about that business at the Wigmore Club? Doesn't that count?'

'Oh, *that*!' His face darkened. We both remembered that dreadful summer's day in May 1988 when a Sunday tabloid splashed the front-page exposé of the Major's secret visits to a notorious vice club in Marylebone, in the heart of London's medical district.

The site, at No. 67 Marylebone Lane, originally established in 1970 as a 'gentleman's steam bath and massage parlour' at No. 82 Wigmore Street, once employed Oriental masseuses imported from Thailand to provide a discreet service in plush surroundings.

By the time my incautious galloping Major rode full-pelt through the anonymous green-painted portals, it was being run by hand-picked girls from Germany, Malaysia and even New Zealand, and calling itself a health club – even though in reality it was nothing more or less than a high-class brothel.

As *The People* story revealed: 'A parade of showbiz celebrities, TV actors, sports stars and eminent businessmen are known to be members of the club ...' Tarty-looking girls with names like Julia, Lorraine, Gina and Yitka stepped forward eagerly to tell how the Major gave them twenty-pound tips for 'services rendered'.

Knowing Ronald as I did now, I couldn't help thinking: Who would dare to cast the first stone? There was just so much hypocrisy around, and enough scandal going on in high places to fill the tabloids every week. Why judge him so sanctimoniously, as so many of them attempted to do?

Of course Ronald had been silly to risk so much – but, as was evidenced by his daughter, veins of incaution ran through the Ferguson bloodstream like fool's gold. He knew it; he had been caught, and he had paid the price.

Now, in response to my question, he shrugged his broad shoulders and said: 'That was all very stupid and unpleasant. I know what everyone thought. But I can honestly tell you here and now that all I had down at that place was what is euphemistically called "hand-relief."'

In the morning, I was woken by a light tap at the door. At first I didn't realize where I was – but when I did, I was out of bed in a flash, scampering into the bathroom. I just had time to slip inside before the bedroom door opened and I heard the smooth tones of Terry the butler.

'Good morning, sir. Your tea ...' The daily papers, headed by *The Times*, but also including the down-market tabloids like *The Sun* and *The Star*, would be laid out on the sideboard in the breakfast room.

There was a muffled 'Thank you' from the pillow, and then the sound of the door closing. I popped my head round – and there on the side table was a silver tray with a pot of tea, a jug of milk, a bowl of white sugar lumps – and *two* cups!

Oh! Now it was common knowledge below-stairs – official. I could only wonder what the conversation would be like in the kitchen that day – the Major and his mistress enjoying their morning cup of tea to revive them after the rigours of the night before?

It had been a wonderful night in the House of York, strange hours stolen from reality. But now the warmth of the previous evening had vanished with the cold light of day.

And in its place was a growing certainty that this whole affair was getting dangerously out of hand.

CHAPTER EIGHTEEN

Gorgeous Charles

As T-for-Tournament Day approached, my social life took off with a vengeance. The good word was spreading. I had formed the International Ladies Polo Association, and offers to hold the Tournament abroad the next year poured in from foreign fields as diverse as Milan, Palm Beach, South Africa, St Moritz and Jamaica.

My committee and I had decided to organize and International Polo Ball to raise funds for charity, although Ronald warned me that it would probably cause me more headaches than the Tournament itself. He was right. But I persisted, and on 24 July the event took place at the Royal Holloway College, Egham, in South London, and raised about £12,000 for the Save the Children Fund, the Faith Foundation and the Trevor Jones Trust. Celebrities like Adam Faith and Gloria Hunniford were there, and it received a favourable Press.

At the Ball I took the opportunity to thank Ronald publicly. 'I cannot explain to you what it is like to see your own dream finally come true,' I told the black-tie audience. 'I had an enormous vision. It strikes me that if one has enough faith in one's dream, then it cannot help but materialize.'

Then I turned to Ronald. 'How can I start to thank you? You picked me up when I fell. You calmed me down when things went wrong. You pointed me in the right direction. You became my protector, teacher and, most of all, my friend. Thank you, Major Ferguson, for believing in me, and giving me strength.'

As the applause rang out, Ronald reached for his pocket handkerchief and wiped his eyes. I had meant every word, and he knew it.

Over the summer we toured the country to appear on TV and radio talk programmes to promote the Tournament. *Wogan*, *Pebble Mill* and the *Gloria Hunniford Show* were just three of the top shows where we popped up together. By the time we had finished we could congratulate ourselves on being a polished and professional double act. Rather more to the point, I paid a media analysis firm to assess the value of all this PR. The final estimate was £256,000.

Another big social event was a charity polo match at the Royal Berkshire ground in aid of the Gulf Day Trust. Prince Charles led one team. Being his polo manager, Ronald assured me he would effect an introduction. He would always refer to Charles as 'PoW', and told me about a running joke they shared. 'We both sleep in separate bedrooms – and sometimes we agree that our marriages seem so crazy the only thing we can do is laugh!'

Crowds gathered early, with picnic hampers in car boots, and a running bar in the public marquee doing a fast trade. The prospect of meeting the heir to the throne had caused me to have precious little sleep, but I felt fresh and excited as the riders cantered around No. 1 ground to warm up.

I couldn't help noticing that the game exhibited a certain amount of 'needle', particularly when Charles was in the vicinity of a dashing young Army rider on the rival side. It was supposed to be a friendly – if such a term can apply when polo teams take the field of battle. But the match finished without any serious harm done to man or mount, and Ronald and I hastened to the VIP marquee for lobster canapés and champagne.

At the party I was introduced to the Army rider who had caught my eye – a Guards captain who said his name was Hewitt. 'Call me James,' he said, with a quick smile. Some months later this same James Hewitt would feature in the sensational 'Dianagate' tapes and be revealed as a close friend of the Princess of Wales, with a pet name for her – 'Dibbs'.

As I saw on the field that day, he was an expert equestrian, and used to give Diana riding lessons. But in August 1992 photographs of James allegedly cuddling the Princess in the stables at Windsor Barracks were reported to be in circulation among Fleet Street's less-than-finest papers.

But all I knew on that summer's day at the Royal Berkshire was that I was in a marquee, sipping champagne and being chatted up by an engaging young officer in his early thirties with wavy fair hair and the kind of crinkly smile that can melt a girl's resistance.

James told me how he had been in the Gulf War and was now stationed in Germany. What he did not tell me was that he had led the Royal Scots Battle Group on a dramatic three-day dash into Kuwait at a critical stage in the conflict.

The quiet hero merely talked to me about polo, and revealed that he was even thinking of giving up the Army to become a professional polo player. Then he asked: 'How is the big Tournament coming along? I've heard all about it – and about you.'

I wasn't quite sure what he meant. 'It's all very exciting,' I said. 'We're having a cocktail party to launch it at the Royal Berkshire Hotel. You must come.'

'I'd like that very much, if I can get away,' said James.

'And in return you must come and visit me in Germany!'

'Oh ...?' I was taken aback by his forwardness, and I noticed Ronald glaring at us from the open entrance to the marquee. His thick brows were knitted, and I hoped to heaven that he wouldn't make a scene. The Major's jealousy had been growing increasingly irrational, though with my new companion it might well have been justified.

'Let me have your phone number, and I'll call you,' James was saying without further niceties. He was full of easy charm, no doubt of that, but a little too quick off the mark for my liking.

'Sorry,' I said bluntly. 'But I'll still send you an invite to the party.'

'I'll call you anyway,' he said, with that winning smile.

As James Hewitt melted away into the crowd, Ronald materialized at my elbow. He bestowed a parting glare on the young officer's back, and said tersely: 'That man has eyes for you!'

'Don't be silly,' I said lightly. 'I think he's rather nice – but harmless.'

'Listen to me,' said the Major, 'I think you ought to know something about James Hewitt. The word is this is the man who has become infatuated with the Princess of Wales, and she has done nothing to dissuade his affections.' The inner grapevine again, way ahead of public knowledge.

The Major added: 'It's all been a bit unfortunate. PoW had no idea that Hewitt was playing, and doesn't find it at all amusing to be seen chasing after his rival in public like this. We all know what the papers will make of it if it ever comes out. He has made his feelings known to me in no uncertain manner.' His voice changed as he looked past me. 'Ah – sir!'

I turned – and there at my elbow was the Prince of Wales himself, looking straight at me with those huge, deep eyes.

'Sir, may I present Miss Player? Lesley is the lady responsible for organizing the Ladies' International.'

Charles extended his hand, and his face lit up with one of the sweetest smiles I had ever seen. His photographs can make him look so solemn. Close to, there is a warmth and a presence about him that is utterly captivating. In short, the man I hope will be our future King is both sexy and gorgeous.

'I am delighted to meet the lady behind all this. Though I must say I was expecting someone slightly older to have taken on such a mammoth task.'

'I am so pleased to meet you,' I said. 'I want to thank you for that terrific foreword for the brochure.'

'Tell me, where are you holding this Tournament?' One of Prince Charles' conspicuous qualities is ability to listen and appear to be genuinely interested in what people say to him. With that unyielding eye-contact and his full attention, the effect is to blot out all other sounds and movement around you – and for those precious few minutes you become the only two people on the planet. There were others pressing around us, but I hardly noticed any of them.

'Right here, sir, at the Royal Berkshire next month. I – er – I hope you can come and watch some of these women. They're really quite good, you know.'

He leant towards me so that he wouldn't be overheard. 'I don't think much of the ground here. What about you, Lesley?'

I found myself muttering back: 'Not too hot, is it.'

More loudly, the Prince said: 'I'm not sure if I'll be able to make it, but I *would* like to know how it all goes.'

'I'll send you some photographs as soon as we have some,' I promised. Out of the corner of my eye I was aware of Ronald making beckoning motions. Other people were queuing for the favour of a royal word, but Charles made no move to end our conversation.

'And do you play polo, Lesley?'

'Yes, sir. I love the game, I really do. But I'm not particularly good.'

'And what position do you play?'

'Er – minus one,' I said, temporarily confused. The Prince raised one quizzical royal eyebrow. 'No, that is – Back.'

Behind the Prince's own back, Ronald was getting frantic. 'I'm delighted to have met you, sir, and I hope to see you again.' I looked over at the Major, who stepped forward smartly to present another couple to HRH.

Charles looked temporarily bemused. 'Oh – yes, of course. Good luck, young lady.'

When I thought about it later I realized that it couldn't be often that a commoner ends a conversation with Prince Charles. And I'd quite forgotten to curtsey to him, too.

Somehow, I felt he would understand.

Next morning the phone rang in my office, and there was James Hewitt's cheery voice. 'Hello, Lesley, it's me. James. I'm off to Paris this weekend for a party. Like to come along?' The cheek of the man! I couldn't help smiling, but aloud I said firmly: 'No, but thank you for asking me. I just don't have the time.'

Over the next week James rang four times, and I listened intrigued as he told me all about himself – virtually his entire life story, but I suspect with salient areas left out, including any mention of the Royal Family or the stable-yard at Windsor. The emphasis was on how he had yet to find a woman who was 'right' for him. He did mention an engagement to some girl in Devon, but that sounded like a passing fancy.

The last call came from his barracks. 'I'm in Germany. Come on over, you'll love it,' he promised.

It was time to call a halt to the game. 'I'm sure I would,' I said. 'But I just don't want to go out with you. Please don't call me again.'

Captain – soon to be Major – James Hewitt took the rebuff like the gentleman he was. And never called again.

Meeting Charles is enough to restore anyone's faith in the Throne, though in fact I have been a life-long supporter of the Monarchy. I think the Queen Mother is just amazing, and I idolize Princess Anne for the work she does and the way she does it: no airs and graces, no fuss, and she doesn't spend a fortune on clothes either! She seems to bring her children up perfectly, and even her divorce was handled with dignity.

The Royal Family have been let down by the 'fringe', and I only hope they survive. Perhaps the 'old guard' are out of touch in some ways with today's society. The only first-hand acquaintance I have had with this side of the family was the day I met Prince Philip at the Windsor Horse Trials in June that year.

Harrods were sponsoring the English Ladies team in my Tournament, and I was in their private marquee talking to Ali Fayed from the House of Fraser when Prince Philip strolled up and joined us. He was told who I was, and fixed me with that beady gaze I have always found faintly condescending. 'Oh, are you?' he said.

There was a brief silence. Then he suddenly launched into a long – and less than riveting – monologue about how he had started carriage-driving when he was a young man. We all listened politely until he was through, when he said: 'Well, you're a very pretty young lady, and I'm delighted to meet you. It's always good to see fresh blood.'

There would be enough of it on the carpet at the Palace soon, I would think later, remembering this one-sided conversation. Then he was gone, and I wasn't sure afterwards whether I had actually said a word to the Duke of Edinburgh or not during our one and only meeting.

I had first been introduced to Prince Andrew on a blustery autumn day in London, at a lunchtime reception I attended with Ronald at the Café Royal for the Trevor Jones Trust. We had exchanged only a few brief words, but I liked this young man immediately. Polite, open and relaxed, he made me feel at ease at once. We talked about his passion for photography until he was dragged away to meet other fund-raisers.

The second time was in the dining-room at Sunninghill Park.

'Hello! What are you doing here?' His voice from the door startled me as I emerged. Andrew stood there, looking confused. Obviously no one had told him about my stay there.

He remembered me, and Sarah had told him about our burgeoning friendship. 'Ah, yes, of course. But we can't go on meeting like this!' He gave me a friendly grin and a quick up-and-down look and disappeared – in the direction of the golf course, as it transpired.

On another occasion, on a cold Sunday afternoon, I

found myself shivering in the drawing-room. The central heating was on – and it must have cost a fortune in that huge place. But the unlit log fire was too tempting. I grabbed a firelighter and a box of matches. As the flames started to catch hold, Andrew appeared beside me, and crouched down, warming his hands.

'Isn't that a lovely sight?' I said.

'Do you know,' he replied, 'this is the first time we've ever had a fire in this house.'

I had been popping in and out of Sunninghill quite regularly at Sarah's invitation, either for afternoon tea, dinner, or just to spend the day with the family. Ronald was always there, the benign granddad, and eventually I came to feel part of the household. I would always bring a bottle of champagne or flowers, despite Sarah's protests.

On my second visit she showed me the princesses' quarters. The nursery was tucked away in one wing, far enough from the main rooms not to disturb the rest of the house, with twin bedrooms, and a bathroom specially designed for youngsters.

One lady visitor had commented scathingly that Beatrice's bedroom, in eighteenth-century French style, 'was enough to give a toddler nightmares'. This expert in child psychology also pointed out that the brass bedstead rails were too easy for a three-year-old to get her head stuck in.

I disagreed completely: the wallpaper design was a glade of cheerful animals, and your skull would have to be the size of a tennis ball to become trapped in the bedstead. Their playroom was a pink paradise, complete with its own miniature table and chairs, even down to a small sofa where the little girls could sit and watch children's TV. 'They love videos,' Sarah confided.

'*Snow White* and *My Little Pony* are their favourites: they'll sit there like little angels and watch them over and over again. I hope you like them too!'

I learned to. I would sit for an hour with little Eugenie on my lap in the 'grown-up' seats – large, comfortable sofas – with Beatrice beside me, and then swap over.

'Fair's fair,' I told them sternly when one complained. 'It's your turn next.'

Both princesses were so cute that they could capture your heart with a single look. Frequently, Sarah dressed them in matching outfits, whether they were on show to the waiting cameras or not. As for character – those two little girls may be out of the same pod, but in no way are they as alike as two peas.

Beatrice is like her mother – forthright, headstrong, wilful, spoilt. 'I want' were two of her favourite words. 'When she gets married,' I told Ronald darkly, 'I guarantee she'll be the boss.' He laughed, and agreed.

For some reason Beatrice took a liking to my long, dark hair. Every time I saw her in Sunninghill she insisted on sitting me down in her nursery and brushing with my own Molton Brown hairbrush – and she would go on until I had to ask her to stop. One one royal trip where I accompanied Sarah and her children to Geneva, little Bea's morning ritual was to run along the corridor each morning crying: 'Les-ley, Les-ley! Have you washed your hair yet?' Then, imperiously: 'I *must* brush it!'

Bea had a habit of giggling when she was scolded, which tended to take the wind out of one's sails. Many was the time that Nanny would say sternly: 'That was naughty, Beatrice', only for the Princess to dissolve in a fit of giggles.

There were tantrums, too, from Eugenie, who had a

habit of screwing up her little face when she was about to cry. Sarah looked at her one day just as a small storm was about to break in the nursery, and said to Ronald and myself: 'Look at that face! It always reminds me of Andrew's expression when he doesn't get what he wants. He pouts just like that! Yuk!'

But they were both highly individual toddlers, and a delight to watch. And efficient, down-to-earth Alison Wardle, their Nanny, was very strict, and wouldn't stand for any nonsense.

Eugenie is a sweetheart. She has her father's temperament. She looks, listens and observes before she acts. You can see her pondering: Shall I do this, or not? Even at her tender age, you can detect a special attitude: If you like me, that's fine. If you don't, too bad! I'm not going to cry to get my own way.

I brought them a little present every time I was a guest at Sunninghill Park – nothing too expensive, but something I had taken care in choosing: matching t-shirts from South Africa with a jungle logo (and one for their mother, too); more t-shirts from the slopes of Aspen, Colorado, this time with a grizzly bear on them; little pink brooches; the obligatory Cindy Doll, not forgetting Patch.

I was intrigued by the way Sarah acted with her children. She left Alison to wield the big stick – only metaphorically, of course, as she would never hit her children – while Sarah would become child-like herself, diving under the table to re-emerge from underneath, prop her chin on the table, and pull faces at them. 'Coo-ee, who am I? Who am I?' She was like a kid herself!

'Lesley, I'm a great friend to them,' she told me on one of my visits. 'I play games with them.' But assertive she was not, unless pushed to the edge.

I always hoped that Andrew would be there on my visits, though more often than not he was away at sea. I
found it hard to keep up with his career through the
Navy, but he was obviously dedicated and destined for
high office.

The ships he had served on had names like *Invincible*
and *Brazen* and HMS *Cambletown*, which had been
based in Devonport, only a couple of hours from
Sunninghill. I knew he had been an officer of the
Standing Naval Force Atlantic, and a Flight Commander
of Lynx helicopters, and there was no doubting his
courageous service in the Falklands. I last heard that
Andrew was commanding the minehunter HMS
Cottesmore.

What always struck me as odd whenever I set foot in
his home was the absence of nautical knick-knacks in
his study. I expected at least a modern galleon in a bottle in his personal wardroom – but there was nothing
unusual to show for his naval career.

There was just one way in which the tide came in
through the portals of South York: in the salty language
which could occasionally be heard in the gangways.
One Sunday afternoon, after lunch, Andrew was watching cricket by himself on the big TV screen in his study.
Sarah was on the phone in another room. Ronald was
reading the paper by the fire.

Andrew saw me enter the drawing-room and called
out: 'Hey, Lesley!' I joined him.

The Sunday tabloids had been full of fresh speculation about the Yorks' marriage. Andrew had read the
papers, just as all the Royal Family do. Now all he wanted was to be left to watch his cricket in peace. 'You
know, Lesley,' he said quietly, 'I don't know what
they're talking about. I don't know what the hell's going

on in my own life, let alone what's in the papers.'

A county match had just begun. As we were settling down to watch, a sudden chorus of squeals filled the room – and in flew two little figures in matching red dresses, to fling themselves on the carpet and crawl around as if they were playing Hunt the Thimble.

'Oi, you two!' said their father amiably. 'Keep the racket down.' He flapped an indulgent hand at the pair to shoo them away. Two small faces gaped at him. 'Quiet!' he started again, only much louder. With tears in their eyes the two small girls obediently trotted off.

Sarah was at the door in a trice. 'Don't you shout at my children like that.'

Andrew didn't try to laugh it off. He simply shrugged his broad shoulders and turned back to the television.

But I couldn't help noticing how the word 'my' was creeping more and more into the conversation when the Duchess of York was talking about her children ... and about her future.

One day, when Andrew was away, I was catching up with some work on the Tournament in his study when Ronald suddenly appeared. 'There's one thing I haven't shown you,' he said.

'What's that?' I looked up, intrigued.

'Aladdin's Cave.' He beckoned. 'Come on – this way.'

I followed him down the passage until he reached a door, unlocked it, and flung it wide open. 'Eureka!'

My eyes widened until I thought they would fall out of their sockets. Ronald really wasn't exaggerating. The room looked like a miniature warehouse. It was piled from floor to ceiling with cardboard boxes, and I could see other shapes wrapped in cellophane stacked against the walls.

'You're not kidding! It is an Aladdin's Cave.'

He laughed at my expression. 'Wedding presents ... gifts from their trips ... They just haven't got around to unwrapping them.'

I remembered some of the mind-boggling figures I had read: 2000 wedding presents from that July day in 1986 when Sarah had promised to love, honour – and obey. Some of the more exotic included six pairs of silver and gold pheasants priced at £80,000 – I hadn't noticed them lying around in the dining-room, so I presumed they were still under wraps – as well as 600 dinner plates and enough crockery and silverware to satisfy the Savoy.

I also recalled the public outrage at the 'Fergie freebies'. Amid the worst recession Britain had endured this century, the public were treated to the unedifying spectacle of the Duchess of York swanning around the world from the ski-slopes of Klosters to the sunshine of Florida, armed with an apparently bottomless suitcase in which to stockpile the goodies offered her wherever she set foot.

Even Andrew himself could not refrain from an uncharacteristic public swipe at his errant wife in that November of 1989 – when Sarah cancelled an appearance at the launching of a £20 million ship in the northeast of England in favour of the six-day jaunt in Texas during which she would fall under the spell of Steven Wyatt. Standing in for her, Andrew said caustically: 'Thank you for inviting me to take over from my wife, who is resting up at the moment – and about to disappear again on another trip, leaving me behind to do all the work.'

The record year had probably been 1987, when Sarah notched up 'fun trips' to Klosters (twice), Barbados, Mauritius, Bordeaux, Paris, Connecticut and Canada.

Add to that the apparent magpie greed, which had the Yorks coming home with so much overweight luggage that it was remarkable that the planes ever took off, and it all spelled Bad Attitude.

At a later date, Sarah, as if reading my thoughts again, commented casually: 'What I say is that if it's free, why pay for it?' She saw my look, and added defensively: 'Also, you insult your host if you're offered something and refuse to accept it. Some of these heads of state take it very personally.'

I nodded. She had a point, I had to admit.

On the desk was a Mercury telephone exchange. 'Let me show you how it works.' She pointed at various switches and lights. 'They're for Andrew and the staff.' When she reached the last one, she said: 'Whatever happens, don't answer that. It's my private line.'

Ronald told me later that it was an open secret among the staff that when the private line rang Sarah would disappear upstairs to her bedroom to take the call.

And that whatever was said on it would affect the Duchess of York's mood for the rest of the day.

CHAPTER NINETEEN

Show Time!

The opening day of the International Ladies Polo Tournament dawned bright and clear. The sunlight dappling the vivid green lawns of the No. 1 ground at the Royal Berkshire reflected my own mood, and Ronald's too.

The Major was in top form, resplendent in double-breasted blazer, dark-grey flannels and sporting the Club tie, as he strolled across the turf giving TV interviews and paying generous tribute to me: 'Lesley has pulled off a minor miracle. In the beginning a lot of our colleagues didn't think this would ever happen.' He added, rightly and without any false modesty: 'It took me four minutes to make up my mind to put my own weight behind her in this enterprise.'

We all gathered in the clubhouse that warm summer's evening in August for a reception to greet the Angels on Horseback – as a TV show had dubbed them – twelve teams from across the globe. The date: 12 August, the Glorious Twelfth. What more fitting date for me, I thought, as the champagne corks popped and the glasses clinked in anticipation of an event unique in the annals of polo. In a quiet corner I touched Ronald's hand and raised my glass to him with a smile that reflected a mixture of pride, gratitude and relief.

He smiled back at me. 'Well, Lesley, you've done it. Congratulations.'

'*We've* done it,' I corrected him. 'I wouldn't have got anywhere without you.'

'Somehow I think you'd have made all the chukkas,' he said with a confidence in me that touched me to the heart. 'But now – go out and show 'em! I'll be with you all the way.'

And for the whole of that frenetic, unforgettable, triumphant week, Ronald was my shadow as I scurried here, there and everywhere, the adrenalin pumping through my veins like hot mercury as I strove to keep ten volatile nationalities under control and under one awning.

They had flown in from Australia, Argentina, America – fielding three sides – France, Italy, Spain, Kenya and Pakistan to join the English and Scots teams. And as they prepared to meet on the field of battle, all the ladies were saying just the right things to the TV and Press representatives who crowded around them.

I myself was able to emphasize that it wasn't brawn that counted in this game, referring to the Argentine men, reputedly the best in the world. 'They're very slim and slight; they don't have big muscles,' I said, 'but they have brilliant technique. Polo is all about being in the right place at the right time – and being able to ride very fast to get there!'

At my shoulder, Major Ferguson nodded approval. 'It is also very dangerous,' he said, speaking with the voice of experience. 'And for the ladies this week will be just as dangerous as for men. But I can promise you they will go all out to win.'

His prophecy would prove correct. England, in the dark-green strip of their Harrods sponsors, had the distinct advantage, not only of being on home soil, but of having their own ponies, whereas most of the other riders had only a few hours to get to know their mounts.

But Caroline Anier, the chic and determined French captain, insisted that her cream-and-white brigade, sponsored by Champagne De Venoge, 'will be proud to bring the trophy back to France'. The trophy was a magnificent silver specimen standing over three feet tall, gleaming in the corner of the clubhouse like the Holy Grail, prior to being taken out to the pitch for the final.

The dramatic raven-haired figure of Sehr (pronounced Sahir) Ahmed, whose family had travelled all the way from Pakistan to cheer her on, declared that this tournament had helped bring glamour to a game which in her country she remembered as 'just being played on a dustbowl ...'

The week was followed with intense and gratifying media interest – possibly, I had to admit, because of the royal seal of approval conferred by the joint forewords of Prince Charles and Princess Anne in the glossy blue souvenir programme.

Reproduced with his Kensington Palace letterhead, the message from Charles said:

> I am delighted that the ladies of the polo world will be having their own International Tournament, the first ever in the history of polo. I am most impressed by the initiative taken by Platinum Polo International [that was me!] and by their foresight and determination in organizing this event.
>
> For a very long time ladies have been seen as the long-suffering wives and friends handing over sticks at the side of the ground to harassed players. It will be interesting to see what happens when the roles are reversed for a change!
>
> I can only wish all the battling ladies taking part

in this historic polo event every possible success, and an accident-free result ...

What more could I ask? Only a message across the page from his sister, on Buckingham Palace notepaper and signed simply 'Anne', which welcomed the teams and said:

> I grew up watching polo and so am particularly pleased to see this exciting sport becoming more popular, especially with the ladies. Polo is the oldest team sport in the world, and it is wonderful to see the birth of this new tournament which I hope will become a regular world championship in years to come.

Oh ... if only! A year later I would hold that souvenir brochure and weep bitter tears at the memory of all the broken dreams it stood for.

But for now the dust rose from thundering hooves, mallets swung, the white ball bounced across the grass, and the air was filled with unladylike cries. 'Take her out of the game!' I heard shouted by Clare Tomlinson, a veritable Boadicea in the saddle as she led the English team out to the final against Boston.

From the crowded main stand I looked around at a scene that was like a pageant from the jousting days of King Arthur. The marquee shone in the sun. The pennants of ten nations fluttered at the top of dazzling white flagpoles.

Throughout the heady week there had been only one irritant: Ronald's habit of pressing little notes of encouragement and affection into my hand, often quite openly, and leaving loving notes on the seat of my car for me to find at the end of the day. 'I love you – R.' The message was always the same.

And this in full sight of the world's Press, who would have gone berserk if they had realized the story that was up for grabs under their very noses. I would sigh to myself and shake my head as I climbed behind the wheel after another tiring day and head for home and a few hours' precious sleep – although I knew the car phone would ring before I had gone five miles. The man would never give up. Yet I could not deny the warmth I felt for this staunchest of allies.

But why couldn't we just stay friends?

On that day of the final, Sunday, 18 August, I sat in the crowded main stand savouring my success. *Our* success. Ronald had been my mentor and guiding star, after all. I was wearing a dazzling outfit of brocaded silk, and felt like a zillion dollars. Nothing was going to spoil this day, which had been my life for more than a year. I pushed the lingering doubts away – they would resurface later, as they had all week – and allowed a surge of pride to replace them as a familiar ramrod-straight figure, as tall in the saddle as the White Knight, came trotting into view below the fluttering banners.

On his magnificent chestnut pony, Pacific, a gift from Prince Charles, Major Ronald Ferguson looked as distinguished as I had ever seen him. He was in his black-and-white-striped shirt that marked the uniform of chief umpire – a position he deserved and, naturally, relished. Beneath the maroon helmet his keen, austere gaze, suitably stern, missed nothing – but now and then I would catch a glance in my direction, and a small nod, imperceptible to anyone else.

Even the TV commentator felt impelled to remark: 'Major Ferguson may look grim, but like the rest of us he must be amazed at the physical commitment of these women ...' Physical it certainly was. England were up in the finals against a keen, strong, totally committed team from Boston, the underdogs whom no one had given a chance of going beyond the first round. Now they were fired up, and straining at the leash.

One girl had already been knocked flying and her pony sent rolling in the grass when another rider crashed headlong into her. Somehow, no one was hurt. Another of our ladies had an eye that was swollen to the size of a plum, and was about the same colour, after the ball struck her. England were still odds-on favourites, but wise old Ronald, summing up our chances, had cautioned: 'Boston will give you a run for your money.'

As usual, when it came to polo, he was right. The Bostonians led by five and a half points to five until seconds before the end. But almost on the stroke of time, Clare Tomlinson galloped through the pack and slammed the ball across the line to win for England by the narrowest possible margin – six points to five and a half. A final blast from the hooter – no whistles in polo – and the game was over, and the Tournament with it.

Thrilling stuff, summed up by my other staunch friend Jilly Cooper in her typically effusive style: 'It was a brave, wonderful, glorious final.' And, about me: 'Lesley has worked and worked – and so did today!' As the trophy, almost too heavy to lift, was presented to Clare, I quietly thanked Jilly.

'You're a treasure,' I told her.

She gave me her famous gap-toothed smile. 'You deserve it,' she said. Then, with strange foresight: 'The problem's going to be – how do you follow that?'

A traditional jazz band had started up on the lawns – five jovial men in straw boaters and striped blazers blaring happily away with trombones and ukeleles. People crowded around me to shake my hand and say: 'Well done ... brilliant ... a lovely week ...' But I felt a sudden pang, a curious emptiness that was totally unexpected in the middle of all the bustle, and therefore all the more unsettling.

Ronald's big frame loomed beside me, and for a moment we were alone in the throng. He saw my face and frowned in concern. 'Lesley, what is it?'

'I don't understand,' I said. 'I feel on top of the world – yet I've got this terrible feeling of anticlimax.'

'Of course you have, my dear,' he said, a gentle giant talking to me like a father. 'Think of it: for a year and two months your whole life has been about giving birth to this dream. You've worked so hard for it, above and beyond the call of duty! Now the work is done, and there's nothing left for you to do. You aren't needed any more. The dream is born, it's alive. Now – just enjoy it!'

The clouds cleared. I was being silly, I knew it. I smiled up at him. 'Thank you,' I said. 'That's what I needed to hear.'

To the strains of 'When the Saints Go Marching In', I walked across the grass with Ronald beside me. There was a spring in my step.

For one brief moment of self-delusion, I believed everything was going to be all right after all.

CHAPTER TWENTY

The Palace and Madame Vasso

The first time the Duchess of York invited me to Buckingham Palace, Ronald said: 'You *must* curtsey to her. When she's in the Palace, that's the form. It's expected of you.'

'Oh God!' I groaned. 'Must I?' Sarah had been most insistent that I should visit her at her offices in the Palace. I suspect it made her feel rather grand. In all I would go there three times – each time, despite her constant avowal of friendship, being made to feel that she was showing off a little.

But curseying! That was carrying protocol a little far.

'It's the form,' the Major repeated.

'All right,' I said reluctantly. 'If it's expected, I'll do it.'

I took the Rolls-Royce. It was the first time I had ever been beyond the great gates, and I felt that I should arrive in style. I wanted to discuss the 1992 Ladies Polo Tournament, and enlist her support. It was still only November 1991, but Sarah's diary was filling up rapidly several months in advance, and it was important to stake my claim early.

I had moved to a basement flat in Fulham and drove the black Rolls through Belgravia to the private entrance at the side of the Palace as she had directed, stopping by the gate for a uniformed policeman to tick my name off on a list. He eyed the car, saluted, and waved me on into the inner courtyard.

After a short wait in an anteroom that reminded me of a doctor's surgery, I was escorted by an elderly footman to an antiquated iron-cage lift which rattled up three floors with painful slowness.

The Duke and Duchess of York had separate suites of offices on this floor. To reach Sarah, I was led along an endless corridor over a red carpet which stretched forever until it vanished into the distance. The aged retainer made the journey seem longer, but it gave me plenty of time to take in the ornate chests and cabinets that lined the walls. The silence was so intense that the shuffle of our feet on the carpet sounded like sandpaper.

Then I jumped at a sudden flurry – and there was Sarah leaping out into the corridor with a whoop to give me a hearty hug and a kiss on the cheek. 'Come into my parlour!' she said with a theatrical leer. The retainer bowed and shuffled off, much to my relief that the old chap hadn't succumbed to a heart attack.

Sarah's 'chambers' were comprised of a traditional lounge with family photos on the shelves, a large office with two desks – one for Jane, her secretary, the other for her – and a connecting bedroom with its *en suite* bathroom.

I remembered my instructions, and started to bend in a formal curtsey. If you're not used to such calisthenics, I can assure you it isn't as easy as it looks. Sarah grabbed my arm. 'What on earth do you think you're doing?' she demanded.

I said: 'Your father told me ...'

'Oh God!' she interrupted. 'Dads! Forget it! Don't you ever curtsey to me, Lesley. You're my friend – understand?' I nodded. She went on: 'Employees curtsey. *You* don't!'

She eyed me fiercely – and then we both burst out laughing. 'I'll have a word with Ronald later,' I assured her.

'So will I,' said his daughter. 'Sometimes I don't know what gets into him.' We sat down in two comfortable old armchairs which had obviously seen a lot of use over the years. Buckingham Palace was steeped in history – and so was its furniture.

Sarah looked at me for a long moment, then said: 'I'm glad to have this opportunity to talk privately about Dads. I'm worried about him.' She paused, momentarily uncomfortable. Then: 'He's not happy at home. I just want to know how you feel about the whole thing, and where you see your relationship going.'

I met her gaze. 'I've been very honest with your father, Sarah. I've told him I'll never marry him. I'm not in love with him, and if he ever leaves his wife and children I will not be there for him. I've told him all that.'

I allowed the words time to sink in. Then I added quietly: 'Don't forget that I come from a broken home, too.'

Sarah nodded. She understood. 'I know. But don't you think you and Dads can ever be together?'

I said: 'Sarah, no. I don't think we could.'

'Maybe one day ...' Her voice tailed off. Then the old Sarah reasserted itself. 'Love will prevail! If you and Dads are meant to be together, you will be. And I fully support you! I just want him to be happy.'

'I do too. You know I do.' We left it there for the moment. And while we were being so open, I took the opportunity to bring up another sensitive subject that had been on my mind. I liked Sarah. I felt protective toward her. I did not approve of her liaison with Steven Wyatt, but who was I to make any judgement? She had no idea of my involvement with him – not then.

I had already suggested an idea to Ronald, and I knew he had mentioned it to his daughter.

Now I said: 'About my flat – you're very welcome to use

it, you know.'

She smiled back at me. 'Dads told me. It really is a kind offer, but it's too dangerous. I gather it's a base-ment, and there are only two exits. If I was caught, I couldn't run anywhere, could I?'

She realized I knew about Steven. 'It just seems to me that things are getting a bit difficult for you,' I said, men-tioning no names. 'I just thought I'd let you know it's there if you want it.'

Sarah leaned across and laid her hand on mine. 'Thank you for the offer. I won't forget it. But I'll sort something else out.'

And she did. Cadogan Square was proving too haz-ardous, but John Bryan's flat in Cheyne Place turned out to be an ideal alternative, as Ronald revealed to me later.

I changed the subject to the official reason for my being there. Sarah studied the rough drafts of the pam-phlets I had prepared, and checked dates in her diary in the office next door.

'Patron to the ILPA? Ummm – you know, I can't stand polo, to be honest. But okay, yes, it'll be fun, and I know it will help you.'

She agreed to everything I asked. She would attend the International Ball I'd planned for July, and the final day of the Tournament the following month. 'That's marvellous!' I cried, hugging her instinctively. I knew that with the Duchess of York's name behind us, we couldn't go wrong.

At that point Jane knocked on the door. 'Excuse me, ma'am. That DHL package to America – are you splitting the contents up? Which one do you want the pho-tographs to go in?'

Sarah turned to me. 'What do you think, Lesley? Do

DHL open packages?'

'They're certainly allowed to. Have you got letters going with it, and will it be obvious who they're from?'

'Umm – yes,' she said. 'I'm sending Christmas presents to you-know-who, along with some letters and photos. What do you think I should do?'

'If I were you I'd split the photos from the letters and send them separately. And don't put anything in with the packages. You've got to be very careful, Sarah.'

'Gosh, I'm glad you're here,' said the Duchess. 'Dads told me how careful you were. I'm afraid I'm like him sometimes – I act before I think! I'd better go and sort this out.' She put a hand on my arm. 'Thank you so much. That could have been a right disaster!'

As I left, she handed me a beautiful bouquet of flowers. 'Don't get lost' were her final words, as I set off on the long trek down the red carpet to the real world outside.

In the Rolls, heading for my office in the City, I pulled in to a parking spot and rang the Major.

'How did it go?' he asked eagerly.

'Ronald,' I said. 'Don't ever ask me to curtsey to your daughter again.'

I went back to Buckingham Palace for two further visits, and to Sunninghill a great deal more. We talked of everything, Sarah and I, and when on one occasion I mentioned my broken marriage she started quizzing me intensely about what it was like to go through a separation. 'I can't recommend it,' I told her dryly. 'It just drains both of you.'

'How do you cope?' she asked. 'I mean – with your friends. They don't want to take sides, do they? It must be very hard for them, too.'

'Oh, it is,' I assured her. 'Very hard indeed. I think those weeks were probably the lowest point of my life.'

She stared at me intently with a searching blue gaze. At last she said: 'All I know is that I don't want to sell myself out.'.

'Tell me about self-hypnosis,' Sarah said one day, as we sat around the fire at Sunninghill Park. Outside, the raw November wind was sighing through the trees, sending spurts of rain sputtering across the windows.

It was a day for warm fires and talk of other worlds.

'Go on,' she urged. 'Tell me how you do it.'

I had already mentioned my interest in the subject, and told her about a course I had taken some years before. Now she leaned forward eagerly as I collected my thoughts and began: 'Well, first you need a safe place where you won't be disturbed. Lock the door. Take the phone off the hook. Then lie down.'

'Yes ...?' I had her undivided attention.

'Then you count from five down to one, aloud, and v-e-r-y slowly. When you reach one you're in a state of self-hypnosis, and that's when you say to yourself: Deeper and deeper ... And repeat it.

'Now comes the important bit: you must never use a negative phrase – words like 'don't', 'can't' and 'won't' are out! Instead you say to yourself: I am totally positive.'

Sarah was spellbound. 'How on earth do you make yourself come out of it?'

'You tell yourself you're going up ... up, that you're getting closer ... closer ... that you're becoming more aware ... Then you count from one to five – and you're back!'

I beamed at her. 'It's really very refreshing. You must try it sometime.'

'And you,' said Sarah, 'have got to meet Madame Vasso!'

Madame Vasso was a middle-aged Greek mystic who ran a stall in an indoor market in Islington, North London, where she told fortunes, read Tarot cards, and promised 'Help for all your problems, no matter how big or small'.

The house where she practised healing was in nearby Southgate Road – a neat flat on a busy street bordered by Victorian terraced houses, with bright murals of windmills and plants painted on the wall by her front door. Madame Vasso was a small, dark-haired woman with sparkling black eyes who had learned her 'powers of relaxation' from her grannie in the harbour village of Nafpaktos.

The Duchess of York had consulted her on several occasions for back and neck pains, as well as for advice on matters of the heart, and pronounced her 'absolutely marvellous'. She had also sent her father along, and Ronald swore by her, too.

Sarah had already told me about some of the alternative medical treatments she had pursued, especially in her struggle to lose weight. She talked of 'Joe the Toe' – no relation to a certain John Bryan, but a 'zone therapist' named Joseph Corvo who massaged pressure-points in the body to promote well-being.

Then there was homeopath Gudrun Jonsson who introduced her to acupuncture, and the Hay Diet, which works on the principle of not mixing certain proteins and starches in the same meal. She used the Alexander Technique to improve her posture, and had even had her hair analysed to find out which foods made her gain weight.

But Madame Vasso had taken over, with her simple

resolve: 'I make people feel happy.' Once Sarah had even had her picked up in a chauffeur-driven Range Rover and brought all the way out to Sunninghill for a 'consultation' that lasted six hours.

Curious to learn more about this little lady who appeared to exert so much influence on the Duchess of York, I went along to Southgate Road, N1 to see for myself.

Madame Vasso wore a long black dress and an apron, and she was cooking stew on the stove of her small kitchen when I knocked on the door. Ronald had phoned ahead on my behalf, and she greeted me warmly, and ushered me upstairs to the 'treatment room' on the first floor.

The room was bare apart from a large hollow perspex pyramid painted blue – the 'healing colour' – and mounted on four wooden legs. Madame Vasso sat me on a stool under the pyramid and began massaging my neck, talking all the while in a gentle, motherly voice as if she had known me all my life.

Madame Vasso was good, I have to say that for her. As her experienced fingers kneaded away at my neck muscles, stretching and relaxing them, her soft voice seemed to fill the space inside the pyramid. So this was what Sarah had experienced. No wonder she was impressed.

Madame Vasso was intoning: 'There's an older man in your life. Be careful, because he is too infatuated with you – but be careful not to chop him off, because he is part of your future.' Then she added: 'There's another man in your future – tall, rich and famous. You're going to meet him, fall in love with him, and have twin boys...'

I sat up so sharply I nearly banged my head on the perspex. My God, I thought, that's pretty drastic!

I left in no doubt that here was a woman of genuine healing powers, though I was less sure of her forecasts. Ronald came through on my car phone. 'Well? How did you get on?'

'She's lovely,' I responded.

'Tell me more, tell me, tell me!'

'Do you really want to know?'

'Yes. What did she really say?'

I told him. There was a silence. Then he burst out: 'Oh, my God! You're going to meet someone else. You're going to have an affair ... and have babies from someone else ...' I had never heard him so distraught.

'Calm down, Ronald. Don't believe everything someone like that tells you ...'

'But I do,' he said. 'And I've got something very special I have to give to you. Meet me this evening at Claridge's – just for a drink, nothing more.'

That worried me. Major Ronald Ferguson, that most generous and misguided man, had showered gifts on me almost from the moment we met. There was the St Christopher medallion, with an inscription on the back in his own handwriting: 'To my darling, your ever-loving R.' He had been insistent then, too, in a note that contained the ominous words: 'As a warning to you, I need to see you for five minutes after the Prince Charles match to give you something ...'

And there was more: two Cartier pens; a gold Cartier travel-clock; earrings; perfume; a ball-gown he bought me in Palm Beach; a polo blazer; a vintage champagne decanter; a painting ... the list went on. He even gave me his polo pony, Pacific, which had been a present from Prince Charles, together with the tack and saddle – though my new four-legged friend remains at Dummer Farm under Ronald's care.

I still have the photographs he took one sunny morning of Pacific – such a handsome boy – at the farm, and one picture in particular, taken in Ronald's own single bedroom: my white Platinum Polo baseball cap on his pillow, and below it a cushion with the words 'Older Men Make Better Lovers' embroidered into it.

I had tried not to accept the presents without hurting his feelings, but he would have none of it. And now came the last and most extraordinary gift of all: a whistle and a clock which had been in his family for half a century, and obviously meant a great deal to him.

In the lounge at Claridge's he opened a small box and shyly, almost reverently, showed them to me. The tiny gold whistle was attached to the clock, which was also made of gold. Ronald had written out the legend for me:

The whistle is 150 years old. It was given to my uncle Victor by his father, General Algernon Ferguson, in 1914. Victor was killed by a sniper's bullet in 1917, and it went to my father, Andrew, who wore it throughout the last war, when he was awarded four medals for gallantry. In 1950 I went to Sandhurst, and wore it until 1970, when I left the Army.

My grandfather left us the following message: 'When in moments of crisis, despair, depression, loneliness or need, blow the whistle to summon my help. You will be blowing for my spirit, soul and support.'

For twenty years it was around my neck. I have blown it on several occasions when you have been away, or in moments of doubt and stress. I will miss it quite dreadfully. It has been part of my life for forty-two years. If you give your life to someone else, then a tangible part of that life has to go with your love and spirit.

When I die please give it to your eldest son. Take it now with my sincere and deep love. May it help you in your future life to achieve your dreams.

And the clock:

This sweet little clock was given to me by my grandmother, Margaret Ferguson, when I went to Eton in 1947. It is of enormous sentimental value. When I die please give it to your younger son.

My hands were shaking. 'I can't take these, Ronald,' I said in a low voice. 'They're too precious.'

The Major pressed them into my hands. 'That,' he said, 'is why I want you to have them.'

CHAPTER TWENTY-ONE

Ratted in Geneva

The morning sun was dancing across the waters of Lake Geneva as our Swissair flight floated down over the Alps to make a smooth landing on the tarmac at the International Airport. From my first-class seat I had watched the mountains slide by, seemingly so close below, with snow still decorating the highest peaks like icing on rows of cakes.

My heart was light with anticipation – or maybe it was my head that was light with the champagne that Swissair had been serving ever since we took off on the 8.15 a.m. flight from Heathrow.

It was September 1991, and I was going to spend my thirty-third birthday with the Duchess of York and her father as part of the royal entourage on a visit to Switzerland – to Geneva, the city which Ian Fleming once listed, despite the legendary dullness of the Swiss, as among his ten most exciting cities in the world.

'I want you to act as my lady-in-waiting,' Sarah had said formally. Then, unbending with a laugh: 'You'll have a whale of a time. I promise!'

My first royal tour! And for the first time I became aware of the goldfish bowl in which the Royal Family live for so much of their lives. It was not something I would want to do all the time.

But for now it was eat, drink and be merry! The visit was to be from 12–15 September. But Ronald had thoughtfully arranged for us all to go out for a couple of days beforehand. He wanted Sarah to have a private break prior to the official functions she was attending in her capacity as patron of the Motor Neurone Disease Association, one of her pet charities.

The official royal party would arrive that evening – the Duchess of York, the two Princesses, her secretary Jane Ambler, nanny Alison Wardle, Inspector John Askew (Sarah's bodyguard) and another security officer. Prince Andrew was 'somewhere at sea' again, aboard HMS *Edinburgh*.

Our host was a polo-playing friend of the Major's, a millionaire businessman named John Manconi, who owned a beautiful schloss-style mansion in the village of Ascona, on the border of Lake Maggiore. He had paid for everything, including the chauffeur-driven Mercedes that was waiting for us at the airport.

The village was two hours' drive away. As we drew closer, spinning along the smooth lakeside highway, I could see the white triangles of small sailing boats dotting the gun-metal waters, and behind them the glorious vista of the Alps rising to fill the entire horizon. Everything was so peaceful, I felt as if we had stepped out of our own time into another dimension.

'This is just wonderful!' Instinctively, I squeezed Ronald's arm, and he smiled down at me, happy that I was in seventh heaven.

'Happy birthday!' he said.

'Not quite yet,' I joked. 'Don't make me old before my time. There's days to go yet.'

As we turned in through the big iron gates, my jaw dropped. The place was incredible: a wedding-cake hewn out of stone, with soaring towers, rambling grass-covered balconies which descended to the lakeside in massive steppes, and a private landing-stage where a sleek-looking speedboat was moored.

'You certainly know the right people.' I shook my head in awe as the driver brought the car to a halt outside the large mahogany front doors.

Ronald's eyes crinkled in amusement. 'That's polo for you,' he said. 'Do you think Sarah will like it?'

'I don't see how she can fail to,' I told him.

A few hours later the Duchess of York saw it for herself, as her motorcade swung in through the gates with sirens wailing and blue lights flashing on the accompanying police cars, fore and aft. The Swiss do this sort of thing rather well, if noisily.

The lakeside guest-house had been newly decorated throughout for the two-day royal presence, and everything was squeaky-clean. A little unreal, I thought, because it contrasted uneasily with the traditional air of the building – but who was I to argue when the world was suddenly our oyster? Nothing was too much trouble for our hosts, and if there seemed to be an unusual number of burly men with bulging jackets hanging around, then that was something I could live with. Ronald and I were staying in a separate lodge reached by a small private walkway. To my annoyance, I found that yet again he had contrived to ensure that we shared the same bedroom. Twin beds, at least. The last time I had shared a bed with the Duchess of York's father had been two months ago – and it would *be* the last time. But Ronald never gave up the chase. The persistence and possessiveness of the man were unrelenting.

Why was I not firmer in demanding separate bedrooms? I have asked myself that question a score of times. The only rational answer is that when you find a virtual *fait accompli* on a VIP tour, and you've already shared a bedroom with your erstwhile lover – who happens to be the father of the royal guest – it all becomes

rather difficult to make a scene. And somewhat acade-
mic, too.

As we were taken to our suite a police launch roared
up and moored off the landing. 'They're very tight on
security here,' Ronald said. 'But they can't afford not to
be.'

We joined Sarah and our hosts for cocktails in the
opulent, antique-filled drawing-room before dinner, and
I could see at once that she was not in a good mood.

She had seen my suitcase being taken to our lodge,
one of a set of Louis Vuitton luggage which Jim had
bought for me when our business – and our marriage –
were thriving. Now she inquired: 'Dads, how come
Lesley's got such nice luggage?' Her own, I must admit,
was surprisingly tacky.

I cut in: 'Oh, I had a nice husband who bought me
things.'

Sarah's instant rejoinder was: 'I wish I had!' I wondered how long it would be before that little wish came
true.

Her tone had been surprisingly sullen. I raised an eyebrow at Ronald. When he had a quiet moment, he murmured: 'She's not happy. Fred [Steven Wyatt] is being a
bore. She gave him the number here, and he's supposed
to have called her. But he hasn't.' So much for Texan
reliability. I wondered where Steven Wyatt was just
then. It was too early for Tramp's.

At least Beatrice and Eugenie were in their element.
The Princesses had been give a special nursery at one
end of the house, filled with toys and games, and they
had a wonderful time running riot through the corridors
and up and down the staircases. When Bea saw me, she
squealed: 'Oooh, Lesley, why are you here?'

'I'm celebrating my birthday, darling,' I told her.

'Oh,' she said. 'How old are you?'

Everyone laughed, and Sarah said: 'Never you mind! Go and play upstairs.' But the little girl persisted.

'What are you doing? Do you want to go swimming?' Beatrice was the inquisitive one, always asking questions.

'It's a bit cold in the lake, isn't it?' I shivered theatrically.

'No, there's a pool here!' cried the three-year-old in triumph. And there was, too, a magnificent indoor pool on the top floor.

'Oh. Well, maybe tomorrow ...'

Finally, the cruncher: 'Do you want to come and see my dolls? Now!'

What could I say but yes? I followed her up to the nursery with Alison, and spent the next fifteen minutes admiring the various toys and dolls which seemed to be everywhere. The Manconis had left nothing to chance.

The phone had remained stubbornly silent, but Sarah relaxed as the evening wore on. She had lost a lot of weight, and was absolutely stunning in a designer outfit of pale blue over a navy silk blouse. Just before we went into dinner, I told her how great she looked, and her eyes sparkled with pleasure.

'Everyone knows I've got a weight problem,' she said. 'I can put it on so quickly if I let myself go.' She glanced quickly across the room at our hostess, who was enviously slim and chic. 'Do you think I'm fatter than she is, Lesley? Should I lose any more weight?'

There was at least a stone in it. But Sarah was always terribly sensitive about her weight, and I was mindful that her father had told me how hurt she had been about the unkind Press jibes aimed at skewering the 'Duchess of Pork'.

Sarah was saying: 'But then I think: I'll show 'em! And I go on a great big diet. I'm very determined when I have to be.'

'I believe you,' I said. 'But you look fine. Absolutely terrific.'

'You've seen me. Do you think I've got a lot of cellulite? You've got to be truthful ...'

At that time, I could be. 'No, honest. You're fine.'

She looked relieved. 'You know my secret? I always drink heaps of water.'

At that moment Jane Ambler came up and bobbed in a brief curtsey. 'I thought you would like to know that dinner will be in five minutes, ma'am,' she said. Ma'am? I frowned in uncertainty. Was I supposed to call her that?

She read my thoughts. 'No, I'm Sarah to you, and always will be.'

'Thank you,' I said. 'That's very nice.' I meant it, too. It made me realize how close we had grown to each other, and how much I was able to be myself, and that was the best birthday present I could have asked for.

Breakfast next morning was served on the upper patio overlooking the lake. The sun was out, the air was crisp and dry, and you could feel it filling your lungs and driving the cobwebs away. I sat alone, as Ronald was indoors discussing plans for a forthcoming polo match with John Manconi. I thought to myself: Now I really do feel lucky.

Maids moved silently around serving fresh warm croissants and crisp rolls, with silver jugs of coffee and hot chocolate. Sarah came out, refreshed and smiling, and sat down next to me. Ronald would tell me later that she had had a long call from Wyatt during the night.

Whatever they had said, it had made the sun come out
for her.

'Isn't this lovely?' She waved an expansive hand at the
incredible view. The yachts were out again, a hundred
white pocket handkerchiefs waving in salute, and the
lake shimmered blue in the sunlight.

I nodded. 'It's beautiful.'

She looked at me questioningly. 'Is anything wrong?'

I hesitated. 'Just the old business – you know, with
Ronald. It still doesn't seem right. I just feel so uncomfortable with the way he behaves towards me ...'

She nodded in sympathy and understanding. 'I've
been through it too, you know. Paddy and I were
together four years.' Of course. Paddy McNally was the
charismatic Formula One racing manager who had cap-
tured Sarah Ferguson's heart, even though he was twenty-two years older than she was, with thinning hair and
spectacles, and could hardly be labelled an Adonis. But
his sense of fun and adventure appealed to women, and
Sarah fell under his spell. She left him when he declined
to marry her.

I heaved a mock sigh. 'Older men! What can you do
with them?'

She smiled wryly. 'I know ...'

I looked her full in the face. 'So tell me – how do you
really feel about us, Ronald and me, knowing that we've
been – well, intimate together?'

There was a long silence. Sarah turned away and
stared out over the lake. The police launch was chug-
ging around a hundred yards off-shore in slow, lazy circles, with watchful eyes at the wheel.

At last she said: 'I don't think we should talk about it.
But whatever you do, don't be pressurized. Dads is like
a little boy, and when he lost Mummy I had to really

take him under my wing.'

'Yes ... I see ... But you know that I can never give him all he wants from me?'

'I know,' said Sarah. 'But he's desperately in love with you.'

'Look, I've always been honest with him. I've always told him I can't be any more to him than I am now. I *won't* be his wife ...'

Sarah sighed, and there was sadness in her voice when she finally said: 'I don't know how you're going to work it out, but you've got to think long and hard about what you're going to do.'

On the first evening we roared out to a local restaurant in three limousines, complete with our faithful police escort. 'When the Duchess of York is in town, nobody sleeps!' I said jocularly. The restaurant was family-owned, justly proud of its cooking, and the Manconis were obviously well known judging by the welcome we received.

A large round table was waiting for us, set for twelve. A menu had been prepared – home-cooked pasta and local Swiss white wine – and the atmosphere was just marvellous.

It was a noisy night, and grew more animated as the wine flowed. At the end, as the bill was presented and Mr Manconi reached into his pocket for his wallet, Sarah held up an imperious hand. 'My treat!' she said. There were murmurs of protest, but she reached over and took the bill from its saucer. Sometimes I thought I would never fathom his daughter, this strange mix of parsimony, calculated avarice – and sudden spontaneous acts of generosity.

On the eve of my birthday we dined at the Manconis'

private residence. The wine flowed and our spirits lightened by the minute. We returned to the schloss feeling just that way – 'I'm schlossed!' as I giggled to anyone willing to listen to my alcohol-induced wit.

'Me too,' Sarah echoed. 'Let's open some wine.'

Ronald headed for the kitchen as our hosts diplomatically made their excuses and retired to bed. There was the happy sound of exploding corks, and he returned with a beaming smile writ large on his craggy features – and two bottles of chilled white wine.

The party was warming up. Inspector John Askew and Jane Ambler sat at a table in one corner sipping nothing stronger than orange juice – neither of them ever lost sight of their position within the household. But the rest of us ... well, to put it mildly, Sarah and I got absolutely 'ratted' – her own word for pie-eyed.

'Right!' the Duchess of York shouted. 'Everyone's got to tell a joke. I'll start!'

And she launched into a long shaggy-dog story which had us in hysterics. Mainly it had to do with her hiding behind a curtain, peering out and pulling funny faces – and although Sarah has a reputation for earthy humour, I can promise that this was clean, simple fun with no bad language or vulgarity. I just wish I could remember the joke or the punch-line, but I'm sorry – I can't. I think it had something to do with a comedian appearing in an amateur contest ... but don't hold me to it!

At the end she tripped merrily out of the room in search of a fresh bottle, and Ronald turned to me, his face beaming. 'This is the first time in months I've seen my old Sarah back. I haven't seen her look so happy for ages. She's really letting her hair down, and I haven't seen her doing this since she's been married to Andrew.'

The jokes flowed thick and fast, and became sillier by

the minute. None of us ladies wanted to go to bed; we were having too good a time. We could have gone on till dawn if Ronald, suddenly reverting to being a real old-fashioned father, had not suddenly boomed: 'Right, girls! Go to bed! It's late, and we'll all have hangovers.'

He was right. Next morning our heads were thumping loud enough to be heard clear across the lake. Still in my pyjamas, I was sitting on the patio with Ronald, nursing my fifth cup of black coffee, when Sarah came along the private walkway carrying something in her hand.

'Happy birthday!' she intoned in a weak voice, and threw it at me with a limp hand. It was a colourful streamer, but it could only land somewhat pathetically several feet from me. 'Oh dear. Is your head as bad as mine?'

'Worse!'

She produced a package wrapped in colourful paper, and handed it to me. Inside nestled a gift-box of Floris bath-oils, lotions, perfumes, and soaps – actually freebies, as Ronald happened to mention later. But the thought was there. And I wasn't complaining – because in London they had presented me with a magnificent gift: a superb video camera with which to record the trip. 'A joint gift from us,' Sarah had said, kissing me. These Fergusons were unbelievable!

She gave me a birthday card that was typical Sarah – on the outside, a cartoon of Buckingham Palace, with the words: 'Her Majesty isn't sending you a telegram this year, but ...'; and inside: 'She would like you to know she's counting! Happy birthday!' In blue ink she had signed it 'Love, Sarah'. In addition to the jokey card, she gave me a second one – a genuine 'Happy Birthday'.

In the lounge they had hung out a banner with

'Happy Birthday Lesley' inscribed on it in large capitals. We stayed in pyjamas and dressing-gowns all morning, slowly recovering – helped by an unexpected cabaret from little Eugenie, who rushed in wrapped in sticky tape wound around her body and legs like a miniature Egyptian mummy.

Before we left we went on an exhilarating speedboat trip across the lake which took our breath away. Sarah had changed into a swimming-costume, and lay back on her seat, drinking in the sun and the spray. Occasionally she pinched her thighs, looked at me, and groaned. The curse of cellulite!

A walkie-talkie message was relayed through to our police bodyguard on the boat. Could we return at once to the jetty. Little Beatrice was missing her mummy. The speedboat made for the shore, and one squealing child was deposited in her mother's arms before we headed back, constantly shadowed by the police launch.

Looking at Sarah cuddling her daughter and laughing out loud as they shared some childish joke together, I knew that here was somebody who might only reserve 'quality time' for her children, but who was a loving mother all the same.

All too soon the two stolen days were over, and duty called. The motorcade appeared promptly at 10 a.m. and by now word had spread that someone special had been staying in the village. As I climbed into the big official car, I had a renewed glimpse of life in the goldfish bowl: the faces staring in through the window, idly curious; the pointing fingers; the traffic being stopped to make way for the royal convoy.

As I watched, a subtle change came over her, a metamorphosis that was intangible yet blindingly obvious

She became the Duchess of York.

Her posture changed. She stiffened in her seat. Even her features tightened. 'Let me see the schedule again,' she said briskly, and went through it item by item as if it were a shopping-list.

Flashing blue lights tend to be tiring on the eyes if you're stuck behind them for too long, and the monotonous dah-dah dah-dah of the two-tone siren was enough to inflict a lasting headache on the deaf. I felt a sense of relief when our police escort reached the imposing portals of the Richmond Hotel in Geneva, where a whole floor had been set aside for us 'for security'.

In her third-floor suite Sarah took me to the window and gestured down at the crowd below. I could make out TV cameras and sound-crews, and saw the bunched figures of professionals who were there to work, not gawp. 'Always make friends with the Press. As you get to know them you'll find your favourites who will really look after you.' Not when there's a major story bubbling away in the cauldron of world interest, I thought, wondering how soon Sarah would find out who her friends really were.

For now, I was taught the rudiments of joining a royal entourage. The Duchess of York's engagements in the land of the cuckoo clock were not desperately taxing: a ball that evening at the Geneva Polo Club which would bring valuable Swiss francs into her motor neurone charity; a polo match the following day; then home.

Ronald and Jane gave me individual pep-talks to bolster my confidence. I would be on show, too, though strictly in the background. Still, there were formalities to be observed. 'Always keep two steps behind her, and be aware of where she is moving next,' Jane instructed.

She was an old hand at the game. 'Be ready to take any flowers or gifts she passes to me.'

The afternoon dragged by. We were trapped in the suite, in our gold-plated goldfish bowl, unable to be like ordinary human beings and walk down openly into the lobby for a stroll around the city. Fame has its price. Instead, Sarah ordered hamburgers and chips, which we shared around as a prelude to the 'smart food' that would no doubt be on our plates in a few hours.

The ball was in a large marquee in the grounds of the Club. As we arrived, Jane said hurriedly: 'I forgot to tell you – just keep walking. Push past anyone who isn't officially being introduced. Make sure you're not parted from the Duchess – and keep smiling!'

'Oh,' I said. 'Right. Thanks for telling me.' She was right, too. Faces pushed eagerly towards us, and you knew that every one of them was there for a personal smile – and, if the fates were kind, even a *word* – from the Duchess. Because I was in the entourage people jumped to the natural conclusion that I was part of 'her circle', and treated me as such. Sarah's speech went down well, as she had known it would, complimenting her hosts by being delivered in their language – a small point, but vital to the cause, which in this case was raising money for her pet charity.

Back at the hotel, Sarah hurried to her suite to make a call to Steven. He was there, and they had a chat – as Ronald put it – that 'left a smile on her face all the next day'.

I was awoken by little Beatrice banging on my pillow with a small but determined fist. Sarah put her face round the door. What would I like for breakfast? Ronald was in the next room finishing off his prune juice, his regular starter to the day. I muttered something about eggs, and dozed off again.

Twenty minutes later Sarah was back with a tray of eggs and toast. As I sat up in bed, still drowsy from sleep, I knocked the plate, and one of the eggs slid off onto the carpet. 'Oh ...' I said, peering over the side – but Sarah had raced into action, grabbed a towel from the bathroom, and wiped the mess clean.

Before the big afternoon polo match, we had lunch in the hotel dining-room. Little Beatrice was feeling particularly mischievous that day, and started to pick bread rolls out of their basket and tear them apart, dropping the pieces on the tablecloth and on the floor. I noticed people at neighbouring tables stop talking, and start to stare.

Sarah scolded her. 'Beatrice, no!'

The little girl ignored her. Sarah tried again.

This time Bea raised her small face petulantly and responded: 'I'll do it if I want to!' The crumbs were everywhere.

That did it! Sarah got up out of her seat, grabbed her daughter's hand, and marched her resolutely across the dining-room to an empty alcove on the far side. I watched Bea's face as her mother gave her a good talking-to: first sullen, then apprehensive – then an eager nod.

I couldn't think what threat or inducement Sarah had made to her daughter – I knew that both she and Andrew abhorred corporal punishment.

But when she brought Beatrice back to the table the little girl raised her face, looked us all in the eye as she spoke, and said in a loud voice: 'I am very sorry for being so rude, and I will not do it again.' Then she sat down in her seat, and didn't say another word for the rest of the meal.

I was curious. When the moment was right, I leaned over and asked Ronald: 'What on earth did Sarah say to make Bea sound so grown-up?'

Ronald eyed his granddaughter across the table from beneath his bushy ginger brows. Quietly he replied: 'Whenever Beatrice is naughty, Sarah always takes her aside and reminds her that she is a very special little girl, and that everyone is watching her. And she must behave, and cannot afford to act like a baby. Otherwise Mummy would have to smack her in public – which would make Mummy even more angry once she got home. So is it worth it?'

How grown-up does a child of three have to be, I wondered? But even if Bea was still a tiddler in the goldfish bowl, she seemed a happy little girl.

As was her sister, equally noisy at our family table. Eugenie was only just over a year old, but possessed a powerful set of lungs for such a wee mite. Suddenly she gave full vent to them. '*A-l-i-s-o-n!*' Her voice rang round the dining-room.

Nanny was horrified. 'Don't be so familiar!' Alison Wardle said sharply, at which the little tot looked suitably abashed, and we all giggled.

We had become aware of two middle-aged American ladies trying to enjoy their own lunch nearby. As we got up to leave, Sarah walked over and apologized for the noise from our table.

'We had to be in here, as there are a lot of photographers outside waiting to take pictures,' she explained.

'Oh, are you somebody famous?' asked one of the ladies. 'We heard the Duchess of York is in town. Are you important as well?'

'Yes,' said Sarah. 'Actually I am the Duchess, and these two are the Princesses.'

There was a silence while the two tourists digested the information. At last one nodded, and said slowly: 'Well, I guess you kind of look like her.'

Sarah dined out on that one for weeks.

The polo afternoon went well, and we returned to the suite to pack for the trip home the next day.

Sarah suddenly threw down a dress she was holding and turned to her father. 'Dads, why don't we stay here another night? I don't want to go back to that place. I just can't bear it. He'll be there...'

Was this really Prince Andrew she was talking about?

Yes, it was. And she went home to him.

CHAPTER TWENTY-TWO

John Bryan

The other Texas ranger riding rough-shod through the life of the Duchess of York was John Bryan. A cousin of Steven Wyatt's through a series of complicated marriages on the part of various aunts and uncles, he moseyed onto the royal prairie in the late summer of 1991, but it was not until some weeks later that his name became publicly linked with hers.

'Johnny' had been born in the East Coast state of Delaware on 30 June 1955, the son of a copper magnate who moved the family to New York when John was still a youngster. He was in his teens when his parents divorced, and was sent to school in Houston, Texas, where he struck up a close friendship with Steven Wyatt, the 'college jock', which would endure for the next twenty years and more.

Both young men were good at sport, became expert skiers, and dabbled in the health-food cult that was part of their up-bringing. They also joined the exclusive clique known as the Texas Longhorns, a group of play-boy bachelors who worshipped the twin gods of hard work and hedonism.

The first I knew of this particular Longhorn was when the phone rang out of the blue one morning in October 1991, and the excited voice of Catherine Loewe shrilled down the line. 'Lesley, there's a new man in my life. His name's John Bryan. You've got to meet this guy – I can't make him out. He's outrageous, he's flashy, he's posey – but he's got something.'

Catherine was a girlfriend I had known for three years whom I first met at a party in Chelsea. I had given her a lift home in my Rolls, to which she reacted with the comment: 'This car is so big you've got to shout from one end to the other to make yourself heard!'

She was a vivacious, attractive girl in her late twenties who came from the wealthy Loewe leather family, moved in society circles, and was on the 'A' list for all the top parties. Just the sort of girl to be targeted by John Bryan, I would discover, in his ruthless quest to conquer the Everests of London's top echelons.

Catherine was a bright young woman with a mind of her own. She had a degree in the History of Art from the University of East Anglia, and had worked in various West End galleries. We found we shared more than one common interest, not least of which was a capacity to organize events – she specialized in conferences – and, when my Tournament was approaching, we would compare notes on what lay ahead.

Right now her consuming interest was this tall, personable thirty-six-year-old American businessman who had waltzed into her life a few days previously at Tramp's, the Jermyn Street haunt of the rich, the famous — and those who aspired to be both.

'Come and have dinner. I want you to meet him. And he wants to meet you.'

'Fine with me,' I said, mildly amused. If she was happy, so was I. We fixed a date for the following Saturday night at 190 Queen's Gate.

I arrived on time, to find Catherine waiting for me – alone. 'I don't know where John is,' she said, with a hopeless shrug. 'But he's like that. I'm sure he'll turn up.'

'Tell me,' I said. 'Who is this man?'

Over the veal and salad, Catherine told me how John Bryan had picked her up.

'I'd gone to Tramp's with another girlfriend,' she began. 'Amanda. You don't know her. She's an actress – a little zany, but a lot of fun. We had been to a party and had grown bored with it, and Amanda suggested: "Let's go to Tramp's." It had been one of those Chelsea parties, and we were both dressed in wild outfits – I was in a leopard-skin mini-dress and looked totally outrageous!

'We were sitting at the bar, and Amanda was being *very* noisy, laughing and chatting with the waiters the way she always did. It can be a very friendly place. She was saying: "Give me another bottle of champagne *now* or I'll tell your grandmother in Sicily!" They loved it.

'Johnny Bryan was standing with a friend at the other end of the bar, eyeing us. I honestly knew nothing about him. I'd never heard of him, and he had yet to make the headlines as the Duchess of York's friend and "financial adviser".

'The pair of them had been laughing at Amanda's behaviour. The next thing I knew, Johnny was standing at my elbow and saying: "Can I buy you a drink?" We were all laughing at nothing in particular, as people do when they're having fun or drinking too much, and then he added the oldest pick-up line in the world: "What are you two girls doing in a place like this?"'

Original, I thought, looking at Catherine's animated face. But she had obviously fallen for it. 'Go on,' I said.

'Johnny invited us both back to a table he had reserved – and all of a sudden the waiters were swarming around us like flies. They just could not do enough for this man. The owner, John Gold, came over and shook his hand and said "Welcome!" And I thought: Who is this guy? But he was terribly entertaining, and charming – and a wonderful dancer, as I found out when he took me on the floor, and waltzed me off my feet, whatever tune they were playing! Okay, he was being terribly forward, as so many Americans are. But fun at the same time, and not at all offensive.'

I was intrigued. Catherine had been around this kind of scene for years now, and was not the sort of girl to be swept off her feet by your average fast-talking American. This man Bryan must have something. He still hadn't put in an appearance, and I was starting to get the feeling that we had been stood up.

It didn't matter. Catherine and I always had a good time in each other's company, and we had a lot of news to catch up on. She was still pouring out her story.

'That night Johnny was on such a high! He had completed some amazing deal – don't ask me what – and he was celebrating. The champagne flowed like water. He kept saying: "It's really major." And he had a spark about him – unlike so many of the wealthy playboys and jet-setters you meet at places like Tramp's who are just plain boring.

'As for Amanda, she was getting more and more outrageous. At one point she said to me: "Come on, Catherine, let's swap clothes – here and now, at the table! Or under it ..."'

Now I really was agog. 'Wow! What happened then?'

Catherine laughed. 'She was all for taking her dress off on the spot. And she wasn't wearing anything underneath! I managed to dissuade her from that – but then she insulted some other woman on the dance-floor by calling her a cabbage! The boyfriend got angry, and she told him to drop dead! Oh dear – what a night that was. But Johnny kept his cool and smoothed things over.

'We stayed at the club until it closed, somewhere

around three in the morning. Then we all piled out into the street and found a taxi to take us back to his place – "Strictly for coffee only, ladies" was Johnny's line. And that night, that's all it was. Poor Amanda was so drunk she fell headlong into a pile of black rubbish bags on the pavement outside the club, but we pulled her out and somehow got her into the cab. We were just a hilarious, happy group having a high old time.'

And John, I asked – how did he behave? I was curious about this man who had suddenly sent my girlfriend's life into a somersault.

'Oh, we were all too tired to do more than sit around and drink coffee and try and get our heads back together. He lives in Chelsea, a top-floor flat with the most marvellous view of the river. We just sat around and talked, and then the sun came up – and he called a cab for us.'

Catherine sighed. 'He really rates himself. But there's something about him that intrigues me. That's why I rang you. I'd like to know what you think of him.'

At that moment I found out. We had reached the coffee stage when there was a bustle of movement and a tall, balding man in a patterned blue and white ski sweater with penguins shuffling all over it suddenly materialized at the table. It could only be Johnny.

'Hi, women!' His voice was a disarming drawl, the blue eyes lazily feigning an apology. Here was a man with total confidence in himself, I found myself thinking, a man who had power over women – and knew it. 'I've just come off the ski slopes!'

That was a novel excuse – but he had, too, as it transpired, and his plane from Geneva had been delayed. And now here he was, Johnny Bryan, the man who by design or chance would cause a royal scandal, sitting down with us and taking my hand as if he had known me all my life. And saying earnestly: 'Lesley, this is a real pleasure. Catherine has told me so much about you.'

I felt the oddest shiver flicker up and down my spine. There are some people you take an instant liking to on sight, even if you can't put a finger on why, but John Bryan was not one of them. Call it a sixth sense. As the night wore on I would tell myself I was wrong. He was an absolute charmer, constantly laughing, always entertaining, with the incisive wit I had found in New York bankers or among the Wall Street whizz-kids I had met in America.

But ... I didn't trust him. As Catherine had said, he was flash, brash, a typical American full of his own success. He had the gift of making a girl feel relaxed, so why did I feel uneasy in his presence?

I pushed my doubts away, and went with the flow.

Johnny called for a bottle of champagne, then said expansively: 'Right, we're off to Tramp's.'

We hit the club as if it were going out of style, whooping it up from the moment we descended the staircase into the bar and called for the first bottle of bubbly. Catherine and John danced the night away – and when the tall Texan persuaded me out onto the floor I found I was in the arms of the Big State's answer to Fred Astaire. Johnny was a mover and a groover, and that night he could have auditioned for a Gene Kelly musical and landed the role.

At our corner table away from the dance-floor, he talked business. He made it clear to us that he was hugely successful, that he ran a film business, and was part-owner of a nightclub in New York. Through a haze of champagne bubbles I also gathered that he was building a hospital in Germany, though I remained unclear exactly how or where. 'I'm going over there in a couple of days, girls. Do you want to come with me?' Straight and to the point was Johnny.

We stayed until the waiters started putting the chairs on the tables, 3 a.m., then back to Johnny's place in his chauffeur-driven Mercedes, which was on stand-by throughout the night. His flat was in Cheyne Place, off the King's Road, and, although he didn't know it, previous near-neighbours had included the artist Annigoni and the film director Joseph Losey, as well as a varied selection of actors, artists and socialites, most of whom frequented the famous Pheasantry Club across the road.

But Johnny was more intent on telling us about his 'good friends' Andy Warhol, Mick Jagger, and a whole host of other show-business names. We were all three of us quite tipsy as we took the lift to his penthouse apartment, and the slightest thing would trigger us off into gales of meaningless laughter. I heard him giving Catherine a nice chat-up line: 'Oh, there's so much electricity between us – I can feel it. Can't you?'

She remained singularly unimpressed, though she had to admit that he did have that certain charm.

His flat, when we walked into it, was a *mess*. A typical bachelor's pad, Catherine and I agreed, the décor a rather vulgar red and grey with two large red sofas in the living-room, a grand piano, and a large red canvas over the fireplace. On the glass-topped coffee table was a book which looked as if it had been left there deliberately – the book that Sarah had written about Queen Victoria. And pinned to the front, a note that said simply: 'To John, love – S.'

The striking feature of that apartment was the south-facing picture window, with a wonderful view of the Thames and the lights of South London beyond it. Now there was a show-stopper!

Johnny was in the kitchen opening a bottle of wine. As Catherine and I stood at the window staring out at the lights reflected in the river, I muttered out of the side of my mouth: 'I hope you know what you're doing. As far as I'm concerned, this guy is a moron!'

'Give him a chance,' she said.

I went into the kitchen to make myself a coffee, just as Johnny weaved his way towards the bathroom. He left the door open, and beckoned Catherine to join him. 'Come on in,' he called, 'and see what we've got here.'

Through the door I saw him produce a plastic bag of white powder from a cupboard, and carefully trickle out a line of it onto a marble shelf. He looked at her. 'Want to try some?'

'Why not?' Catherine said. She would tell me later: 'It's no big deal. I don't smoke dope. I've never tried anything harder than coke, and I never will. I'm really not into drugs.' And in the eighties, she added, most of her girlfriends had tried substances of one kind or another.

I didn't see it that way. Johnny waved a hand at me. 'You want some of this?'

'What is it?' But of course I knew.

'Coke.' He took out a thin wad of ten-pound notes, selected one, and rolled it up into a tight tube.

'You must be joking,' I told him curtly. 'I've never taken anything like this in my life, and I don't intend to start now.'

'Okay, fine,' was all he said.

To me, it was anything but okay or fine. I think the whole drug sub-culture is wrong, and I don't find people who indulge in drugs particularly clever. My main thought was for Catherine.

But she was a grown-up girl, and I left them to it. I

marched into the living-room with my coffee, took off my earrings and shoes, and curled up on the sofa to watch a video on the TV. But I couldn't help glancing back.

Through the bathroom door I saw Johnny push the ten-pound note into one nostril and sniff up a whole line of the powder. Then he laid out a second line and passed the rolled-up note to Catherine. 'It's all yours,' he said.

She told me later that she hadn't touched the stuff for a long time, at least seven years, and certainly wasn't going to get hooked on it. But she followed suit, though with markedly less enthusiasm.

Catherine explained to me when we compared notes: 'Really, Lesley, it did very little for me, apart from making me feel quite alert, just as if I'd had ten cups of coffee. But Johnny – he was in seventh heaven!'

That was for sure. After ten minutes he came breezing in, talking nineteen to the dozen – and without warning grabbed me, picked me up bodily from the sofa, and marched into the bedroom!

Crikey, I thought, remembering a similar experience with Steven Wyatt. Here we go again! These Texans get very – physical. There was a large four-poster bed in the middle of the room, and he dumped me down none too gently and bent over me.

'Ignore me!' he said. 'I just want to make love to you...'

'No, John!' I said firmly.

'Come on,' he urged. 'Don't be so prudish ...'

At that moment Catherine appeared in the doorway. John's eyes lit up. 'Come on, Catherine!' he called. 'Come and join us. Let's all have fun!'

I put a hand up against his chest. 'I said *no* – and that means no!'

He didn't argue. 'Okay,' he said. 'If that's how you feel ...' And he straightened up, turned on his heel and walked out of the room.

'Excuse me,' I said. 'I'm out of here!' I got off the bed, smoothed down my dress, and followed him out. 'I've got to get home.'

Catherine was watching the video. John shrugged his shoulders, gave me a quick, humorous look, and said: 'Take my car. The driver's downstairs.'

'Thank you,' I said. Actually it was hard to be angry with him. 'I'll send him back.' To Catherine I whispered: 'He'll be back in an hour. Will you be all right? Will you phone me?'

'I'll be fine,' she promised.

I rescued my shoes, and jumped into the lift. The Mercedes was waiting downstairs, the driver dozing at the wheel. As we eased out into the King's Road and headed east, I remembered my earrings, still lying on the coffee table in Johnny Bryan's apartment.

As far as I was concerned, that night they could stay there.

The next morning I waited anxiously for Catherine's call. When it came, she told me she had stayed for a further hour watching TV and chatting, before – as they say – making her excuses and leaving.

'Johnny is okay,' she said. 'He's not dangerous. I never felt threatened with him, and I don't think any girl would either. He's not that type.'

Catherine kept me posted. I must admit I was agog to hear how their affair progressed. In a strange way I felt both curious and protective. But Catherine could take care of herself, and was happy to confirm that John always played the gentleman to the hilt. Ambitious – yes, he was that. A social climber? No doubt. And already he was breathing the heady air of royal approval.

Catherine mixed in the kind of circles where you rub shoulders with the aristocracy, big business and the art world. As she pointed out: 'When you get an American on the make, there's no stopping them. John told me how determined he was to crash the royal inner circle, and it was blatantly obvious how both he and Steve Wyatt set out quite deliberately to do just that. "You've got connections," he kept saying. "Who can you introduce me to who would be useful? Just one foot in the door – that's all I need."'

And further: 'John constantly questioned me about the gossip going on in those circles. "What's the latest – who's doing what to whom?" he would ask with that boyish grin. He even asked me if I had had an affair with anyone in that crowd – I told him quite truthfully that I hadn't! But he was quite openly using me to try to further his climb up the social ladder.

'At least he was discreet enough not to talk openly about Sarah. But he was definitely making plans to become an accepted part of the royal circle and inveigle himself into the ranks.

'As for me – his line to get me back to his flat would always be: "Come back and watch videos."

'I told him: "John, you must be able to do better than that!"

'And he would just give me a wicked smile.'

Catherine went out with John Bryan for two months, and resisted all his advances until the final night they were together. 'The truth is that I really didn't fancy him as much as he fancied me,' she declared. 'When I rebuffed him he was very polite – but my goodness, was he persistent! I knew he would keep on trying until he had worn me down. He would never give up!

'In some ways he could be astonishingly naive – but in others, Johnny was nobody's fool. He could show a girl a very good time. But I wasn't interested in having a casual fling – if I have a relationship it has to be something a good deal more serious.

'He's a playboy, and I knew I wasn't the only girl in his life. Once I asked him if he had a steady girlfriend, and he merely said he "saw somebody" from time to time.

'Eventually I spotted a small story in *The Times* which stated he was "financial adviser" to the Duchess of York, and I was quite shocked. I called him up to tell him: "So you've finally made it." But he wouldn't take my call.'

When he finally ditched Catherine, she understandably saw him in a new light: 'Sneaky, devious, King Rat ...' were some of the choicer epithets she used. But she had to admit: 'Johnny Bryan loves adventure, loves the fast lane in everything. He's fascinated with speed, whether it's aeroplanes or fast cars. That's how he lives his life.'

It was also, she surmised, why he had taken coke with her that night. 'It gives him a buzz,' she said.

There was never any hint that Sarah ever took drugs, and I'm quite sure she didn't. She was patron of the Chemical Dependency Centre in London, and did much good work for charity in that field. But, ironically, among her friends were alcoholics and addicts – people like the Marquis of Blandford, her skiing chum Guy Wadsworth and various other people had all been reportedly involved in drug abuse of some kind.

Catherine and I sat down to analyse the man who was snapped frolicking with a topless Sarah at that sunlit villa in the South of France, the little-known Texan who overnight became a household name himself, and set tongues wagging around the world.

'John Bryan loves a challenge. It turns him on,' she said revealingly. 'He wanted me – and the more I ran away, the more he wanted me. He's that type of person. He was pursuing me so relentlessly that in the end I thought: Oh, go on, you can have it! It took him two months, that was the length of our affair. And the day after we went to bed together – he lost interest.

'We only slept together once. It was on a Saturday night two months after our first meeting, and he had taken me to Annabel's for dinner. Then we headed for Tramp's, in what was becoming a familiar route, before we went back to the penthouse in Chelsea. I have to say that John Bryan was very good in bed – though I never enjoyed the royal treatment of his toe-sucking speciality! I have never been to bed with an American before. But Johnny was very much into fitness – he was Action Man between the sheets, a very aggressive, very active lover who could keep going for a long time. I felt at one point he could go on for ever and ever!

'That's probably one of the reasons that Sarah became so attached to him. She's a very sexy lady. But I cannot believe for one minute that Johnny Bryan is in love with Sarah.

'What we had between us was a kind of mind game. He was toying with me, like mental foreplay. I was the last girlfriend he had before he moved his attentions over to the Duchess of York.

'But was Johnny a show-off! He would throw his money around like water. And my goodness, how he would drop names. One night at Annabel's they played a Frank Sinatra record, 'Strangers in the Night', and Johnny said: "Oh, I remember when Frank was singing this for me. I was just a boy, and he was chasing my mother for a long time, and sang this special song for me in front of her.'"

I laughed at that. I could just hear Johnny regaling his audience with it. But the clearest image I retain of the Texan Longhorn is one of self-seeking egotism and ambition. And, in the dreadful break-up of the marriage of Sarah and Andrew, I share Catherine's verdict: King Rat.

The fact is that all along Johnny had nothing to lose – while for Sarah, whatever her headstrong foolishness, everything was in jeopardy.

And for Catherine? 'Johnny was like so many men,' she told me, with the brittle benefit of hindsight. 'To him everything was a goal, everything was an achievement. A woman was there to be conquered. That's how he thought.

'I would hardly call us lovers – though I'm sure he would have liked me to fall in love with him, but at least I was spared that indignity. There are so many men like him, the privileged rich who manipulate women for their own ends. It really is just a game with them.

'John is into all the things that men like him want in life: power, money and status.

'I sometimes think we probably could have had a proper, longer-lasting relationship if John had not been so hell-bent on achievement – through the Royal Family or anybody in high society.

'But ... I also wanted to see how he would react to me afterwards. I found out the hard way. After I left his flat that Sunday morning I never heard from John Bryan again.'

I leaned forward and took Catherine's hands. 'After all that, looking back, what did you get out of it?'

She thought for a long moment. Then she tossed her ash-blond hair back, tilted her chin, and replied: 'A bit of a thrill, that's all.'

CHAPTER TWENTY-THREE

Goodbye, Mother

My mother once said: 'If you really want something, Lesley, you'll get it. But you've got to really want it.' As her health deteriorated, and her mind occasionally wandered, she gave vent to the most hurtful statement I ever heard from her.

'You don't want me to live, do you? So I won't.'

It was so far from the truth that I was momentarily speechless. Then came my predictable reaction. 'How could you say something like that? That's a dreadful thing even to think ...'

But as in so many families, my mother and I could rub one another up the wrong way in seconds. Often all it took was one chance remark, and we were caught up in a blazing row – which thankfully would be extinguished almost as soon as it erupted. Yet deep down I know she loved me, and she knew that I loved her, and that was all that mattered.

Irene and Ronald got on famously. They would go shopping together, and discuss our relationship quite openly. He would laugh when I confessed that 'She knows how to press my buttons, and can wind me up in minutes!'

'That's what happens in families,' he said. 'Sarah and I are the same. Don't concern yourself over it – Irene is a fine woman.'

Mother knew how Ronald felt about me, but never took it upon herself to counsel either of us against the obvious dangers in such a reckless affair. In that respect she was incredibly open-minded, and I loved her for it. She was a shoulder to cry on when I needed one, and she had been with me all the way during the trauma of the abortion. That had been one secret she had been able to keep from Ronald.

The first hint I had of anything seriously wrong came on a grey, damp morning in December. Some dates you never forget, and this would turn out to be one of them: Tuesday, 3 December 1991.

I had had an early meeting with the caterers who were taking care of everything during the next Tournament: the cocktail party, the International Ball, afternoon teas throughout the week, the various receptions. It was a huge contract for them, and they were as anxious as I was to get every little detail planned, down to the colour of the table linen and the motifs on the menus.

I was due back in my office at 11.30 a.m. to see the company printing the ILPA Year Book. Another printing firm was due to show me proofs of the Christmas cards I had ordered, which would be going out to 2500 of our clients. I was also waiting for confirmation from Ronald that Harrods would be sponsoring the English ladies' team again next year.

In the afternoon a group of musicians would be waiting for me in a studio in Knightsbridge to play me their proposed theme tune for my Katchy Kid launch. And in the evening I was due to see one of the organizers of the Children's Ball, and personally sign seventy-five letters we were sending out.

All in all an average day, I thought wryly, as I sipped a much-needed morning cup of tea at my desk. But I could handle it: I was in the fast lane, and if there was a little too much traffic on the road I still had the energy to stay with it.

Then, at 9.30 a.m., came the phone call. Sam knocked at my door. 'I'm sorry to interrupt, Lesley, but I've got a hospital in Peterborough on line four insisting they speak to you. They won't give me a message.'

My stomach went into a spasm. I grabbed the phone. 'Yes?'

'Miss Player,' said a cool female voice. 'It's Peterborough Hospital. As you know, we have your mother here for a check, and she's a bit poorly this morning. We think it advisable that you or your sister come up at some point today to sit with her and give her moral support.'

I knew Mother had been feeling tired. When I had expressed concern, she had replied in her usual brisk way: 'It's all right, Lesley – I'm not worried, so there's no need for you to be!'

Peterborough was only an hour away. 'She only came in for tests on the tablets she's taking. What's wrong?' I asked the sister.

'It's not critical, or anything like that,' she assured me. 'There's nothing to worry about. She's just a bit under the weather, that's all.'

'We'll be there later today.'

I called Nicola, my sister, and told her the situation. We decided she would take the first available train from King's Cross, and that I would join her later. I instructed Sam to cancel all my afternoon appointments, and was snatching a hasty lunchtime sandwich when the phone rang. Ronald was saying: 'Lesley, I've heard from Harrods. There's good news and bad.'

'Oh, no,' I said. 'Tell me the worst first.'

'They won't sponsor the ladies' team next year. But the reason is that they would rather go with your children's clothes idea – as sole sponsors. Isn't that fantastic?'

It was, even if it meant that I would have to go scratching around again for a new polo sponsor. 'Thanks, Ronald,' I said gratefully. Then I told him about my mother.

He was instantly concerned, and said: 'I'll be here if you want anything. Just call.' That was all I needed to know.

The phone rang again, and this time it conveyed the message I dreaded hearing. It was the same sister, but now with an edge to her voice which she could not disguise.

'Miss Player, I'm sorry. It has become critical. Your mother suffered a heart attack, and it took the emergency team over half an hour to revive her. She is in a coma in Intensive Care, and I'm afraid your sister went into shock when she saw her. Would you please get here as soon as possible?'

I fled. I left a plate of half-eaten sandwiches on the desk, grabbed my handbag, shouted incoherent instructions at Sam and the rest of the staff, and ran into the street to flag down a taxi.

I remember very little about that journey from King's Cross. But staring out at the wintry landscape sliding past the windows on the fifty-minute run to Peterborough, my last conversation with my mother filled my mind. It had taken place on Sunday, just three days before.

'Please don't bother to come and see me. I'm taking all my Christmas cards in with me, so I can write them there. And, darling, don't send any flowers either. There's really no need. I don't want any fuss.'

'What's wrong, Mummy?'

'Oh, it's my feet, they're so painful. I hope these

bloody doctors can sort it all out at last.'

'And are you still not smoking?' She had smoked for years, and one lung had finally collapsed some months ago. This created circulation problems, hence the painful feet.

'Oh no, I'm not smoking. Don't you worry your head, I've been very good. Now – will you stop nagging?'

That was better. She sounded more like her old fighting self.

'Mummy ... I really love you. You know that, don't you? You really are the very best in all the world.'

And her laugh, short and brittle. 'What's wrong with you? You silly thing, I'm just going in for tests to make sure I'm on the right medicine. Silly girl!'

But I knew she was pleased, and I was grateful to Jim, my ex-husband, for persuading me to utter the words Mummy wanted to hear. 'Make sure you tell Irene how much you really love her, every time you speak to her,' he admonished. 'Even if you don't feel like it, tell her. She won't be around for ever ...'

When something like this happens, your mind can play tricks with you. All the way from London I had run through the possibilities, persuading myself that this was only precautionary, wasn't it? And the moral support which Nicola and I would give her just by our presence would bring our dear mother through this minor crisis. Then we would take her away for a holiday in the sun so that she would become her old self all over again. Majorca, perhaps. Or the Greek islands. Or let's go mad and waltz off to the Caribbean ...

The moment I walked through the glass doors of the hospital and found a nurse waiting for me, I knew I had been deluding myself. She had been ordered to wait by the reception desk until I arrived, and to take me straight up to Intensive Care.

I managed a small smile. 'Is it very serious?' Someone had to be strong, and that person was going to be me.

'Follow me, please,' she said, in a voice that was kindly, yet gave nothing away.

I felt the chill in me deepen. Nikki was on a chair outside the Intensive Care ward, her face pale. She looked crumpled and helpless, and instinctively I ran over to kneel beside her and put my arms around her. Wordlessly, she stared at me, and I saw the tear-stains on her cheeks. She clung to my arm, and would not let go – Nikki would not let me out of her sight during that long night, even when I went to the bathroom.

The nurse indicated the ward, and I went slowly through – to be faced with the most pitiable sight I had ever seen. My mother lay in the first bed, suspended like the victim of some ghastly scientific experiment: tubes uncoiling from her neck; respiratory equipment leading from a huge hole in her trachea; pipes, wires, pumps, catheters, bags, hypodermic syringes. And, amongst all that, my mother – helpless, quiescent, with no sign of sensibility, only the humming machinery and computers keeping her alive.

Feeling like an intruder, I opened her handbag, which was hanging from a chair beside the bed. Inside I found her address book. There were people who should know, and I set about the business of phoning relatives and close friends to alert them.

The nurse said that Mother could probably hear what we were saying. Looking down at the still, ashen face on the pillow, I was less optimistic. But even the slightest spark of hope was worth the effort, however useless – and in the long, desolate hours that followed I was never to feel more useless in my whole life.

So Nikki and I sat by the bedside, chatting with artificial brightness about our week, telling Mummy what the weather was like, how the plans for the Tournament were progressing, giving her Ronald's love – God, even telling her what we had had for lunch. Anything but mentioning her condition; anything but begging her not to die.

My younger brother Neil arrived, and a junior doctor talked to us outside the ward as we sat in a row on plastic chairs lined up against the wall to listen to him. I felt as if I were back at kindergarten. The poor man did his best.

'Now, I take it you three are the next of kin. And who is the eldest?' he began.

'I am,' I answered mechanically. My thoughts were in the next room, beyond the glass windows.

'So you must be Lesley, is that correct?' A trolley appeared at his elbow. 'Ah, here's the tea. Who would like sugar?'

'Yes, it is,' I said. It was all getting a little unreal.

'Sorry, was that yes to sugar?'

'No, it was yes to me being the eldest. And, no, I do not want tea!' I felt I was caught up in some black-comedy film-script. My temper was beginning to fray at the edges.

'Oh, yes, of course,' the young doctor said hastily. 'Now, to explain the situation with your mother. This morning she seemed quite calm, but occasionally out of breath. The ward sister kept a careful eye on her, as requested. But at 11.30 a.m. she suffered a major heart attack. The crash team were immediately sent for, and took just over half an hour to resuscitate her, at which stage she was brought straight to Intensive Care.'

'And now?' Somehow I felt we weren't being given the whole story.

'Well ...' He sounded reluctant. 'She is having problems with her heart function, so we are drip-feeding her stimulants to keep it beating. The rest of her organs seem fine at the moment. I can't quote you percentages of recovery, but time will tell ...'

'What kind of idiot do you think I am?' I interrupted the smooth flow with a rudeness that startled him. 'Half an hour? You've conveniently forgotten to mention one major organ – the brain. Half an hour is a very long time to have no oxygen to the brain – so why don't you just come clean with us, Doctor, and tell us the truth? We're all over twenty-one. We can cope. Honest!'

He stared at me, appalled by the venom in my voice. But it was my mother in there, wired up, helpless, probably dying. I had to know.

'All right,' the doctor began hesitantly. 'It's true that if she begins functioning on her own, it is more than likely that she has suffered a certain amount of brain damage. Her kidneys, lungs and liver will be affected, too.'

'So she'll be on a machine for ever ...?'

'I can't say that. I have to give you some hope. I can't just give up.'

Suddenly he looked so young and uncertain that I couldn't help taking his hand and giving it a squeeze. We were all on the same side, after all.

One thought kept circling in my head: ever since I could remember my mother had made me promise that if she was ever so ill that she was a burden not only to herself but to others I should take the responsibility of giving her an overdose of sleeping-tablets, or 'pulling the plug', as she put it so bleakly and calmly.

She had meant every word, and in those early, healthy days when death belonged to another time and place, it was easy for me to agree, though with a slight shake of my head. 'Mummy, don't be so morbid. It will never happen.'

'But if it does, you've got to promise.'

'All right,' I said. 'I promise.'

Now, though she couldn't speak or communicate even by the slightest flicker of an eyelid or the tiniest movement of a finger, my mother was holding me to it. I knew it. She must have known it too.

The doctor was speaking again, his voice solemn, the words carefully spaced. 'I need a decision from you all – but ultimately from you, Lesley, as the immediate next of kin. All that is keeping your mother alive are the drugs and machines. Without them she will surely die. We cannot give her anything else that would change her condition.'

'Thank you, Doctor. We understand. Give us a little time, please ...'

'Of course.' The white-coated figure slipped away, leaving us to stare at one another, then to turn to the glass barrier and the lone figure in the bed, pathetically linked up to the wires that spread from her like huge, obscene insect legs.

I shook my head in despair.

The three of us kept a bedside vigil until the early hours, then, exhausted, were given rooms to share in the hospital for the remainder of that awful night.

There is an expression: dying in dignity. The form I had to sign permitted the hospital to stop giving my mother any more drugs, but left the painkillers and the oxygen linked up. They unplugged the machines and took them away, and quietness descended on the ward, broken only by her harsh, uneven breathing. She would die in dignity, and without pain.

It took two days for her to pass from this life to the

next. I sat alone with her, holding her weak hand, and began to cry for the first time. The tears came without any prompting, my throat hurting with the sobs. It was not self-pity but a total, unyielding despair as my mother's life ebbed away.

The others came in, silently filing around the bed as the curtains were drawn, and the three of us stood close and held something of her – her hands, her arms – and prayed together.

I bent my face to her, and whispered my final entreaty: 'Mummy, you're not alone. God loves you, and He's waiting for you. There are people waiting to greet you on the other side, and they love you. And Granddad and Grandma are there. They are so looking forward to seeing you ...

'Please don't be afraid. Your next life will be fantastic, because you deserve it. Thank you for being the best mother in the world ... we are all sorry for hurting you occasionally, and not always doing what you wanted ... Dear God, look after our mother ...'

I kissed her dry lips, and Nikki and Neil did the same. Nobody needed to tell us the exact second our mother died. The respirator carried on breathing for her, but we all knew that the life had flown away from her body and that her soul had gone with it.

She had always been there to love me, and seldom to judge me. I found myself thinking: Mothers do that kind of thing – their unconditional love is like no other. No matter how stupid, cruel, thoughtless, unkind or whatever else you are, your mother will still love you. Now that love and the security that went with it were only a memory, and I felt devastated by their loss.

It was Ronald who took charge of the funeral arrangements in Sussex. He was the tower of strength I needed in those dark, empty days that followed.

And it was Sarah who phoned with words that were soft and gentle and kind; words that helped give me new heart to face the future – and forget the terrible guilt that consumed me from the moment I kept my promise and put my signature to my mother's death warrant.

CHAPTER TWENTY-FOUR

Palm Beach

There is nothing like a spot of winter sunshine to cheer one up. So when the Duchess of York asked me if I would like to accompany her to Florida in the middle of that cold, gloomy January in 1992, I didn't have to think twice before accepting.

It would be a short, four-day visit to Palm Beach, Thursday to Sunday, 16–19 January. 'But it sounds like fun. You can be my lady-in-waiting again. How would you like that?'

'Oh, yes,' I said. 'Count me in!'

Sarah paused. Then, rather more deliberately, she said: 'I do want you to come. But you must understand you've really got to *be* with Dads this time.'

'Oh?' This was one irritant I could do without – the pressure from both of them to get me to restart our affair. We would be together under one roof again, staying at the mansion of a banking tycoon named Robert Fomon, who was a friend of Steven Wyatt's, and his wife, Lewis.

Was it really such a good idea?

But I was desperately low that Christmas after the traumatic death of my dear mother. Ronald had tried to console me, and had been very supportive. His help with the funeral arrangements enabled him to do what he did best – organizing people, cars, timetables.

The only argument came after the funeral when he wanted me to drive back with him in his car to London. 'Ronald, please. I have to be with my brother and sister, don't you see?' Grudgingly he acceded, and drove off alone.

Now I thought: Yes, I'll go. I could do with a change; I had been looking very pale, and the sunshine would bring colour back to my cheeks. I could fly out to Aspen for Christmas, and go on to Florida afterwards.

Like her father, Sarah was also very sweet, understanding the grief of my loss, and was delighted when I agreed. 'When you come to Palm Beach we'll have lots of cuddles, and if you want to talk about your mother, you can. You have all my love. Keep your chin up!'

Our party consisted of Jane Ambler, her bodyguard, Chief Inspector John Askew plus another protection officer, Major Ronald Ferguson, and myself, proudly listed on the official itinerary as lady-in-waiting.

In the days before I flew off to Aspen, I found myself prey to a feeling of growing unease. Ronald had obviously asked Sarah to invite me. He seemed, if anything, to be more possessive than ever, constantly asking me about other men in my life.

'Is there anyone on the horizon?' Then the gruff voice would scold itself, saying: 'Never mind, it's just Old Mister Reliable here.'

The pressure was amounting almost to emotional blackmail, and the messages on my answerphone grew ever more harassing. 'I have always accepted that sometime in the future I will have to take second place, and will be put through a horrific test of character, which I dread. I pray that we will be able to go away somewhere without looking over our shoulders.

'You have been adamant to keep your private life to yourself, but you have been very unkind and cruel as you cannot imagine how it has affected me. Remember I am so in love with you – and so desperately need you...'

I agonized for days. Sarah, if anything, grew more insistent. 'You *must* come!' she said fiercely.

Oddly enough, Ronald voiced his concern that I might be drawn into becoming a general dogsbody for his daughter's notorious whims. There had been some initial doubt whether Jane Ambler would actually go on the trip, as she was on the point of retiring from her post. I was asked if I would be happy to do her work as well.

I didn't mind – but Ronald did. 'It's fine if you're a lady-in-waiting, but that's different from being a secretary. I never want you to be a servant to Sarah. Once a servant, never a friend,' he growled. In the end Sarah persuaded Jane to have one more fling on the royal bandwagon, and she came along.

I was more concerned with being a virtual prisoner with Ronald as my keeper. Before heading off for the snows of Colorado, I cornered Sarah one afternoon in the lounge at Sunninghill Park.

'Look, I really am worried.' I gave it to her straight. 'Don't you think it's really foolish of you to condone your father taking me with him like this to Florida?'

She tossed her thick red hair in annoyance. 'You're not going with him,' she said. 'You're going with me, as my lady-in-waiting. It's official, so what can anyone say?'

For the hundredth time I thought: Why, oh why, Ronald, can't you and I be just good friends? Aloud I said: 'But supposing the Press get a whiff of it? Wouldn't they have a field-day revealing how the Duchess of York always wants to take her father's mistress with her on trips abroad? Can you imagine the headlines?'

'Relax,' said Sarah. 'It won't happen.'

'How can I relax,' I demanded. I was quite heated by now, and realized how agitated I had been getting over recent weeks.

Sarah put a hand on my arm. 'Lesley,' she said. 'I need you with me on this trip. Things haven't been too easy here recently. Please ...'

She did look a little odd, I could see. I took her hand. 'All right,' I said. 'I'll go.'

When Ronald heard about it, a delighted fax came churning through the machine in my office, outlining the itinerary. He had compiled it from a reconnaissance trip he had made with his protection officer, John Askew, the previous month. A welcoming cocktail party and dinner on the lawns; a polo match for the William Holden trophy, which the movie star's great friend Stefanie Powers would present to the winning team; several receptions; a ball. The fax also told me what I would be expected to wear, and the kind of clothes I should take for that time of the year – it would be pleasantly warm in Florida in January.

There was further useful information. Buckingham Palace would take care of my luggage, and my ticket from Aspen to Palm Beach would be paid for. I should fly into West Palm Beach airport, where I would be picked up and transported to the residence of Mr Robert Fomon.

I couldn't help smiling. If this was the royal gravy train – roll on! And if you were in the hands of Major Ronald Ferguson, you never needed to worry about a thing. He was one of the world's great organizers.

Who else would know how to phone me in the first-class lounge at Los Angeles airport at the precise time I was nursing a glass of champagne in the stopover between Aspen and West Palm Beach – to break the news. 'There is something I should tell you, Lesley. They've run out of bedrooms at the house in Palm Beach, and we're going to have to share a room.' I was furious and he knew it. But it was too late to turn back.

But the beckoning sunshine as I stepped out into the early evening warmth of Palm Beach lightened my mood. And when I looked out of the windows of the stretched limousine and glimpsed the sumptuous mansion where we were to stay, I couldn't help feeling a great lift in my spirits. The others had already arrived, flying from Miami International Airport to the local West Palm Beach air terminal, and then in a motorcade that whisked them in a siren-wailing convoy along the six-lane highway to their destination.

In this land of the mega-rich, Mr Robert Fomon was gold-plated. A silver-haired tycoon of sixty-six, he lived with his somewhat younger third wife in a pink and white stucco mansion set close to the Atlantic on South Ocean Boulevard – a sprawling estate which oozed wealth out of every brick. As I was driven up the long private road between other equally opulent properties, the chauffeur pointed out a huge castle with mock turrets which I can only describe as a monument to bad taste. 'Donald Trump's place,' he said laconically.

'Oh, really?' There was little else to say.

But then I really did catch my breath. The scene ahead was like something out of a *Starsky and Hutch* movie – or, more appropriately, seeing where we were, *Miami Vice*. Six squad cars were awaiting us – four parked outside the high electronic gates, two inside the drive. Uniformed police officers patrolling the manicured lawns seemed to be behind every shrub, their holsters looming large on their belts.

Other limousines were easing their way through the gates, and I caught the flare of flashlights as photographers jostled to get shots of the dinner-suited occupants.

Celebrity night! There were even TV crews swarming at the windows.

Craning forward, I could see a huge striped marquee on the far lawn, with a crowd of people in evening-dress milling around. I glanced at my watch: 6.45 p.m. Supper time! I've always said they eat far too early in the States.

The very presence of the Duchess of York ensured that high society was out in force, and anyone who was anyone would kill to be there tonight. If there seemed to be more media than the occasion warranted, I would soon find out why.

My limousine cruised slowly into an inner courtyard. Clustered around the front door stood several large men in shiny suits, all wearing dark glasses and looking anywhere but at me as the limousine cruised to a halt on the gravel drive.

'I thought they'd brought me to the White House by mistake,' I joked to Sarah when we met over champagne cocktails later. 'I suppose you're used to this sort of thing. But I'm certainly not.'

'You never really get used to it,' she replied shortly.

I eyed her curiously. She looked upset – Sarah was never able to hide her feelings terribly well.

But now I heard a squawk from the courtyard, then another. Two multi-hued parrots with questioning, beady eyes were perched amid a froth of greenery that looked like a miniature jungle. This night was getting to be full of surprises.

Ronald came hurrying up. 'Lesley, I'm so glad to see you! You have got exactly fifteen minutes to get showered and dressed and join the cocktail party. Sarah is there already and doesn't want to stay long.' I caught a worried edge to his voice. He saw my look. 'I've got a lot to tell you – later.'

The Fomons were Steven Wyatt's friends. Over the next four days, as we sat around the pool or sipped champagne, I would learn from Sarah how Steven had persuaded her to stay with them because, he knew, it would help their business and social credibility enormously. They knew it too.

The ripple of anticipation heralding the Duchess of York's visit had swollen into a frenzied tidal wave of excitement among the social hierarchy by the time our convoy rolled up. It was the day the circus came to town.

To have an actual Royal on their doorstep sent flutters through the geriatric jet-set in the élite golf and yacht club community. To have one under their roof assured them of a place in heaven.

That first night I trotted obediently after Ronald while a servant took my case from the car. He showed me our room, and the first thing I noticed – with some relief – were two single four-poster beds, something I had never seen before in one room. The *en suite* bathroom was very ornate with Italian tiles, and the windows looked out on to magnificent front lawns.

It was a view I wouldn't see again throughout the duration of our stay. Ronald snapped the curtains shut. 'There are photographers out there with their cameras trained on this place night and day,' he said. And from that moment on the curtains stayed firmly closed. Shame, I thought. So much for the price of fame – or notoriety.

'Fifteen minutes!' Ronald ordered. 'I'll see you in the marquee.' He knew me too well to hang around while I was changing. I jumped in and out of the shower, and was in a fetching black cocktail dress with my hair freshly blow-dried within the time. Outside my room,

the house was totally quiet. As I made for the staircase I
noticed that the passage was lined will tall cupboards. I
couldn't restrain my nosiness, and peeped in. Shoes!
Dozens of pairs of women's shoes, at least two hundred, I judged, as I opened the cupboards one by one.
Many were in exactly the same style but different
colours – and had obviously never been worn. Weird!
The Marcos syndrome must be catching!

I hastened through the deserted mansion and out on
to the lawn in the direction of the music and the buzz of
the crowd. Pondering over Ronald's obvious agitation, I
started to feel uneasy myself.

At the back of my mind, whenever I was close to anyone connected with Steven, was the constant anxiety
that Sarah would find out about our affair. Why it
should concern me so, I didn't know – but it did. I had
learned to live with it, so why shouldn't she? But I just
didn't want any more unpleasantness in the growing
turbulence of her marriage problems. There was a hur-
ricane brewing, and I was in the eye of it.

That first night in Palm Beach I was convinced she
had been told. Up to now she would usually rush over
to me the moment she spotted me, even in a crowded
room, and hug and kiss me. But this time, when I
appeared in the packed marquee, caught her eye and
smiled and waved, she didn't do more than acknowl-
edge me with a curt nod.

My immediate reaction was: Oh my God, she knows!

Ronald noticed it 'Just ignore her,' he said. 'She's
emotional and upset ...'

Proof of just how emotional and upset came later,
when the four of us had returned to the private beach-
house which was reached through a thirty-foot under-
ground tunnel. On the patio, Sarah suddenly turned on

her father. Apparently he had earlier unwittingly left her
alone for a few moments to talk to a group of local
socialites.

Sarah's volatile red-headed temper snapped. 'Don't
you ever do that again to me!' she practically screamed
in front of Jane and myself. 'You just can't *do* that, leaving me talking to people I don't even know! You've got
to protect me ...' And she turned and marched off into
her room, slamming the door behind her.

Ronald was shaken by the tirade, though it wasn't the
first time he had had a tongue-lashing from his daughter, and I suspected it wouldn't be the last. 'I should be
used to it by now,' he said to me later. 'She gets these
moods. I just let her get over it.'

As usual in these circumstances, he went very quiet,
his shoulders sagging, looking for all the world like a
small boy who has been ticked off by his mother. The
complex intensity of their relationship was such that any
ripple on the water would cause Ronald grief and agitation beyond all reason. He lived his daughter's emotions
from day to day – which was why, as the thunder-
clouds gathered over the marriage, his attitude to
Andrew actually hardened.

'But why is she so upset?' I was baffled. 'She should
be in her element here.'

Ronald took me by the elbow and guided me into a
corner away from any eavesdroppers. In a low voice he
said: 'Just before we flew out they found some photographs in Steve Wyatt's flat.'

'Who did? What sort of photos?'

'Some cleaner. He handed them over to the police.
But the papers are on to it.' Ronald gestured at the high
wall. 'Why do you think there are so many of them
hanging around out there?'

He shook his head. 'The pictures are only holiday snaps, taken at Wyatt's villa in the South of France a couple of years ago. But they show that Texan fellow in a basket-chair with his arm around her – and the one that really annoyed Andrew was little Beatrice with no clothes on being cuddled by him. Andrew's hit the roof.'

'Oh,' I said. No wonder Sarah looked so drawn. 'Why was he so angry if they're only holiday snaps?'

'He thinks they're having an affair,' said Ronald.

'Oh,' I said again. 'Has Sarah been a silly girl?'

'I'm afraid so,' said the Major. 'A very silly girl.'

CHAPTER TWENTY-FIVE

Flannel Flight!

When those holiday photographs were finally published three months later in March by *Paris Match*, the papers would go to town. Under headlines like 'Fergie Dude and Nude Bea' they proclaimed: 'This is the holiday snap that finally wrecked Andy's marriage'.

But in those sun-filled days in Florida, what was going on seemed to me more like a damage-limitation exercise. Of course it was a strain on the marriage, and on the Monarchy as a whole, to face the potential scandal threatening the future of the Queen's favourite son, even if it would seem like a mild shower compared to the storm that would be unleashed with the later, infamous toe-kissing pictures of a topless Sarah with Steven's successor, the frightful John Bryan.

Having been away from the hothouse of intrigue that was South York for a few precious weeks in the cooling snows of Colorado, I was unaware of the 'considerable concern' those photos and Sarah's imprudence were causing in royal circles. Major Ferguson was swift to enlighten me on that first night.

Sarah had gone to bed. Jane was in a neighbouring room, and the bodyguards slept within earshot close by in a separate lodge.

When I opened the door to our bedroom soon after midnight, tired and desperately ready for bed, I found a red rose on my pillow. The last of the limousines had disappeared up the drive, and the electronic gates were shut on the outside world. Ronald followed me in.

'Thank you for my rose.' I kissed him on the cheek, but slid away when he wanted to take it further.

'Won't you give me a cuddle?' he asked, the gingery eyebrows raised hopefully.

'You know I didn't want to share a room with you,' I said, controlling my exasperation. 'And I'm exhausted. It's been a very long day.'

Ronald accepted it. Instead he sat on his bed and heaved a sigh. 'Lesley, things are coming to a head now. They've really done it this time, those two.'

'Surely it will blow over?' I said. 'It's news today, but tomorrow ...'

The huge, grizzled head shook in anguish. 'Not this time. Those photos ... I don't think much can be done to stop the rippling effect. It's already begun.'

'Go to sleep,' I said quietly. 'It will all work out – one way or another.'

I awoke to the sound of squeaking from the floor. I opened one sleepy eye and focused on the table by my bed: my watch said 7.30 a.m.

The squeaking sound came from the end of the bed. I sat up – and there was Ronald, crouched on his knees in his pyjamas doing his early-morning exercises with a small wheel with handles on either side, pushing it backwards and forwards on the carpet. *Squeak! Squeak!* I wasn't going to get any more sleep, so I got up, peeked through the curtains at the beautiful Florida sunshine, and went into the bathroom for a shower.

Sarah was her old breezy self that morning. When I saw her by the pool, she gave me a quick hug. Nothing was said about the previous night. But she looked well rested and ready for the day – and for the 'Bushpress', as she called her tabloid persecutors and the paparazzi

we all knew would eagerly be focusing their long lens-
es on anything that moved within the walls of the
Fomon residence.

That day: high drama! The schedule was blessedly
light, with plenty of free time for us to soak up the sun
around the pool and top up our tans. Around mid-
morning I was lounging on a sun-bed on the patio by
the beach-house, with Ronald and Jane nearby, when I
saw that Sarah was still inside, sitting on a settee in a
blue swimsuit with her legs tucked under her and a
mobile phone to her ear.

Her father noticed it too. 'Why aren't you in the sun?'
he called.

'Bloody photographers, Dads. Do you know what
happened earlier today? Some little man climbed over
that hedge' – she pointed to a high and very prickly
hedge by the pool – 'and managed to get a shot of me
on the phone before he fell. I hope he bloody well hurt
himself.'

Jane later told me that Sarah had hurriedly finished
her conversation, flung the phone down – and freaked
out while the man was frog-marched out of the grounds
by security guards.

'Dads.' Sarah had an anxious note in her voice. 'Don't
go near the balcony of your room – the Bushpress are
all out there. They're on the neighbouring property.'
She sounded really angry now.

'I'm sorry, sorry, sorry,' was all Ronald could mutter.

And then the phone rang.

We were sipping champagne and squinting through
the morning haze at the yachts far out at sea when the
shrill buzz of the mobile phone broke in. Sarah
answered it – and all hell broke loose.

She started screaming down the phone: 'What? Where

are they? You've got to find them!'

After further heated conversation along these lines, she banged the phone down, and turned to us with a face like thunder. 'That was Steven. There are more photos.'

'Oh, my God,' said her father. 'This is dreadful. Dreadful. Where are they?'

'He's left them in his apartment in Washington, and he's worried sick that someone's going to find them.' Sarah sounded as if she'd been talking to an imbecile.

Doubly careless, I thought, but kept it to myself. Aloud I asked: 'What are they?'

'Holiday snaps,' Sarah said. 'But you know what the Press will make of them if they fall into the wrong hands. They're like the others – only, well, closer ...'

What she meant was that they were more obvious, and therefore more incriminating. A huge hoo-ha broke out. Sarah shouted: *'Jane!'* Her secretary jumped up from her canvas chair by the pool and literally ran barefoot to the open glass doors. 'Jane, we can send you. The housekeeper can give you the key to the apartment. You can go today ...'

'Wait!' Major Ferguson raised a hand. He could be very assertive at times. 'Everyone just calm down! Get back to Steve and work it out with him.'

Sarah, normally so dominant over her father, acquiesced at once. She spent the rest of the morning on the phone, and by lunchtime the crisis was over. A trusted friend – I never found out who – was despatched to dig out the photos and, presumably, destroy them.

As for Ronald and me, we settled for the bay shrimps.

The afternoon dragged. Unable to sunbathe, Sarah spent the hours flicking restlessly through glossy magazines, occasionally asking me if I liked this or that outfit she'd spotted – then ripping the page out, and ordering her secretary: 'Jane, ring them up and order this one – straight away, will you?' Which royal command Jane dutifully obeyed, knowing that most of the designers had Sarah's measurements on file.

She disappeared into the bedroom for half an hour – speaking to Steven, I heard later – and emerged a different woman: lively, laughing, the clouds lifted. 'Dads, he's wild, he's absolutely *wild*!' she exclaimed, pirouetting towards the champagne bucket.

I looked at Ronald with a questioning glance. He leaned across. 'She means wild in bed,' he muttered.

The final act of betrayal with John Bryan and the toe-kissing shots from the South of France was yet to come. But unknown to any of us the seeds had already been sown, and the game – if you'll forgive the pun – was afoot, unfolding like some Shakespearean drama. Or tragedy.

Next day we had our first official engagement – with Sarah visiting the Connors nursery for drug-addicted and AIDS. In the car on the way to the clinic, Ronald quietly advised her that this was a chance to improve her personal public-relations standing, and that she should ensure that she had as many photographs as possible taken of her holding the children, pictures we all knew would go round the world.

And so it proved. Sarah, decked out in her favourite pink, smiling and sympathetic, brought a ray of sunshine into the wards. She unhesitatingly cuddled babies with full-blown AIDS, moving one misty-eyed nurse to tell the assembled media: 'I've met ambassadors and royalty here, but never anyone as caring as the Duchess.' As I followed Sarah through the wards, it brought a lump to my throat to see the tiny victims, cruelly orphaned from normal life by the dreadful virus that was not of their making, reaching out their small hands to her as she passed.

Outside, an hour later, as the stretched Cadillac slid through the applauding throng, she even ordered the driver to stop so that she could have a word with a child in a wheelchair. The cameras snapped away like crickets.

Finally Sarah relaxed back into her seat. 'Thank God that's over,' she said. 'Who's for a swim?'

First came lunch, at the colonial-style home of another Palm Beach worthy. The dining-room was set out in tables of eight, and Sarah and I found ourselves seated on the top table, where the average age could not have been less than the late seventies. Sarah cast one look as we took our seats, and muttered to me behind her hand: 'Oh, my God! Let's get this lunch over quickly – it's going to be incredibly tedious. You know I can't stand Americans at the best of times – and this is a bunch of American geriatrics!'

But we were in for a pleasant surprise. We had been placed on either side of an elderly aristocrat who introduced himself as Mr Francis Kellogg, from the cereal family, a gentleman who would later make his own headlines by escorting Princess Diana's stepmother.

He turned out to be a delightful old boy, keeping us in stitches with hilarious anecdotes about the people he had met in his long and illustrious life – neither corny nor flaky, as I murmured to Sarah on the way out.

Sarah was still watching her weight, even to the point of not wanting to succumb to the temptations of the cook's pride and joy: chocolate brownies, personally presented to her by the lady herself, who emerged from the kitchen with a large tray loaded with extra calories.

Mr Kellogg noticed Sarah's look. 'You don't really want to eat that, do you, my dear?' he said.

'Can I slip it on your plate?' asked Sarah gratefully.

'Of course you can, my dear.'

A few minutes later the hostess cast her eagle eye in our direction. 'Oh,' she exclaimed. 'I'm delighted you like our brownies. Cook will be so pleased. Here – do have another!' And she passed a fresh one to Sarah, who just had to eat it to avoid causing offence.

That afternoon we went shopping. The Duchess of York was due to host a small but select barbecue at her beach-house that evening for the Canadian Prime Minister, Brian Mulroney, and his wife Mila, who were holidaying in Florida. She needed shampoo and hair conditioner from a pharmacist. In addition, she had decided to wear a short dress – which meant I had to find a new one for myself, as my wardrobe was exhausted. Ronald and I were duly despatched into town. 'Also, I want you to get Cindy Doll and Cabbage Patch outfits for Bea and Genie,' she called as we set off.

It was the weirdest shopping trip I had ever embarked upon. Somehow word had spread through the grapevine, and every salon not only knew we were coming but actually had dresses waiting for us in my size. I could only imagine that Jane Ambler had mentioned our foray to Mrs Lewis Fomon, after which the phones started buzzing. Glasses of champagne were offered to us in three of the boutiques and were gratefully received, and the Major was repeatedly asked for his autograph. 'A little birdie told us!' one blue-rinsed assistant whispered to me. What a spree! We returned in triumph to the beach-house with bulging shopping bags.

That night we were on our best behaviour for the

Mulroneys – a delightful couple who reflected the pleasant informality at which the Canadians excel.

On that last night amid the mega-bucks and high-society hype we were treated to a wonderful farewell dinner at the Everglades Country Club, with mountains of food that no one could hope to get through in a month of Sundays. This was a venue that caused some outcry in the Press, with allegations that the Club discriminated against blacks and Jews! Oh dear! None of us, least of all Sarah, had any idea whatsoever of possible racial impropriety when we went there. We were simply responding to yet another example of good ol' Southern hospitality – and that's a fact.

But for Sarah, her visit was to rebound on her return to Britain, when she found just how much sensibilities in certain quarters had felt insulted by her visit to the Everglades. Amazing, the hackles that rise over a totally innocent situation where no slight was ever intended.

Afterwards, late at night back at the Beach House with champagne flowing, the party got extremely merry. Well, let's be truthful, some of us were quite drunk. Ronald and I decided we need some fresh air. We left Sarah at the Beach House, and strolled back to the patio by the pool.

Passing the Fomons' private suite, we heard voices through the door, and recognized our hosts. On that quiet, still Florida night, the voices carried.

They were talking about the royal party – not surprisingly, as it was probably the biggest week of their lives. But it was what they were saying that shocked us.

Mrs Bobby Fomon was talking. 'Who the hell does that little madam Sarah think she is? I'll tell you – she thinks she's God's gift! We've put everything on for her, but her father keeps dragging her off and won't let us near her.'

That, I had to admit, was partially true. But before I could pursue this further, I was hearing the redoubtable Mrs Fomon continue to dig a deeper hole for herself. 'Don't you think it's a weird relationship between the Major and Sarah?' Ronald was transfixed outside the door, like a model of himself in Madame Tussaud's. He put a warning finger to his lips.

Our hostess was adding her own appreciation of the house guests who would make the Fomon name live for ever on the social lists.

Ronald was livid. His knuckles were white as he restrained himself from breaking down the door and saying something very rude to our most generous hosts.

Finally, his face set in stone, he went off in search of a bottle – and it wasn't milk that he had in mind.

We sat in our room talking long into the early hours. Ronald was still upset, but he was fortified by a bottle of chilled white wine he had brought up with him from the kitchen. I had followed him in, and seen a new arrival in the Fomon household – a sweet baby parrot in its cage in one corner. I gave it a few drops of water, and it squawked its thanks with a series of tiny little burps.

Back in the room, I started to worry about the bird, for no real reason. But I kept asking Ronald to go down to the kitchen and see if it was all right – it was that kind of night. He obediently shrugged into his dressing-gown and trotted downstairs. Throughout what remained of the nights I kept waking up, worrying about the baby bird. Each time I got Ronald out of bed to go and inspect it. Each time he did, showing the most extraordinary patience – but with the same caustic remark:

'That fucking Fomon parrot!'

Next day, Ronald was captaining a British team against a local polo side from Palm Beach. The scene was familiar: pennants fluttering on the grandstands, marquees with long tables groaning with food and bottles of beer, wine and soft drinks. I was re-introduced to Stefanie Powers, a vivacious, delightful woman with enormous zest. I mentioned that I was recovering from my own mother's death, and she gave my hand a sympathetic squeeze. 'She knows she was loved,' she said. 'That's all that matters.'

Before he swung up into the saddle, Ronald said: 'I'm going to play the best polo, just for you. So you'd better cheer me – or else!' He gave me a cheery grin from under the peak of his maroon helmet. Sarah was happy, so her Dads was too.

His mood was catching. 'I'm your number-one fan,' I laughed back. 'What do you mean? Of course I'll cheer you.' There were serried ranks of photographers covering this event, and the constant clicking of cameras sounded like a chorus of cicadas on a warm Florida night.

Ronald gave me a mock salute, dug in his heels, and cantered off into the fray. Sarah had arrived by now – but in a bad mood. She looked stunning in a short black skirt and white jacket, but the hem of her skirt had come down during the drive from the Fomon estate. There had been some panicky moments before Jane had found safety-pins to repair the damage.

But she recovered her humour quickly, and leaned across to say to me: 'You just watch Dads, he's so good. I really am very proud of him.' She had cause to be. Sitting tall in the saddle, the galloping Major was in his element as he led his cavalry charge across fields that hadn't seen anything like it since the Civil War.

On our way to West Palm Beach Airport in our motorcade, Ronald mentioned to his daughter the conversation we had overheard. I thought she was going to hit
the roof!

At the airport she marched straight into the private
suite they had kept for us by the first-class lounge, and
made for the phone.

'Would you stand guard outside the door and make
sure no one comes in please, Lesley?' she ordered in a
tone that brooked no argument. When the 'redhead', as
some of the royal advisers called her behind her back,
was in a rage – get ready to duck! Anyway, I *was* her
lady-in-waiting that week. So – I waited.

Ronald and I started to fidget. The plane was being
held up, but still Sarah stayed on the phone. A young
lady came up and introduced herself as Joan Collins'
private secretary. Joan happened to be at the airport,
catching another flight. Could she pop in and say hello?

Knowing his daughter's mood, Ronald said diplomatically: 'I'm awfully sorry. She's very tied up, and then
we're running to make the plane.'

'Oh,' said the secretary, unimpressed. 'Joan will be
very disappointed.' She turned her back and marched
off.

Ronald glanced at his watch, frowning. Then he
tapped gently on the door, and put his head round.

'Sarah ...'

I heard her voice screech like a banshee. 'Get *out!*'
Her father hurriedly closed the door again, and looked
at me with a hopeless shrug. What could he do? When
Sarah was in one of her moods, as I had seen, she was
impossible.

Finally the door of the VIP room opened. Holding her
head high, but looking pale and biting her lip, Sarah

emerged. Ronald hastened over, put an arm around her shoulders – and then to our consternation and embarrassment she burst into tears. The two of them walked together through the departure hall, and I saw Sarah wipe her eyes with a wan smile and a shrug.

Later I heard that she had called both Steven and Andrew. She had given Steven a blast over his tacky Florida friends, but her conversation with her husband had ended abruptly with harsh words. I didn't have to ask why. The papers were still having a field-day with those photographs.

On the flight, first-class Miami–Heathrow, champagne eased the mood considerably. After an hour, Sarah, seated next to her father, became her old frisky self. A wet flannel hit me on the side of the head. I flinched, and looked up to see Sarah's grinning face across the aisle. More wet towels and tissues went whizzing around the cabin as Jane and I joined in the flannel fight. Suddenly peanuts were raining around us like hailstones as the Duchess of York got into her stride.

Other passengers ducked instinctively or buried themselves under newspapers and tried to ignore the fracas. The stewardesses took it all with indulgent smiles – poor things, what could they say to the Queen's daughter-in-law? But I wonder what would have happened with ordinary passengers?

Then Sarah pulled a sick-bag over her head and started making telephone noises into it! We shrieked with laughter like silly schoolgirls – it seemed the funniest thing ever.

But finally the burly form of Inspector John Askew appeared at Ronald's elbow. He bent down and murmured something in his ear. The Major frowned, nodded, and called a halt to the frivolity. 'That's enough now!'

The sharp-eyed bodyguard had noticed a passenger two rows back making notes – and sure enough, it turned out to be a member of the Bushpress, and the story would duly appear in the tabloids the next day.

Back in wintry Berkshire, we learned that Steven had been on the line to Florida within minutes of Sarah's furious call. I don't know what he said – but I do know that the phone was ringing at Sunninghill Park that night and a female voice was whinging down the line: 'We're so sorry, there's been a terrible misunderstanding. We didn't really say anything *like* that.'

That was according to Ronald, who told me all about it with grim satisfaction. Sarah was at her iciest – and when she wanted to, she could sink the *Titanic*. 'Excuse me,' she said coldly. 'But it was my father who heard it all.'

That was one high-society name wiped off the Yorks' Christmas-card list. I could almost hear the wailing from South Fork!

But for me, it entailed an unpleasant postscript: something I had dreaded all along. During that exchange of words Steven must have told Sarah about us.

It was the last trip I ever made with her. Indeed, it would be her last official visit abroad before her separation.

Why else would Sarah shortly turn her back on me, refuse to answer my letters or take my phone calls, and begin to 'chill me out' the way she in turn would be chilled out by the Royal Family a few months later?

CHAPTER TWENTY-SIX

Bad Day at South York

The Yorks' marriage was in the eye of the storm. By late March 1992 the situation was volatile in the extreme, though a strange, uneasy calm had descended. Lawyers had been called in on Sarah's initiative to set the wheels in motion for a formal separation. An announcement had been made from Buckingham Palace on Thursday, 18 March, stating brusquely: 'These discussions are not yet completed, and nothing will be said until they are.'

Now it was official, and the whole world knew about it.

Yet both Andrew and Sarah kept up a brave public face of normality to conceal the anguish of what was going on behind the scenes. Two nights later they even went out together to a party at Elton John's house in nearby Windsor.

But the undercurrents of tension between them were palpable, and within the walls of Sunninghill Park the façade was showing the stress-cracks.

An invitation reached me to spend Sunday, 22 March, the first Sunday after the bleak announcement from the Palace, with the family at the House of York. The summons came by the usual courier – Major Ronald Ferguson. But long-distance, all the way to South Africa ...

The previous year I had established contacts for future polo tournaments in Cape Town, and had paid them a flying visit. Now I went back again to snatch a fortnight in the South African summer sunshine, and also to pursue a new project I'd had in mind for some time: starting up a small company to manufacture children's clothes. I would use cheap, good-quality cloth and the skilled local labour that was crying out for work. The name: Katchy Kid.

It had been a busy two weeks trying to sort out the problems facing the launch, putting a quart of work into a pint of time as I raced against the clock to get the project off the ground.

But no one could possibly have missed the reports of the crisis in the Yorks' marriage. Rumour was rife, filling pages of newsprint as well as the airwaves on South Africa's somewhat limited TV and radio programmes. Ronald phoned me practically every day, and though he kept telling me 'Don't believe everything you read', I knew that he was a worried, saddened man. I kept my mind on my work, and pushed gossip and speculation away. There would be time to catch up when I got home.

My two weeks were up. As I was packing in my hotel room on the Saturday afternoon for the night flight home, the phone rang. Ronald was on the line. 'Come and spend the day with us. I'll meet you at Heathrow, and take you straight to Sunninghill. We can have a relaxing Sunday lunch.' There was a catch in his voice as he added, almost beseechingly: 'It will do Sarah good to have you around. And I know Andrew wants to hear all about South Africa.'

'Of course I will,' I said. 'I'd be delighted.'

'What a wonderful girl you are,' said the Major, and the line went dead.

By a bitter twist of fate my own life was only four weeks from falling apart at that very moment. But as the South African Airways Jumbo slid through the early dawn sky, and I stared out of the window to marvel at the first flush lightening the English countryside below, I just felt it was good to be home again.

I couldn't know it then, but two weeks previously, the day after I had flown south, the Queen had paid a secret trip to Sunninghill for Sunday afternoon tea with Andrew and Sarah to discuss their marital problems. The Duchess of York had apparently told Her Majesty that she felt that the marriage could not be saved, and the die seemed irrevocably cast. Yet, as in all matters of the heart, nothing is ever quite as it appears.

All I knew was that I was going to spend Sunday with a couple of old friends who were in trouble – whatever their title, rank or position in the social strata. If I could help, I would. If not, maybe at least I could inject some cheer into the day.

I was idly mulling over these thoughts as the plane nosed over the fields of Berkshire, the pilot giving us an incredible view of the Thames – ironically, Windsor Castle was just below, as was, presumably, Sunninghill Park, although I failed to locate it. Sarah would be asleep. Andrew might be up and about and heading for the golf course, depending on how late the Saturday night had been.

Thankfully, I had no idea of the turmoil that was about to be unleashed on so many of the players in the dangerous games we had all been playing. All I wanted after the twelve-hour flight was a long soak in a good hot bath.

Ronald, dependable as ever, was there to meet me in the arrivals hall. He gave me a big, unashamed hug, took my trolley, and headed for the car park.

'Tired?' he said.

'Not too bad,' I assured him. 'There's only a couple of hours' time difference, so I don't get jet-lag. But I could do with a nice hot bath.'

'That you will have,' he promised.

Behind the wheel of his BMW Estate, he lapsed into an uncharacteristic silence. 'Are you all right?' I queried. 'Is it that bad?'

He shrugged. 'The usual. I suppose you've read the papers. Things are a bit taut. In fact they're pretty desperate. I just feel sorry for Sarah.' The loyalty of the Fergusons again, so touching – yet so misplaced.

'Oh, yes,' I said. 'Of course.' Then: 'Who's going to be there today?'

'The whole family – Andrew, G.B., the kiddies ...' He paused. 'Alison Lobel, I think you've met her.' I had – Alison was a tawny-haired divorcee, a close friend and confidante of Sarah's, recently separated from Norman Lobel, who had originally opened the Royal Berkshire Polo Club with Bryan Morrison 'to bring polo to a wider audience'.

Ronald hesitated again, keeping his eyes on the road as he turned off the M3 at Virginia Water and headed into the leafy country lanes. At last he said: 'And – er, John Bryan will be there, with his sister.' He added gloomily: 'I don't know why the fellow's there at all, I really don't. He's supposed to be advising G.B. on her finances, but ...' His voice tailed off.

There was no one around at the entrance at that hour. The policeman from the Thames Valley force saluted us through the gates, and I entered the portals of Sunninghill Park House for what would prove to be the last time. It might have been my imagination, though I don't think so because I have always been very sensitive to atmosphere, but I could sense an air of brooding tension hanging within the great house as I followed Ronald over the grey and white tiles of the empty hall to a guest room where I could change and have my long-awaited bath.

'No one's down yet,' said the Major. 'Except Andrew – he's out on the golf course. The rest of them are still in bed. Late night – they were at Elton John's celebrating his divorce or something.' It transpired that Sarah and Andrew had left in separate cars to fool the handful of reporters and photographers camped outside the gates, joined up a few miles down the road, and then Andrew had driven his wife in the family Jaguar to Elton's sprawling mansion outside Windsor to join a party for twenty of his special show-business friends.

Among them had been Billy Connolly, Sting and his wife Trudie Styles, Barry Humphries, Kenneth Branagh and his wife Emma Thompson, and Rowan Atkinson. Elton, of course, was a long-standing friend of both the Yorks, and had been a guest at their wedding. The couple had stayed four hours, and returned to Sunninghill around 2 a.m.

Now Ronald shook his grizzled head in bewilderment. 'Sarah is supposed to tell me everything, but sometimes I can't make that girl out,' he said. 'One minute they're talking about splitting up – the next they're out on the town together.'

In the guest suite I took my time, soaking luxuriantly in the bath and using the 'S & A' monogrammed towels that had been laid out for me by Terry, the faithful Jeeves, who himself would not stay much longer in that house of growing shadows. Eventually I dressed in blue jeans, a light sweater and a hacking jacket, and made my way to the dining-room for breakfast.

The balding figure of John Bryan was the first person I saw, turning from the mantelpiece by the fire to stare at me as I walked in. His jaw went a little slack, but he recovered himself swiftly and managed an uncertain smile. Given that the last time I had seen him he had been sniffing a curious white substance, after which he had tried to take me to bed, I could hardly blame him for looking shaken.

'Lesley has just flown in from South Africa,' said Ronald, as he made the introductions.

'We've met,' said John uncomfortably, extending a hand. 'How was it down there?'

'Hot,' I said. Somehow the very presence of this man in Sarah's home made me feel uneasy. Then I added brightly: 'Oh, yes, John. You've still got my earrings!'

'Hello! What's going on here?' Andrew appeared in the doorway, freshly showered and changed from the golf course.

'Oh, yes,' I said brightly. 'John and I have met before, through a mutual girlfriend. I left my earrings behind on his coffee table.'

'Oh, God!' John exclaimed. His cheeks flushed, but he recovered well. 'So you did. I must send them back.'

'Yes, give the girl her earrings back.' Andrew's tone was amused, and slightly sardonic. His demeanour was quiet but outwardly cheerful.

He retreated to his study, and I saw him start writing at his desk. Sarah and John vanished to another part of the house, presumably to talk about her future, financial and perhaps personal. My own surmise is that they did not actually make love until the Yorks' marriage had irrevocably broken down and the couple had split, but it is impossible to believe that nothing of a more intimate nature happened when those damning pictures were taken in the villa in the South of France.

Meantime I contented myself spending the hour before lunch playing with the little Princesses. We sat on a Persian rug in front of the fireplace, with Beatrice and Eugenie looking like child models in their matching Sunday-best tartan dresses. They really are the cutest kids, I thought again. Ronald relaxed in an armchair nearby, smiling down fondly at his grandchildren.

It was like any happy Sunday family scene – except that this was like no other family I knew, and, alas, they were anything but happy.

I devised a new game. Beatrice had produced a jig-saw puzzle with big wooden animals that fitted into each other. 'Tell you what,' I said, 'let's try it this way.' And I threw the pieces onto the floor, scattering them across the rug.

'Right!' I ordered, consulting my watch. 'You've got two minutes to pick up as many pieces as you can and bring them back to me. Ready, steady, *go!*'

Squealing with laughter, the little girls fell on their knees and scrambled around, peering under chairs and tables, clutching the wooden animals in their small fists, rushing back when I called: 'Time's up!'

This was fun. This was great. There's nothing like the sound of children's laughter to enliven a place, and the atmosphere lifted immediately.

All too soon it was time for lunch. Andrew came in from his study, and squatted down to help me pick up the pieces. Nanny Alison took Eugenie away to her place at the far end of the dining-room table, while I counted the animals. One was missing.

'Where is it?' I asked Beatrice.

'Don't know, Lesley.' She was the pert one, and could be cheeky, too.

I said: 'Well, it must be somewhere. We've got to find it before we go in to lunch.'

Andrew echoed: 'Yes, come on, Beatrice. You've got to find it.'

The little girl started snivelling, then all at once burst into tears. 'I don't know where it is, Daddy!'

Suddenly Sarah was standing over us, hands on hips. 'What are you doing to my daughter?' she demanded, her voice full of anger. Then she swept Beatrice up and marched out of the room with her. I noticed that the sobs miraculously stopped.

On my knees on the floor I looked at Andrew. He looked at me. No words passed between us, but there was an unspoken message. Bloody hell!

Then he simply shrugged his shoulders, and followed his wife out into the dining-room.

As the lunch progressed, and Terry carved roast lamb for the guests from the sideboard, I had the oddest feeling that nobody really knew why they were there. The atmosphere was desperately tense, but also artificially bright, with Andrew pretending that nothing had happened, and Sarah doing the same.

For myself, I recognized that the party was almost over. Sarah had begun to distance herself from me after Palm Beach, and from then on I had started to sense the famous royal 'chill' that Steven Wyatt had fallen victim to before me. Only Ronald's continuing infatuation kept me in the camp, while Andrew seemed impervious to everything around him.

Conversation was stilted, to put it kindly – frequently punctuated by those awful silences in which you can hear yourself chewing your own food, and in which the clink of knife and fork on a plate sounds as loud as Big Ben. When someone did venture a remark, it took its usual course – veering towards the Press, and how rotten the tabloids were to the Royal Family.

It was Sarah who dominated the discussion. 'Isn't it terrible what they write about Diana?' she said – and this was eight weeks before the Andrew Morton book was published.

John's sister Baby, who had arrived shortly before lunch said loudly: 'If I were Diana, I'd leave him!' Her own parents had split up, I recalled. In fact, looking around that table, I realized that every single one of us, apart from Andrew, had come from a broken home. And the Princesses, of course – their turn was to come, poor mites. It gave me a slightly shivery feeling.

'They always kick you when you're down,' said Sarah bitterly at one point. At this there was a general murmur of assent. At least they're in accord about something, I found myself thinking.

I was sitting next to Andrew, who took refuge from murky waters by questioning me closely about South Africa and my Katchy Kid idea. 'It sounds wonderful; I'm sure it will work and make you lots of money,' he enthused. I wasn't so sure, but I wasn't going to put any more of a dampener on the day.

I nodded vigorously. 'I hope so.'

On my other side was Alison Lobel, who lived near-by and who had recently split up with her own husband. Norman Lobel was looking after the children for the weekend, which had given her the chance to drop by and console her old friend. Alison knew all about my own background, and murmured quietly: 'It's terribly important to get out of a dead marriage, don't you think?'

Later that afternoon I had a chance to remark to Sarah: 'You seem to be surrounding yourself with people telling you it's good to leave your husband.' Her blue eyes flamed briefly in what might have been anger or resentment, but after a moment she merely shrugged and turned away.

Lunch was over at last – two of the longest hours I have ever spent. I remember Sarah once saying to me: 'Andrew doesn't like people drinking.' From where I sat that day, which was next to him, that statement couldn't have been further from the truth. He seemed to have no objection if other people wanted to drink, and the wine had flowed pleasantly enough, while he drank lemonade. Ronald had manfully kept up a conversation at his end of the table, while I chattered away to Andrew as best I could.

Afterwards, Sarah, the Major and I relaxed around the fireplace, chatting about the children, always a safe and happy topic. Sarah began playing with the girls, but, happy as they all looked, I couldn't help remembering what she had told her father once: 'My daughters are my passport to security ...'

Ronald was in the middle of a sentence when, without warning, Sarah suddenly sprang up and disappeared into the study where Andrew was working at his desk. Through the open door I saw her rummage through the shelves of LP cassettes and discs, before picking one out. She put it on the hi-fi in the corner and turned the volume up.

The opening fanfare of 'Joseph and the Amazing Technicolor Dreamcoat' resounded through to the speaker in the lounge, loud and clear – blaring trumpets, crashing cymbals. Very loud and clear. Sarah came back to join us, swinging those full hips of hers and snapping her fingers to the beat as the voice of the narrator, Tim Rice, filled the room.

'Jo-seph ... a fine example of a family man ...'

Andrew frowned, got up from his desk and went to turn it down. Next thing Sarah had whirled round and was back in the study, turning it up even louder. It came blasting through into where we were sitting. I saw Andrew jump up like a scalded cat and turn it down again. Sarah turned it up – and it was now so loud that even her father and I went: 'Oh, *please*!' But she was determined to show who was boss. It was a battle of wills – and Sarah won.

'Jo-seph ... Oh, how he loved his coat of many colours ...'

'Joseph' stayed in the tape deck, and we stayed sitting on the sofas around the fireplace going rapidly deaf, trying to control our expressions until the first track was over. Conversation was impossible. Even when Ronald looked at his daughter appealingly, she simply tossed her red hair and ignored the silent message.

John Bryan jumped up and approached her, extending both hands. 'Shall we dance, ma'am?'

Sarah inclined her head in acceptance. And without a word, John took her in his arms and they danced together in a kind of old-world courtly intimacy around the living-room of Sunninghill Park. Although no words were spoken, their body language was patently sensual, and my mind instinctively leaped to an image of Rhett Butler and Scarlett O'Hara in *Gone with the Wind*. Then the little girls joined in, and the four of them held hands and whirled blithely around the floor.

I glanced through to the study, and saw Andrew turn and give his wife and children and their dancing partner one long, steely stare before his lips tightened and he turned away and went back to his work.

When I next looked he had his head in his hands, as if to blot out the music, or the familiarity that was being displayed in his own home, or both.

As the music ended John took her hand and performed an exaggerated bow. 'Thank you, ma'am,' he drawled.

'Thank *you*!' said Sarah. And with a laugh she led the way out of the room to continue their 'financial discussions' elsewhere.

Ronald told me later: 'He has advised Sarah to go for a house for herself in England where she can bring up the children, and to hold out for £5000 a week income for herself – for life.' He added that Bryan had reassured his daughter: 'Don't worry about anything. It's all going to be all right.'

'What about this place?' I queried.

'A lot of people are under the impression that the Queen gave it to them as a wedding gift. But she has absolute ownership of it. They pay a nominal rent.' So it would revert to the Monarch if and when Andrew and Sarah divorced. No wonder Sarah and her adviser were spending so much time in such intense discussions.

On that uncomfortable day at Sunninghill Park, filled as it was with tension and the scoring of petty points, it was obvious to me that Sarah felt more relaxed in the company of John Bryan than she did with her husband. It was there in her every look, in her manner, in her very deportment.

Ronald wanted me to stay the night, but I shook my head.

'Ronald, I just can't. I don't feel at all comfortable in this atmosphere,' I told him.

He was unhappy about it, but he understood. As dusk fell and the lights came on in the big drawing-room, I got up to go. I tapped on the open study door, and Andrew turned and gave me a wan smile.

'Andrew, I've got to get home.'

'Already? That's a shame.' But somehow I felt he was glad to see me go. It had not been a happy day inside Sunninghill Park.

Andrew held me close in a brief hug, and kissed me on both cheeks. For a fleeting moment I remembered what he had told Ronald. 'That's a very, very sexy woman you've got there!'

I liked Andrew a lot. I knew that his mother was the Queen, his brother the future King, and that he had a formidable sister in Princess Anne. But to me he was just very sweet and impressionable, and never wanted to do harm to anybody.

I admired him for his patience and his resilience under the almost unbearable strain that he, Sarah and the whole Royal Family were enduring through those lurid months in 1991 and 1992, when hardly a week passed without some fresh scandal, real or imagined, breaking in the tabloids.

Andrew was kind, a responsible father – despite a career that took him away from his home and children so often – and, above all, a gentleman. He had been infatuated with Sarah, and held a torch for her to the bitter end. But with John Bryan and his sister under his own roof as invited guests, he could hardly say: 'Take your hands off my wife!' – even if he was seething inside. He had been brought up, like all the royal children, not to confront, whatever the provocation.

Over the eight months I was with them, I watched Andrew grow more strained and unhappy – and, worse, less confident in himself as the weeks wore him down. In the early days he had still been a confident young man, excited about life. Now, on the last day I would spend with the Yorks, he was so low that I wanted to reach out and hug and console him.

As for the Randy Andy image – when he was younger, why not? But in all the times I met him at

Sunninghill, I was not to see a single trace of it.

If anyone was the fall-guy in the break-up of their marriage, it was Andrew. He was the innocent. I am convinced that he had little or no idea of what was going on with Steven Wyatt. If he did suspect – in the later stages, prior to the discovery of those compromising photographs, first in Steven's flat, then with John – then he chose to ignore it. But when the pictures from the South of France exploded into print, even patient, controlled, infatuated Andrew could not ignore *that*.

John Bryan had left an hour earlier, with a brief wave in my direction. He seemed glad to be on his way. Ronald was walking me to the car through the dusk when there was a rush of footsteps behind us. Sarah ran up, her face pale and tense.

'Dads! Oh ...' She saw me, and stopped.

'What is it?'

'I've just had a phone call. From the Castle. Andrew and I have got to go over there. The Queen wants to see us.'

'When?' her father asked.

'Right now.'

She looked at me. 'Will you be here when I come back, Lesley?' There was a plea in her voice. Suddenly even the stoic Sarah, shameless as she might be in so many ways, seemed small – and scared.

'I'm sorry,' I said. 'I can't. I've been away for two weeks, and I've just got to get home.'

She nodded, her face downcast. Then the old Sarah reasserted itself, and she reached out and gave me a hug, kissed me on both cheeks, and said: 'Please stay in touch. We'll see each other very, very soon.'

That was the last time I saw her.

CHAPTER TWENTY-SEVEN

Wolves at the Door

The speed with which a life can be turned upside down, or totally destroyed, has always filled me with a mixture of fear and a kind of awe. Fate comes in so many forms to play her tricks on the unwary, from the potentially lethal to the totally absurd: a car out of control ... a careless cigarette end ... wet leaves on a pavement ... or a piece of soap left in the bath ...

In my case I can pinpoint the moment to a phone call that changed my life.

Up to Easter that year, 1992, everything in my garden looked particularly rosy. My chauffeur-hire business was thriving, I was gaining new clients every week in the high-powered world of banking and commerce, and I was able to open up spanking new offices for Katchy Kid in Battersea, which I could rent with a four-bedroom house attached.

On the social scene, too, things were buzzing. A Katchy Kid ball I had organized at the Langham Hilton in aid of the Variety Club of Great Britain was confirmed for July. Moreover, my two little princess friends, Beatrice and Eugenie, were all set to be there – wearing matching ball-gowns in royal burgundy silk we had already designed for them, much to the delight of Sarah, who would be escorting them to their very first official public function.

The Tournament was on course, together with the International Polo Ball that would be staged a few days earlier – with the Duchess of York agreeing to attend both in aid of her pet charity, the Motor Neurone Disease Association. My sideboard in Battersea was full of gold-edged invitations to society functions, and my phone did not stop ringing.

It was one call on that same phone which shattered all my dreams.

It came at 2 p.m. on a weekday in April, when I was in my workshop supervising the final touches to the fashion show that was to be the highlight of the Ball. A reporter from the *Sunday Times* was on the line – and his words left me dumbstruck. He was investigating, he said, alleged misconduct concerning last year's International Ladies Polo Tournament.

'Misconduct?' I repeated in bewilderment. 'What are you talking about?'

The questions that followed left me reeling: Was it true that the charity had received only £2000? Had I misled the sponsors? How much was the hotel bill for the competitors? And finally: 'Miss Player, where do you bank, and what is your account number?'

The story that appeared on the front page the following Sunday left me devastated.

The Charity Commission was apparently investigating discrepancies in the amount of the proceeds that should have gone to the Save the Children Fund – certainly the first I had heard of such rumours, and, as it turned out when I called them the next day, the first the Commission had heard of it too. My lawyer instantly arranged an appointment for me to meet them, and when two impressive-looking gentlemen in dark suits arrived I gladly turned all my papers over to them on the spot.

Eight weeks later they exonerated me completely – a fact I did not see reported anywhere. It was too late.

The damage was done and, despite my protestations, the mud stuck.

The Fund had received £8000; sponsorship had raised £70,000. Question: where did the rest of it go? Answer: to pay for the Tournament. You try hosting an event for forty-eight professional polo players, with hotels, transport – including helicopter hire – insurance, ground fees, ground staff, horses, meals, refreshments, hospitality ... along with 1001 extras like polo shirts, flags, first-aid kits and brochures – even a new zip I had to buy for one of the ladies! – and see how much change you get!

Platinum Polo International, the company I had formed for the event, in fact made a small loss – which I was able to wear with equanimity since this Tournament had been the first attempt, and a rehearsal for the years to come.

The article had also impugned my character, suggesting that I had posed as an official lady-in-waiting to the Duchess of York. My name had certainly appeared on the Buckingham Palace itinerary for Palm Beach as 'lady-in-waiting' – but I had never pretended to be in anything other than an acting capacity. Besides, official ladies-in-waiting get paid!

From that moment, my world fell apart.

Ronald rang me the same day. 'I'm sorry for you,' he said. 'It's terrible.'

'Can we do something – anything – to put it right? It's all lies, you know ...'

'You don't need to tell me that. But really there's nothing I can do.'

I couldn't believe what I was hearing. 'But surely all it would take is a letter from you – or, even better, from Sarah – to put the record straight and clear my name,' I implored.

'It's not that easy,' he said bluntly.

'Can't you at least ask her ...?'

'Lesley, I'm sorry.' There was a silence on the other end of the line. Then his gruff voice came through with a harsh finality I had only ever heard directed at other people, never at me. 'Sarah has enough problems of her own right now without having to be troubled with yours.'

That evening I wrote my first letter to the Duchess of York. Her problems were on every front page of the nation's tabloids, and looked set to stay there. After expressing my genuine sympathy for the situation, and offering any help I could give to someone who had always vowed that they would be my true friend, I explained my own predicament. 'One letter would solve everything – addressed to me, pledging your support, putting the record straight about acting as your lady-in-waiting.'

One by one my sponsors for the forthcoming Tournament started to fight shy. The first hint of impending disaster was a phone call to Ronald from Harrods – they apologized, but from now on they would not sponsor anything with which my name was involved. 'I can't say I blame them,' was his bleak reaction.

Next to fall out were American Airlines, followed a day later by Regina Royal Jelly, then all the other sponsors. Always the same pattern – a brief, impersonal call to my office, no excuses, and always because of That Story. One or two senior executives had their secretaries call to cancel appointments that would have brought in big business.

And from Sarah – silence.

I sent her another letter and left two messages at

Sunninghill, without response. Ronald's calls became a
rarity. Every time I raised the subject of his daughter, he
became noncommittal.

I headed down to South Africa again. My Katchy Kid
project was on line with production, and I took my
London manager with me to check on everything. We
had been there three days when lightning struck twice.

Six o'clock on a warm April evening in the southern
hemisphere. Autumn in Cape Town, spring in London.
Lights started to appear like glow-worms crawling
across the city.

The phone by the bed rang behind me, making me
jump. Ronald's voice, low and shaky, came through.
'Lesley, I have some very bad news for you. Please sit
down.'

'Oh my God, Ronald. What's happened now?'

'There has been a very damaging story in the *News of
the World* suggesting you and I are having an affair. This
is going to ruin us both.'

'*What!* I don't believe it.' I fumbled for the bed behind
me, and sat down. 'How do you know? Are you sure?
Who sold them the story?'

'My sources tell me it was one of your staff who did a
deal with them for £5000. There are people who are out
for the kill ...'

The faxes! I closed my eyes for a moment, imagining
the scene as one of my trusted employees photocopied
Ronald's indiscreet outpourings of love – and held on to
them until the time came to use them.

His voice was almost a moan. 'It will be the breaking
of us.'

And it was – as far as I was concerned. The story
broke in Britain's most widely read tabloid that Sunday,

and from that moment the wolves were howling at my door.

I flew home next morning, walking calmly through a knot of Press men waiting at the arrival gates, my head held high, handbag swinging. I had taken a gamble that they had had no pictures of me wired through yet, and would be on the look-out for a furtive woman in dark glasses and head-scarf trying to slip through the net. The gamble paid off, though I was repeatedly called on the tannoy to respond to phone calls, which I ignored.

Sarah had warned me about getting the Press on my side. What she hadn't told me was how to get out of the goldfish bowl when the sharks arrived to eat you for lunch!

Back in London, I surveyed the wreckage of my life.

One by one my sponsors for the forthcoming Tournament dropped out, and soon the trickle became a flood. Katchy Kid closed down because every single order placed was cancelled that week. We lost our offices – and my home with it. One person opened his front door to me: my brother Neil, with a sleeping-bag and space to lay it out on the living-room floor of his East End council flat. It is still the only roof I have over my head in Britain.

Plans for the Ball were cancelled. I wrote a final letter to Sarah, to her office in Buckingham Palace – and this time I got a reply. A formal note from her Equerry informed me: 'Her Royal Highness the Duchess of York thanks you for your letter, the contents of which have been noted.' That was all, and my phone calls came up against a similar blank wall.

Now I knew what it was like to be 'chilled out'.

Ronald had told me that from now on our only contact

should be by phone, and that those calls should be circumspect in the extreme. During one of them I told him about Sarah. 'I'm sorry,' he said glumly. 'It hasn't been easy for me, either.'

'But she wanted us to be together!' I found myself half shouting, close to tears.

'I know,' was all he said.

A few invitations still filtered through, but I had become a virtual social outcast. The tap had been turned off. The worst moment was a call from a senior executive of one of the sponsors of the Guards Polo Club asking me kindly not to attend any further functions on the hallowed turf of Smith's Lawn as I would make other guests feel 'very uncomfortable'. I fought back the tears until I put the phone down with as much dignity as I had left in me – then I sobbed my heart out. After all I had put into the sport ...

On 5 June 1992 the Charity Commissioners issued a statement to the Press:

> The Commissioners have been inquiring into the International Ladies Polo Tournament 1991 run by Platinum Polo Ltd in support of the Save the Children Fund. They are satisfied that the charity has received all monies due to them under the agreement with Platinum Polo Ltd, and that the agreements between Platinum Polo Ltd and the sponsors were also fulfilled.

As I said, it came too late.

But at one cocktail party given by an old polo friend at the Dorchester Hotel, who should come bursting through the crowd to embrace and kiss me as if we were long-lost sisters but Jilly Cooper.

She had already sent me a lovely letter of support: 'Keep your chin up. Don't worry about it.' She had endured the onslaught of the media with her husband, Leo, and knew just what I was going through.

'Bastards! I'm so sorry for what they've done to you,' were her opening words. Dear Jilly. It was good to have one ally in the camp, at least.

She voiced her opinion in typical style. 'I know the Charity Commission have cleared you, and it's just terrible that nobody's printing it,' she proclaimed loudly. 'As for that other business, I wonder how many people in this room can really point the finger and not feel guilty themselves?'

A few heads turned, and a few weak smiles were directed my way. But once you've been branded a scarlet woman, the scar tissue takes an awfully long time to heal.

Jilly chuckled suddenly. 'I have to tell you, Lesley, that I nearly came to blows with Sue Ferguson at the Cartier's match last week. I'd been speaking out in your favour, and she rounded on me in the bar, and hissed: "How dare you support that Lesley Player in public!"

'I snapped back: "I'll support who I like!" I thought she was going to punch me on the nose – and I'd have done the same to her! Luckily we kept control, and just glared at each other before walking away.'

Jilly apart, I felt the big chill deepen. Away from the social scene, it was worse. My business funds had been swallowed up by the disastrous Katchy Kid venture, and the agency was struggling to survive.

At least, I thought wryly, I had my Rolls-Royce. The market value was so low it would have been a crime to have sold it.

Finally I decided to make for the place where I had found peace in my life.

The sun is blinding my eyes as I sit on the patio looking out at where two oceans meet. The sea is turbulent today, crashing on the rocks below as I write the final words of my story. Diana, the friend who lent me her villa on the outskirts of Cape Town, will be back in a few days, and I will pack my case and head back to London.

I think of Sarah, and remember how someone once described the way she learned to ski: 'She was always fast and furious. She tended to ski outside her limit, taking chances, which is when the adrenalin starts running. It gives you a high which some people might find orgasmic.'

That was the way she lived her life, and probably always will. If it really does look like fool's gold running through the veins of the Fergusons, maybe it buys them happiness anyway.

And Ronald? I realized that once the newspaper articles appeared, I would lose a lot. What I didn't count on was losing the one thing I needed most – the support of two people I had counted as friends.

I treasure the exquisite clock and whistle, but they are his for the asking if ever he wants them back, and he knows it.

We had one last conversation before I left London.

'So it has come to this. You really have to go.' His voice was choked.

'Goodbye, Ronald.'

'Goodbye.' He slowly put down the phone.

The book is now written, and to a certain extent I feel cleansed. As I evaluate myself in its pages I realize that of course I made many mistakes. If I felt that this book was unnecessary, and that my life could be put right without it – believe me, I would destroy it here and now.

In being truthful, the agonies and personal analyses have at times brought me even closer to the edge. At social occasions I am still the target of judicious stares.

But I know that virtually all those with whom I come into contact avoid me because of what they have heard. The best piece of news I have had since all this began is the knowledge that my story can now be publicly told.

I know that many will still condemn me for it. They may say I was in it for the money. But whatever I earn, it will be as nothing compared to what I lost.

A huge container vessel is far out to sea, churning through the swell, its bows sending creamy spray high into the sky. The sun's rays have formed a spotlight dancing on the water around it as it ploughs steadfastly on, heading east out of the murky waters of the Atlantic into the clear blue of the Indian Ocean.

I think I'll follow that ship.

Dear God – please give me another chance in life. I just want to be happily married, have a lovely house, two sets of twins, a cat and a dog. That is all I have ever really wanted.